IN THE
GRAY AREA
a marine advisor team at war

An Association of the U.S. Army Book

IN THE GRAY AREA

a marine advisor team at war

Lt. Col. Seth W. B. Folsom, USMC

NAVAL INSTITUTE PRESS
Annapolis, Maryland

Naval Institute Press
291 Wood Road
Annapolis, MD 21402

Library of Congress Cataloging-in-Publication Data
Folsom, Seth W. B., 1972-
In the gray area : a Marine advisor team in Iraq / Seth W. B. Folsom.
p. cm.
Includes bibliographical references and index.
ISBN 978-1-59114-281-2 (acid-free paper) 1. Folsom, Seth W. B., 1972- 2. Iraq War, 2003—Personal narratives, American. 3. Military assistance, American—Iraq. 4. Iraq—Armed Forces—Training of. 5. United States. Marine Corps—Officers—Biography. I. Title.
DS79.766.F65A3 2010
956.7044'34--dc22
                                    2010020180

Printed in the United States of America on acid-free paper

15 14 13 12 11 10   9 8 7 6 5 4 3 2
First printing

For my girls:
I've been away too long.

I could be bounded in a nutshell, and count myself a king of infinite space, were it not that I have bad dreams.

—William Shakespeare, *Hamlet*

Give me six hours to chop down a tree and I will spend the first four sharpening the axe.

—Abraham Lincoln

Had he known nothing of what had gone on? In that case, he must be an idiot. Had he been part of it? In that case, he must be a criminal. Had he known, yet done nothing? In that case, he must be a coward. The choices—idiot, criminal, or coward—left him depressed.

—Joseph E. Persico, *Nuremberg: Infamy on Trial*

You sign on for the ride you probably think you got at least some notion of where the ride's goin'. But you might not. Or you might of been lied to. Probably nobody would blame you then. If you quit. But if it's just that it turned out to be a little roughern what you had in mind. Well. That's something else.

—Cormac McCarthy, *No Country for Old Men*

Contents

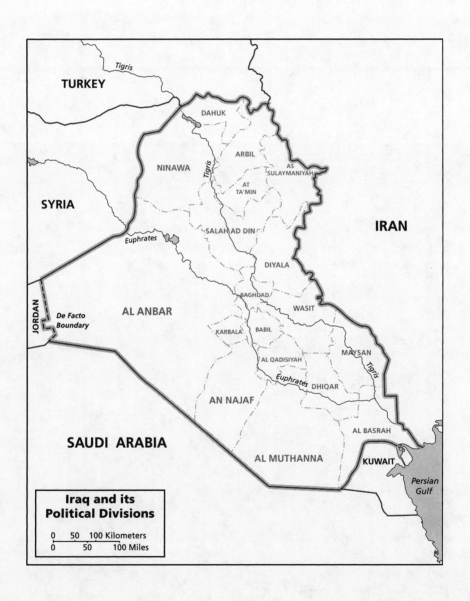

TURKEY

Tigris

DAHUK

ARBIL

NINAWA

Tigris

AS
SULAYMANIYAH

AT
TA'MIN

SYRIA

Euphrates

SALAH AD DIN

IRAN

DIYALA

JORDAN

BAGHDAD

WASIT

*De Facto
Boundary*

AL ANBAR

KARBALA

BABIL

AL QADISIYAH

MAYSAN

Euphrates

DHIQAR

Tigris

AN NAJAF

SAUDI ARABIA

AL BASRAH

AL MUTHANNA

KUWAIT

*Persian
Gulf*

Iraq and its Political Divisions

| 0 | 50 | 100 Kilometers |
| 0 | 50 | 100 Miles |

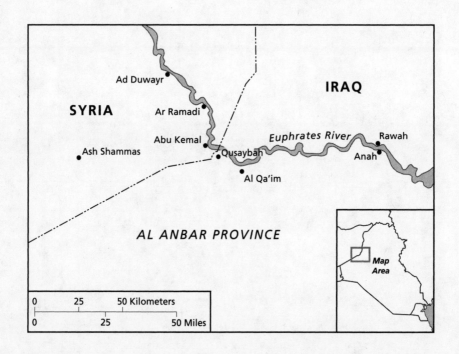

Author's Note

As with my first book, the principal source for this writing was the journal I began at my deployment's beginning. I supplemented my writing with information gleaned from discussions with my Marines, photographs, after-action reports, and my team's official command chronology. Where appropriate I have included information detailing events that occurred elsewhere in Iraq to give the reader a picture of what transpired in areas of operation other than my own.

I have once again chosen not to change names in this book. The reality of war is such that people make mistakes as often as they succeed, and to redact such information would sap the credibility of this writing. It is a memoir—an account as *I* remember it. My recollections of events and conversations are only as accurate as I could record them in my journal. As always, any mistakes or opinions contained in this writing are my own.

Prologue: Nightmare

I'm sitting in the rundown wooden prison of my hooch when Sergeant Frazier calls me on the radio. "There's a commotion going on outside," he tells me. "Over on the eastern side of the Iraqi compound." I step outside from the comfort of my air-conditioned hut into the unseasonably warm spring day, and as I exit my team's compound two Iraqi army gun trucks—Chevy "LUVs"—packed with soldiers speed past me. The young men are frantic, waving their arms wildly and jabbering to each other, attempting to don their body armor as the trucks turn the corner. They are driving so recklessly that they nearly collide with each other as they compete for the small opening in the tall sand berm encircling the camp.

I call for an interpreter, and as Mason shows up Lieutenant Davidoski also appears with Isaac. An IA—our common term for Iraqi army personnel—appears out of nowhere and tells us that a rifle has gone off in the Iraqi compound. A *jundi* (soldier) has been injured. Ski and Isaac race off to find out what has happened. I radio for Doc Rabor and tell him to come running with his medical bag, and then I call the team's Combat Operations Center (COC). "Prep the reports for a CASEVAC [casualty evacuation]," I tell them. "We don't know what's going on yet, but get ready for the worst." Together Mason and I make our way across camp. We aren't prepared for what we'll find.

By the time we arrive at the other edge of the compound a massive swarm of soldiers has already formed. They crowd each other, and they are electrified by what has happened. Ten *junood* ("soldiers") struggle mightily to hold down one *jundi* who is going apeshit with grief. He wails and cries out, throwing his hands skyward as if pleading with Allah to deliver him. He is out of control, and his comrades can barely contain him. Lieutenant Ski walks up to me and tells me that a *jundi* has been shot in the head. The howling soldier is the cousin of the *jundi* who has been shot.

Staff Sergeant Leek and Doc Rabor arrive, panting and nearly out of breath. But their efforts go unrewarded; the soldiers have already rushed the wounded *jundi* to the hospital in Husaybah. I remember the two gun trucks and the way they sped uncontrollably out of the compound, and I wonder if they will make it to Husaybah without getting into a wreck.

We turn back to the crowd, and as we do we see four soldiers escorting a shocked *jundi* away from the melee and toward the camp detention facility. The shooter is limp, lifeless, as if all energy has been sapped from his small body. His head hangs low, the knowledge of what he has done sinking in, draining his spirit. He walks with the weight of the heavens crushing down upon his shoulders. He is placed in the camp's "*jundi* jail" for his own protection; we think the frenzied soldiers may tear him apart if they get their hands on him.

Mason and I walk to the battalion commander's hooch to discuss the incident. As I begin speaking through Mason, I quickly realize that Lieutenant Colonel Ayad does not know what has happened. A captain walks into the office and quickly briefs Ayad. "A *jundi* was joking around with his AK-47," he says. "He didn't realize it was loaded. He put the muzzle in his friend's ear and pulled the trigger."

I return to the scene of the accident with Ayad. He walks into the *jundi*'s room, then quickly exits, his dark complexion suddenly pale and featureless. As Ayad moves away shaking his head I enter the room. The smell of cordite still hangs in the air, competing with the rich odor rising up from a giant, glistening puddle of bright-red blood that canvases the floor. Arterial blood. It has not yet begun to congeal into the clotted, brown mass it will soon become, and I mind my footing to make sure I don't step in the glossy mess. Bloody hand- and footprints decorate the floor and walls like a child's grisly finger paintings, and a Kalashnikov rifle lies discarded off to one side, unconscious of what it has done. The crimson puddle and the bed next to it are riddled with tiny shards of white skull fragments and small gobs of grayish brain matter. I know immediately that the *jundi* will not survive his injury.

The soldiers lock the door behind me as I leave, making my way back to Ayad's quarters. He is visibly shaken, and his eyes well up with tears. He tells me this is the first time anything like this has happened to one of his *junood*. I too have lost a Marine before, and so I feel for Ayad and attempt to share his anguish. I offer my condolences and then take my leave; Ayad needs to grieve in peace. Tomorrow he will go to Karabilah to see the *jundi*'s family. The *jundi* will then be buried according to Muslim law.

The battalion commander launches an investigation, and the shooter remains isolated in *jundi* jail. A squad of soldiers safeguards him to protect him from tribal justice. The battalion mourns the *jundi*'s death, and life goes on.

I have not yet completed my first week as an advisor to the Iraqi army.

IN THE
GRAY AREA
a marine advisor team at war

Chapter 1
Advisor Duty

Upon my return from Iraq after the 2003 invasion I reported to Naval Postgraduate School in Monterey, California, to become a South Asian foreign area officer (FAO). After a year of master's study and another year of language instruction at the State Department I prepared my wife and seven-month-old daughter for the biggest leap into the unknown our family had yet taken. In the summer of 2005 the three of us boarded a packed airliner for the seventeen-hour flight to New Delhi.

Our year in India was a special time for my family, and we shared unique experiences few Americans will ever know. Our home was a walled-in residence in an upscale (by Indian standards) neighborhood called Vasant Vihar, and there was never a doubt in our minds that we were living the good life. At first, the notion of hiring "domestics" (the guilt-ridden American euphemism for servants) went against the grain of our sheltered upbringings. But after learning that we would be shunned in the local community if we did not share our wealth by hiring servants we embraced the idea, and the housekeeper and nanny who worked for us became treasured members of our family. Our daughter, Emery, thrived with the attention she received from Shireen and Sharmain, and the work both women performed around our household enabled Ashley and me to explore the disorganized, albeit harmonious insanity that is New Delhi and India. My family traveled throughout the country with me, and there were times during our travels when Ashley and I would look at each other and say, "I can't believe the Marine Corps is *paying* us to do this." I often wondered exactly what the catch was.

But my tour in India was not all exotic excursions and sightseeing. I spent countless hours locked in my study, absorbing the politics and history of that complex, multifaceted region, as well as attempting to refine my tenuous grasp of the Hindi and Urdu languages. Over the course of our stay there I also spent an inordinate amount of time closely following the war in Iraq. Monitoring troop deployments and redeployments, as well as the ever-dwindling public opinion and support for the war that was touted by the media, I often grew frustrated with my circumstances and distance—both physical and emotional—from the war. As during my two years of postgraduate and language school, I longed to be back in the fight with the Marines. My only hope was to return to the operating forces and somehow find my way to an infantry battalion to be an operations officer or executive officer (XO), the only billets worth having at that level for a major like myself.

My hopes brightened when I received orders to report to the 1st Marine Division staff, and in the summer of 2006 we bade farewell to the country that had mesmerized us and returned once again to Southern California. I was happy to be back with the division that I had fought with in 2003, and it seemed for once that things were going according to plan. I assumed the duties of the division's training officer, and it was quickly evident that my work was cut out for me. The division staff had been sucked dry to support enduring personnel commitments in Iraq and elsewhere, and I had only a skeleton crew to support me in the training shop. It wasn't the kind of job on which I had banked. Sensing this, my boss told me up front, "Give me one year of hard work, and we'll get you down to an infantry battalion to be an XO."

So I worked hard, harder than I probably ever had during the course of my career. Staff work was mundane, punctuated by stressful, exasperating days and frequent late hours. I repeatedly questioned whether my work would make any difference in the long run or if I was simply spinning my wheels into obscurity. But the carrot of being an infantry battalion XO was always there, dangling in front of me as the coveted reward for a job well done. For fifteen months I toiled away as opportunities arose for me that were subsequently quashed by my superiors. Offers from battalion and regimental commanders for me to join their units were overridden or discarded, my services making me far too valuable in my current position. I often wondered aloud if that carrot would ever be placed in my hands, or if it would end up inserted somewhere else.

Throughout all of this there was always the continuous chatter among the division staff about the increasing requirement for advisors and transition teams in Iraq. At the time I knew next to nothing about what the transition teams were doing. All I understood was that vast numbers of junior and midlevel officers were required to man the teams and that they lived with and trained the Iraqi army. And all I really knew about the Iraqi army came from my brief experience observing them in Ramadi and Fallujah in 2004: they had been a shoddy, ragtag force that was corrupt and more than likely penetrated at all levels by insurgents. Now the concept of working with and living in close quarters with the Iraqis seemed to me a suicide mission. I thought back to how the ill-fated Fallujah Brigade had cut and run in 2004 and how many of the Iraqi soldiers had gone over to the side of the insurgents once fighting started. I also poured over reports about an Army transition team that had been kidnapped and executed in Karbala in early 2007. I was not impressed.

And so it was with no small degree of surprise on my part when, one day out of the blue, my boss informed me that I had been selected to lead a battalion-level military transition team (MiTT). The promise of an XO slot vanished in the instant it took to pull my name from a personnel roster, and I knew there was no fighting the decision. The transition team mission had been touted as the main effort, an assignment so critical to American disengagement and ultimate success in Iraq that it had become one of the Commandant's top priorities. In theory it demanded that the transition teams be manned by only the best the Marine Corps had to offer. But theory and the reality on the ground seldom match.

My position on the division staff afforded me visibility over the process by which Marines were being selected, and one thing was certain: the cream of the crop was not being picked to man the teams. Rather, the personnel officers of the division and other major subordinate commands within I Marine Expeditionary Force (I MEF) were merely going down the list of their master personnel rosters, selecting to serve on the teams any and every available company and field-grade officer, staff noncommissioned officer (SNCO), and junior Marine not already spoken for within the force. It was a departure from the spirit and intent of the advisor team mission concept, wherein highly trained senior officers and SNCOs would be able to fuse their experience and technical know-how to assist the fledgling Iraqi military in getting back on its feet. Instead, the teams were often being staffed with the leftovers, officers and Marines like me who may or may not have already served in Iraq. But there was simply no other way to do it; priority for personnel manning was directed toward combat forces slated to deploy, and there just were not enough Marines to go around. The Marine Corps manpower pool was approaching rock bottom, and everyone knew it.

While I was more than aware of all this, at the time I was selfishly more concerned with my own future. I had reached a tipping point in my service where suddenly I had to be concerned about the potential impact any particular assignment might have on my career progression. It was widely believed among field-grade infantry officers aspiring for future command that failure to serve time in the fleet as an operations officer (S-3) or XO was tantamount to a flashing neon sign that blared, "Your career ends here." My consignment to a MiTT team was, for me, just that: an indication that

I had not passed muster. I was particularly concerned about the impact of my previous FAO training. During the three years I had been studying and traveling abroad, my peers had been performing in more visible, "critical" billets, jobs that often guaranteed them duty preferences and made them more competitive for selection to future command. A position in an infantry battalion was my last, best hope for serving in a billet that would similarly increase my own competitiveness for battalion command. But it was not just my ambition to become a battalion commander that had driven me to seek out a job as an XO or S-3. I missed being operational, being where the rubber met the road, being around the Marines who were slugging it out in the streets of Iraq and the mountains of Afghanistan.

Quietly stewing over the decision, I continued with my staff assignments, endeavoring not to let my emotions and feelings about the assignment betray me or affect my work. But as the weeks grew closer to the time when I would report for advisor training, I began to hear stories from officers who were returning from tours with transition teams. In most cases the reports were positive ones, and the common theme was how rewarding the duty had been. One lieutenant colonel I met cornered me, telling me in no uncertain terms that being on a MiTT team was *the* place to be, and that I absolutely *had* to get myself on one.

Another young lieutenant colonel with whom I had struck up an acquaintance in the previous months had likewise just returned from seven months as a battalion MiTT team leader. A bright, youthful officer, he had earned my immediate respect, and I quickly learned to trust his opinion. One day I informed him that I would be taking a MiTT to Iraq, and I asked him what he had thought about the assignment.

"Best job I have ever had in the Marine Corps. Hands down," he said without pausing. "I would do it again and again if I had the chance."

His words altered my perspective, and from that point forward I tried to forget my bitterness. I scoured through after-action reports from other MiTT teams, and I paid particular attention to the ever-changing roster of Marines who eventually would be assigned to my team. Thirteen Marines and one Navy corpsman would be joining me, and as far as I was concerned only the most outstanding would do. But there were gaping holes in the roster, billets that had yet to be filled. My questions about who would fill the gaps were answered by the division personnel officer, who simply told me to pick who I wanted on my team. Easier said than done. I began calling around, seeking out the services of the best and brightest of the men with whom I had served. In every attempt I failed. Marines who wanted to deploy with me and my crew were prevented by their commands from joining the team, and others were just not interested. I even went so far as to seek out my former XO from my time as a company commander. In the process of completing his service with the Marine Corps, he was on terminal leave when I sought to convince him to return to Iraq with me. That effort also ended in disappointment. Ultimately I accepted that I would have no say in who joined my team, and I patiently waited for the holes to fill before our training began. My inability to find anyone willing to join or any command willing to release its people was, for me, an inauspicious first step and not the optimal way to begin training. I wondered what it was about being on a transition team that seemed to chafe people at the very idea of it. But then I remembered my own vicious avoidance of the duty, and I again understood.

The days and weeks passed by, and as advisor training drew closer and closer, MSgt. Norvin Deleonguerrero became a frequent presence in my office. Slated as the team's senior enlisted Marine and logistics chief, he had taken charge of the personnel roundup for our team and began keeping me informed about new Marines reporting aboard. Originally from Saipan, and with a short, powerful build, Deleon—as we tended to refer to him for brevity's sake—drew from an impressive bank of experience, including previous tours as a Marine security guard and drill instructor. With his expertise and quiet but professional demeanor he was exactly the kind of Marine officers wanted assigned to them: someone whose role behind the scenes is so important that his absence from his routine duties hurts. Deleonguerrero was also a big fan of 1980s rock music, and on a regular basis he tended to casually flash the rock band sign with his thumb and index and little fingers extended. He never seemed to get spun up about anything; his most common display of anger or frustration was a casual uttering of "What is this fucked-up trash?"

My office phone rang frequently with calls from a captain named Todd Hanna, a logistics officer who had departed the service just two years earlier. He had deployed to Iraq in 2005 with an infantry battalion before entering the Individual Ready Reserve (IRR), that pool of reserve Marines whose recall prior to 2001 was an anomaly. Like thousands of others in 2007, Hanna had been summoned to active duty for deployment to Iraq, and he had striven to find a meaningful job for his year of active service. His name had been passed to me by another officer on the division staff, and the minute I heard there was a captain who was not only willing, but actually *wanted*, to be on a transition team, I jumped at the opportunity to welcome him aboard as my logistics advisor and, later, my team deputy. A tall, prematurely graying Texan from Austin, he was a polished and highly intelligent graduate of the University of Texas. His age and late entry into the

Corps gave many people the impression that he had served as a prior-enlisted Marine, and his maturity made him an asset to the team. He brought with him genuine experience from the business world, and in time I would come to realize that he was associated with more famous and important people than anyone I had ever known. A subject-matter expert in logistics and an ultraprofessional, he was a natural fit as my second-in-command. Hanna's phone calls became more and more common, and he routinely asked me what was required to get him to the division and on the team as soon as possible. I wondered what his rush was, and it wasn't until later that I learned he feared the possibility of getting snatched up to fill a different billet than the one for which he had volunteered. His fears weren't unfounded; when he checked into the reserve mobilization center aboard Camp Pendleton a personnel officer had attempted to reassign him to the headquarters staff of a deploying regiment.

I also began to field calls from a young first lieutenant named Andrew Grubb. A short, tough-talking native of New Jersey, his personality matched his Italian heritage. He sported an indestructible, continuous five-o'clock shadow that gave the appearance of rarely shaving, and he walked with an ambling gait and shoulders squared off as if he was always looking for a fight. He had led a rifle platoon in combat operations in Ramadi during the previous year's force surge, and he came highly recommended from his command. A creative thinker who often devised irregular, unconventional, yet effective solutions to problems, he had dedicated himself to training and preparing for selection to the fledgling Marine Special Operations Command (MARSOC). Bringing several Marines with him from his battalion, Grubb would be joining the team as my headquarters company advisor and training officer. Like Hanna, his phone calls came regularly, and he began appearing unannounced in my office. Grubb's Marines needed additional training before reporting to the advisor course, and the brusque, matter-of-fact way in which he made his demands rubbed me the wrong way. I began to wonder how my relationship with this young officer would pan out. As a company commander I had often been at odds with my lieutenants, and the last thing I wanted to relive was a power struggle between me and the officers on the team. It wasn't until later that I learned Grubb's battalion—like many others providing personnel for transition teams—had been reluctant to allow its Marines to go until the last possible minute. His pleas for me to arrange training for his Marines had been a futile effort to get them released from their parent command as soon as possible.

With the addition of my training assistant, an intense, pensive captain named Jason Flynn who had also volunteered to join me for the deployment, the core of my team had been formed. Advisor training was next. I forgot about my petty career complaints and the stifling atmosphere of staff life, and instead began to focus on what my job as an advisor would entail. Unfortunately, learning exactly what it was that we were supposed to do during our upcoming deployment would prove to be far more elusive than I had imagined.

Chapter 2
Contractors

As I climb off the helicopter that has ferried me deep into Iraq, one of the first sights that greet me is the throng of contractors. They are everywhere, and they come in all shapes and sizes, all walks of life, and all nationalities. They are overweight, middle-aged men. They are young women sporting cell-phone earpieces and conspicuously unmmilitary clothing. And they are third-country nationals, or TCNs—mostly Indians, Bangladeshis, Pakistanis, and Sri Lankans. They provide instruction on new communications systems. They troubleshoot satellite links. They manage the legions of contracted interpreters. They also make food, cut hair, man the desks at Internet cafés, and do laundry (with a pride rarely seen anywhere in the United States).

Looking around at any of a number of forward operating bases (FOBs) throughout Iraq, I realize that the contractors often seem to outnumber the frontline combat troops. The Americans among them roam the FOBs clad in some unwritten, universal dress code of contractors: polo shirts, hiking boots, and cargo trousers. I analyze the necessary services they provide, and I wonder how any war in the past was ever won without them.

But then I think about the war I entered five years ago, and I try to remember if I ever saw any contractors back then at the beginning. All I can remember is filthy, sweating Marines and sailors to my left and right. There was no chow hall staffed by TCNs subcontracted by Kellogg Brown & Root. Instead, we dined on meals ready to eat (MREs), if any were available from the overtaxed supply lines, and when we couldn't eat we chain-smoked cigarettes and chewed tobacco to suppress our hunger. No Internet cafés were strategically placed along the highway to Baghdad, nor were any phones available to call loved ones after returning from patrols. If you were lucky you befriended an embedded journalist who occasionally let you use his satellite phone. If you were unlucky—like me—the only reason you got to call home was to deal with the aftermath of one of your Marines having been killed.

Walking around one FOB I notice a sign advertising step aerobics for all interested parties on Tuesdays and Thursdays. At another FOB the TCN at the gym makes me show my identification card and sign in. I have no cause to complain; he is following the rules he has been forced to memorize. But then a rear-echelon first sergeant brusquely informs one of my Marines that his physical training uniform does not conform to the gym's standards. As the offending Marine storms away, pissed off at the pogue first sergeant and the contractor and whoever wrote the rules, I remember that there was no gym when we invaded this country. The only exercise for me was pulling apart the heavy feeder assembly of my LAV's (light armored vehicle's) main gun, or changing a tire shredded from the razorlike splinters of artillery shrapnel that littered the highways, or lifting onto a stretcher the heavy deadweight of one of my wounded Marines. I didn't gain muscle back then—I lost it. It melted off my body from the sauna of my chemical suit like butter in a frying pan. One day I looked in a mirror and didn't recognize the filthy, emaciated stranger staring back at me.

One of our contracted interpreters mouths off to my Marines and refuses to participate in the daily grunt work that the team doesn't even seem to think about anymore. When I order him to participate with the team, he casually informs me that he is not a Marine. And then I realize that no, he is *not* a Marine, and that simple fact angers me that much more, because I realize he is not here in Iraq for the same reasons my Marines are. He is not here because of a calling to serve his country. He is not here to rebuild and return security to the country that we leveled five years ago. He is not here because he knows his fellow Marines are sacrificing themselves and he in turn wants to sacrifice himself as well. He is here in Iraq for one simple reason, the same reason why most of the other contractors have made their way to Iraq: money. He gets paid more than most of my Marines, and suddenly I am glad that my pay is a pittance, because I know that one thing I am not is a mercenary.

But then, frustrated by what I see transpiring around me, I log in to the Internet, turn on the webcam, and suddenly my wife and two daughters are looking at me, and I am looking at them. My daughters are sprouting like weeds while I am gone, but because of the contracted Internet service I can watch them grow in my absence. I think back to the time five years ago when the only picture I had of my wife was a wrinkled, sweat-stained snapshot that I had laminated to protect it from the elements. But now I don't need that picture to remind me of her—I can see her beauty and hear her laugh in real time as I chat on the Internet. I see my family, I talk to them, and then I thank God for the contractors who provide the Internet and the satellite dishes.

I realize for the hundredth time that this is not the conflict I lost myself in half a decade ago. It is, literally, a different war. And, despite my frequent distaste for the contractors, despite my frustration at the self-licking ice cream cones that the FOBs have become, I realize that we could not fight and win this new Long War without the contractors. They sustain the force, they elevate morale, they free Marines to fight. They serve a purpose, and my experience here would be very different without them.

My thoughts turn to a future war that we may fight, and I wonder if the contractors will be there for that one as well. I wonder if my Marines and I have grown too accustomed to their presence and the services they provide. I wonder if my Marines will be able to fight again as we did five years ago—shivering in the mud-rain of a desert *aajaaz* (sandstorm), not showering for weeks on end, subsisting on survival rations, nicotine, and caffeine, cut off from all communications with family. But then I watch my men return from a patrol outside the wire. I study their faces, dirty and burned from the desert sun. My eyes follow them as they shoulder their gear back to their huts and begin to clean their weapons. They are smiling. Their jokes and gestures confirm their love for hardship; through their actions they demonstrate that they have *not* grown too soft. I realize that the Marines will continue to fight with or without the contractors. But, more important, I realize that they will continue to win. They are, after all, Marines.

Chapter 3
Training

The headquarters building for I MEF's Advisor Training Group (ATG) was a rundown shell of a building overlooking Camp Pendleton's placid Del Mar boat basin. Dubbed "the crack house," the ATG headquarters came to represent to us in the early days of our training everything that was wrong with the Marine Corps advisor program. During the course of our six-week training regimen—and again during countless briefs throughout our deployment—we would hear that the advisor mission had become the main effort of the American strategy in Iraq. But one look at the bare, cracked concrete floors, the shoddy furniture, the putrid restrooms, and the broken-down drinking fountains that spewed water unsafe for human consumption told us otherwise. The advisor mission, at least in Camp Pendleton, California, was an afterthought. Classes packed with advisor trainees were being pushed through at a seemingly unsustainable rate, and the substandard working conditions of ATG's headquarters indicated to us that while our mission may have been important, it was perhaps not important enough to rate decent instructional facilities.

But we had become the main effort, or so we were told on numerous occasions during our first days at ATG's Advisor Training Course. Packed tightly into a rundown classroom and seated around folding tables, the Marines on my new team eyed each other like dogs preparing to mark their territory. As always, I dreaded this first day of school, one that was sure to be marked by Marines warily observing each other, seeking weak links in the chain, scoping out the alpha males in the pack, assessing the competition for who would be top dog. During our first break I jumped at the opportunity to gather the team and give them my welcome-aboard brief. Prior to meeting them I had carefully crafted my presentation and rehearsed what I would say. Hard experience had taught me that my first impression with my Marines would be the lasting one, and in preparing my brief I had sought to avoid the pitfalls that had so often nearly sunk me as a company commander. As I stood in front of the team, their cold eyes and vacant stares challenged me. *Impress me*, they seemed to say. *Tell me something I've never heard an officer say before.* So I did just that.

"I'll be completely honest with you," I said, leaning casually against a lectern. "I didn't volunteer for this mission. Like many of you—or most of you—I was 'voluntold.'"

As I continued, several of the Marines looked at each other with raised eyebrows. I knew I had taken a chance by admitting that fact to them up front. The possibility existed that I would set the wrong tone for the team or would be perceived as a whiner, someone who didn't want to be there. But the alternative was equally precarious. The Marines would be able to sniff out a fraud in a heartbeat. Any attempt to convince them that I had eagerly volunteered to be an advisor would be shrouded in insincerity, and they would pick up on it immediately. So I told the truth, and doing so set me free. Something in that simple statement enabled me to cross a threshold I had never before been able to traverse. In finding complete honesty and candor within myself I was able to express it to my men. It wasn't honesty in the sense of simply telling my Marines the truth, but rather a newly discovered ability to reveal myself wholly to my team. I had always been taught that an officer must be a great poker player—a great actor. He must be able to appear angry when he is not, and happy when he is anything but. And perhaps that was true, but no longer was it so for me. I had spent my career hiding my true self from my Marines, and I had grown tired of it. As a company commander my inability to convey my true feelings for my men, my unwillingness to openly grieve after the death of one of my Marines, and my compartmentalization of my emotions for so long had nearly crippled me after my return from the war, and I had resolved not to let it happen again. I doubted my ability to negotiate another patch of dark ice like the kind that had blocked my path in 2003 and 2004, and I likewise doubted my family's ability to suffer through it again. And so, with that simple statement, I set the tone for my transition team. My briefing was short, and I ended it with some basic guidance. Anything else would have been superfluous.

"Gents, transition teams are based on the Special Forces advisor team model. For a team to work properly, it requires everyone to know everyone else's job, it requires flexibility, and it requires teamwork. Everyone works on this team; there's no room for anything else. Our job requires us to be able to operate on our own with little guidance. You have a lot of responsibility ahead of you; exercise it, make sound and timely decisions and recommendations, and be accountable for your actions. If you want to be part of *this* elite unit, if you want to be treated as the elite, I will expect you to act and make decisions accordingly."

The die was cast. With our training under way, I waited patiently to see how the team would progress. It wasn't long before I began to like what I saw.

Advisor training alternated between the fascinating and the mundane, between brief episodes of valuable instruction and worthless tall tales spun by our instructors. The majority of the ATG staff had served as advisors earlier in the war during a period in which MiTT teams were responsible less for transition than they were for basic training and shepherding of the new Iraqi army into combat. It was common for instructors to regale us with accounts of leading Iraqi soldiers into firefights with insurgents and dodging improvised explosive devices (IEDs) and indirect fire barrages in places like Fallujah, Ramadi, and Al Qa'im. The stories were interesting, but in the greater scheme of things not exactly helpful. In fact, the storytelling, combined with several blocks of specialized, contracted instruction (including a close-combat shooting course), created a false impression of the atmosphere in Iraq into which we would be entering.

The war I had known was one filled with open combat, one characterized by endless columns of armored vehicles, cannon fire and artillery, and punishing air strikes. With his experiences in Ramadi the previous year, Lieutenant Grubb's recollection of Iraq mirrored my own, as did the memories of my fire support advisor, 1st Lt. Matt Bates. A chiseled, shaved-headed Naval Academy graduate from Oklahoma, Bates had served his first Iraq deployment the previous year in Al Qa'im. Quick-witted and intense, he took his job as an artilleryman seriously. But he also expressed his lighter side by routinely repeating random bits of movie dialogue and scenes from *South Park*. His tour in Al Qa'im had been one punctuated by both fire support missions and provisional infantry operations. Like Grubb and me, Bates was used to the kinetic environment that had been common during the force surge the previous year. It took significant effort on the part of Captain Flynn, my operations advisor, who himself had served on a MiTT team the previous year, to convince us that our role as advisors was not to wage war with the Iraqi army, but to instruct *them* on how to wage war. The surest way for us to lose our jobs, Flynn informed us on several occasions, was for the MiTT team to be kicking in doors. It was our job to make the Iraqis do it, to *teach* them how to do it.

Yet as the course progressed we heard more and more war stories from the instructors. Our training in close-combat marksmanship did little to alter our perception of the dangerous situation we envisioned ourselves walking into, nor did the training we received in subjects such as machine-gun employment and combat first aid. For three days the team was instructed in battlefield trauma management by a former Navy chief—a veteran of multiple tours with Force Reconnaissance units—and his curvy, buxom wife. We learned the graphic art of applying tourniquets and pressure dressings, and we practiced inserting nasal pharyngeal tubes—"nose hoses"—deep into each others' nasal passages and throats. We rehearsed procedures for treating sucking chest wounds, and we practiced the application of needle thoracentesis by inserting heavy-gauged needles into filled sandbags that simulated the chest cavity of a casualty suffering a tension pneumothorax—a sucking chest wound. Exercises included work with fake blood and "moulage" kits that realistically simulated horrible wounds. It was grim instruction and practical application, but at the same time it developed a confidence among the team members that told us we would be prepared to treat each other properly if the shit hit the fan. The training far exceeded that which my Marines and I had conducted prior to the invasion five years earlier. And as the team rehearsed the procedures again and again I found myself wondering if my single Marine casualty during the war's beginning might have been saved had my company undergone such rigorous, realistic preparation.

The gravity of the training aside, our first-aid course was not without humor. On one occasion, as the team stood in a semicircle practicing with the composite graphite and Velcro tourniquets we had been issued, SSgt. Shaun Leek was having difficulty getting the device's strap to fit around his massive quadriceps muscle. Leek, the team's gravel-voiced operations and fire support chief, was an avid bodybuilder with a forceful personality. With a previous tour on the drill field under his belt, he quickly found his niche as the "hammer" on the team. He was an SNCO capable of unleashing drill instructor hell on the Marines, yet instantly being able to transition to the role of mentor. Beneath his hulking, hard-assed exterior lay a warmhearted father and leader. But on this occasion, as another Marine struggled to fit the tourniquet around Leek's leg, frustration set in. I summed up the situation.

"It's easy, Staff Sergeant," I said. "Your leg's too fucking big."

He looked at me, perplexed.

"But sir," he replied. "You told us with all the extra gear they would be issuing us that we needed to hit the gym hard to be able to carry it all."

"Well, maybe not *that* hard," I suggested, laughing.

And Leek was correct: the extra equipment was causing difficulties for all of us. The Marine Corps had begun issuing its new generation of body armor, and even in training the weight was killing us. Named the Modular Tactical Vest (MTV), the new armor was a bulky monstrosity that attempted to crush us beneath its suffocating weight each time we donned it. It wasn't long before we began aching for the days of our old flak vests. The issuing of the MTV, which was advertised to provide the ultimate degree of protection against bullets and shrapnel, as well as the multitudes of other specialized equipment handed to us, only enhanced our perception that we were going to Iraq to fight it out again in the streets. We were wrong, and it wasn't until the team deployed to the Marine desert base at Twentynine Palms, California, for our final training exercise that we began to gain a greater appreciation for what lay ahead of us as advisors in Iraq.

Mojave Viper was the capstone exercise for all Marine battalions deploying to Iraq. For four weeks the force would train in counterinsurgency tactics, and the evolution culminated in a three-day final exercise. In the preceding years the training and exercise evaluation staff aboard Twentynine Palms had filled the high-desert passes with artificial Iraqi towns and populated them with Arabic-speaking Iraqi-American role players. It was as close to being in Iraq as you could get, and once immersed in the "Iraqi" village of Wadi al Sahara it was easy to forget that it was merely a training exercise.

As part of this, our team was attached to an infantry battalion for the final exercise in December 2007. We embedded with a "battalion" of the Iraqi army, and for three days we forged working relationships with the role players acting the parts of the battalion staff and the soldiers. It was an eye-opening experience, and we quickly learned that our role as an advisor team would focus more on the development of an Iraqi battalion staff than it would on conducting routine operations such as patrolling. Over the course of three nights I quickly developed a relationship with the "Iraqi colonel," Abu Fayehdi, himself a genuine Iraqi in real life who had left his home country before Saddam Hussein's rise to power. His advice was simple: *Build a relationship with your counterpart; the Iraqi army will do nothing with you or for you until they really know you. Mistakes will be made, but learn from them and continue forward.*

Mojave Viper was an important evolution for the team in another regard. For two weeks we froze our asses off as we lived and worked out of an unheated aluminum Quonset hut aboard Twentynine Palms' Camp Wilson. It was among the coldest training exercises most of us had ever endured, and I waited for everyone's true character to be revealed. I was pleasantly surprised. The Marines worked together in the harsh, high-desert environment with a sense of purpose, and in their misery they still found time for humor. Shivering together in the icebox of our hut, huddled around coffee pots and space heaters, they traded jokes, played cards, and passed around tins of tobacco and packs of cigarettes. During the final exercise, when our Iraqi army compound came under frequent enemy fire, the team would don their heavy gear, hurry to their battle stations, and rush outside the wire to chase down the attacking insurgents.

In the preceding months, despite the hours and days of mindless classroom instruction and field events, the Marines had molded themselves into a real team, and I found absent in myself the misgivings and concerns that had hounded me as a young, uncertain company commander prior to my deployment to Iraq in 2003. A new dawn had risen for me as a leader, and as we gathered in the Officers' Club after the exercise, drank beers together, and congratulated ourselves on our crushing defeat of the enemy in Wadi al Sahara, I genuinely looked forward to deploying to combat with this group of men.

Chapter 4
Gear

The convoy roster lists my name, and even though it is just another admin run to Camp Al Qa'im I prepare to don the same gear as if going into a full-scale urban assault. Death seeks everyone here, not discriminating between logistical convoys and combat patrols.

I begin by pulling on the tan, fire-retardant Nomex flight suit. The suit has a peculiar quality—during the winter its thin material lets the cold in, and during the summer it somehow manages to keep heat trapped against the body. It is the same kind of suit my father wore when he flew during Vietnam and the Cold War. And in its bagginess and pocket-lined sleeves and legs I imagine myself in his shoes, flying patrol after patrol, each time not knowing if my men and I will come back.

My boots are next. Hundreds of years of modern warfare, entire textbooks cataloging countless revolutions in military affairs, and one maxim continues to stand firm: Your boots are your best friend. I know from hard experience that if your feet are miserable, *you* are miserable. And I refuse to go through that hell again. So I change my socks every day and shower my feet with Gold Bond's medicated foot powder. I worry each time the warm advance of a blister rises to the surface, and I redouble my efforts to keep my feet clean and dry. But I am fighting a losing battle, because the weight of my gear keeps constant pressure on my feet, causing them to sweat and grind against the insoles of my boots. And I resign myself to the fact that my feet will never be the same.

Hanging on a wooden cross in the corner of my hut, my body armor waits for me to once again shoulder its crushing load. As I contort myself into unnatural positions to pull it over my head and secure it firmly against my torso, I immediately feel the rigidity across my chest, the pulling on my shoulders, and the worrisome tingling in my lower back. I begin to sweat, and I haven't even ventured outside into the stifling desert heat yet. The flight suit and the armor trap everything in like the chemical suit I once wore, and beads of sweat run down the length of my body and rest in pools in my boots.

My body armor barely resembles the vest I wore during the war's beginning. I remember how the old vest was little more than a Kevlar blanket, not much different in concept or degree of protection from the even older flak jacket I wore when I first joined the Marine Corps. I remember my complaints about its weight and the heat, and I remember that back in 2003 at the war's beginning almost no one had the ballistic plate inserts designed for the vest. At the time I wondered how anyone would be able to move around with the added weight of the plates on the chest and back.

But, again, the war has evolved, and with it so has my body armor. Everyone has the ballistic plates now; that was guaranteed after it became an issue during the presidential campaign of 2004. Only now the body armor has additional plates hanging along my ribs, and more than ever movement is constricted. The side plates force my arms out from my sides; this is made even worse by the bulky first-aid kit fastened under one arm and the utility pouch under the other. I walk around with limbs outstretched like a gorilla. Magazines of rifle and pistol ammunition are strapped to my chest because that is the only way I can get to them, and my handheld radio hangs next to them for easy access too. My pistol rests in a drop holster on my thigh, and extra gear I have deemed essential lines both the holster's mount and the padded utility belt I wear around my chafed hips. I constantly adjust and readjust my gear, seeking the perfect solution that maximizes comfort and equipment accessibility. But each time I come up short. I make a mental note of what's wrong, where my gear pinches, what I cannot access, and I promise myself to correct it the next time I make adjustments.

My Kevlar helmet waits for me to don it, and like the rest of my gear it is not the same model I wore five years ago. I am thankful, because the old helmet was heavier and too uncomfortable. I remember hardly ever wearing it because it gave me headaches. The new Kevlar is lighter and padded on the inside like a football player's helmet. It fits on my head with the snug comfort of a weighty baseball cap. And even though it retains heat, makes my head sweat, and still causes headaches, I don't remove it at the first opportunity like I did before, because there were no IEDs in 2003, and there were no snipers.

My Nomex flight gloves and ballistic glasses go on last, because I don't want my hands to burn or lose my eyesight if an IED detonates next to me. I also wear pads to protect my knees inside my Humvee, because I can't take the bumps as easily as I used to. And because I know what it feels like when an armored, two-hundred-pound Humvee door closes on my leg.

Loaded up with all of my gear, I grab my rifle and night-vision goggles from the armory and waddle to my vehicle. My thoughts turn to a study I once read. I think about the underlying theme of the study, that as the fighting load and protective equipment escalates, your chances of getting hit and dying actually increase rather than decrease. I also remember one of the first books I ever read as a lieutenant—S. L. A. Marshall's *The Soldier's Load and the Mobility of a Nation*—and how it talked about the ridiculous weights that men under arms are forced to carry. That book was written in the 1950s. I think about the lip service that has been paid to it over the decades, and yet the fighting load has gotten heavier, hotter, and bulkier.

Squeezing myself into the cubbyhole of my Humvee, I feel the pressure of the body armor shift from my shoulders down to my lumbar spine, and I know I'll be lucky if I don't have back problems for the rest of my life. As the convoy leaves the wire I hope I will not have to dismount the Humvee until I reach my destination, because walking even the shortest distance is exhausting. I wonder if I could run wearing all this gear, and the thought makes me laugh, because as it is I can barely walk. My gait is more like a waddle, and I think about that study once again.

I realize that, at age thirty-six, I am getting too old for this crap. My knees, shoulders, and back are worn out from years of this—from humping body armor and Kevlar helmets, from lifting weights and bouncing around in armored vehicles. I understand why so many old, retired infantry Marines walk gingerly and slightly hunched over, because I know the kinds of grinding abuse their bodies have endured. I wonder if that will eventually be me, and I am sure of one thing: if my body armor and fighting load gets any heavier, I am guaranteed to spend my twilight years just as they do, nursing sore joints, tired bones, and sleepless memories.

Chapter 5
Transit

As February drew to a close an Army CH-47 Chinook helicopter dropped me and my team off at the bustling hub of Camp Fallujah, a sprawling American camp that was home not only to Multi-National Force-West (MNF-W; the I MEF headquarters for all Coalition units in Al Anbar province), but also Regimental Combat Team 1 (RCT-1) and numerous other military units. Five years earlier my company and I had been in Kuwait, uncertain of our future as we prepared to march north into Iraq. Now I found myself back in the same country I had invaded, only this time I had come as an advisor, not as a liberator or an occupier. Pausing to catch my breath, I reflected on the previous two weeks since the team and I had departed the United States. Our transit from Camp Pendleton to Iraq had been fraught with aggravation, with long flights and even longer periods of frustration. I was relieved to have the brief respite.

On the morning of 13 February my wife and three-year-old daughter drove me and my mountain of equipment to the armory that overlooked the ATG and the Del Mar boat basin. In the previous weeks the team had been victims of the same cruel yo-yo game of shifting departure dates I had encountered in 2003, and as before the unknown had played havoc with me and Ashley. For months we both had attempted to prepare Emery for my approaching extended absence, and in doing so my wife and I had expended so much energy that we had found little time for ourselves. Our youngest daughter, Kinsey, had been born a scant three weeks before my departure, and the requirements of a newborn only lessened the time Ashley and I were able to spend together.

As it always did with the approach of a pending deployment, time slipped away from me, and before we knew it my departure date was upon us. Leaving Kinsey in the care of my sister-in-law, the three of us piled into our car and made what was for me an agonizing fifteen-minute drive to Camp Pendleton. As I had done before my previous deployments I walked Ashley around to see the team members one last time, and then I steered my two girls toward the car. Ashley knew it was coming and didn't protest; she had become a pro at it by that point. But this time my exit was infinitely more significant. In the past I had only Ashley to worry about, and she had only me to do the same.

Now I was the father of two children, one too young to even know who I was and the other at an age where she knew I was going away but couldn't understand why. The only way Ashley and I could explain it was to tell Emery that there were some soldiers in another country who needed help, and Daddy was going there to try to help them. I couldn't simplify it much more than that, and I silently thanked my fortune that I didn't have to say what so many other Marines and soldiers had had to say to their children in the preceding years—that Daddy had to go away to fight the bad men.

As I kissed Ashley and Emery good-bye one last time, I leaned in to buckle my daughter's car seat. Smiling, she looked at me and spoke, her words catching me off guard.

"Don't go out there . . . and get in trouble with the boys, Daddy."

"What the . . ." I said, turning to Ashley, my voice catching in my throat. "Did you hear that?"

Ashley put her hands to her mouth, her eyes beginning to glisten with tears.

"I don't know where that came from," she said.

I was flabbergasted, speechless that a child so young and so innocent seemed to suddenly understand everything. Her words crushed me, and I realized my life had just reached a new milestone: I was leaving my children for the first time. It shouldn't have affected me. After all, I had endured numerous deployments by my father; they had shaped my childhood, had been the keys to my eventual entry into the Marine Corps as an adult. But now, knowing that my wife faced seven months of taking care of two small children, knowing that my daughters faced what to them would be an eternity without a father, I understood the burden my parents had shouldered in the years my father had served in the Navy. In the moment that my wife and child pulled away from me and drove out of sight I empathized with my father, and admired my mother's strength even more. For the thousandth time I hated myself for what I was putting my family through, and then I turned and headed toward my team and our waiting buses. My moment of sorrow and grief had expired, and I locked my emotions in the dark recesses of my subconscious, preparing myself for the daunting task ahead of me. My compartmentalization had begun.

A swift departure from March Air Reserve Base in Riverside, California, eluded us, and hours after our arrival we learned that our plane had broken down somewhere on the East Coast. Feelings of elation, of "Let's get on with it," were smashed as we were ferried to the Riverside Marriott, where we would remain overnight until our flight arrived. One night turned into three, and we waited as prisoners in a four-star hotel, forbidden to venture out into town in our camouflaged utility uniforms. Some Marines arranged for daily visits to the hotel by their families or girlfriends, each day spent having one last lunch together, only to be stuck there one more day. Others, like me, chose not to invite wives and children to the hotel. One good-bye was enough for me. I had already ripped off the Band-Aid and didn't wish to go through it again. Ashley sensed my frustrations during my nightly calls home, and I believed she understood why I was not asking her to come meet me.

To drown their sorrows the Marines spent the evenings crowded around the hotel bar, drinking and celebrating each "last night home," only to find themselves once again stranded and immobile the next day. By the third night we had grown tired of the revelry, and most of the men spent their last evening sobering up, praying that we would leave the next day. Our wish was finally granted, and on 16 February we boarded an airliner for the twenty-hour transit to Kuwait. The ball was finally rolling.

We landed at night, as all American service members do when arriving in Kuwait. For years Kuwait International Airport had been the principal point of entry for troops heading to Iraq, and the same charade played itself out every night. Exhausted, bleary-eyed men and women were hustled off crowded, stinking airliners and into blacked-out buses, then shuttled to a cantonment area an hour outside the airport to await transportation into Iraq. It was no different for us, and as a Marine corporal shooed us off our bus at Camp Virginia and into a barren classroom tent we were greeted by the video image of an Army general loudly proclaiming that we were now in a combat zone. Audible grunts of "Yeah, right" and "Whatever" reverberated throughout the tent. As we suffered through a stern video lecture by a sergeant major extolling the virtues of proper uniform wear and shunning such unforgivable sins as wearing sunglasses on the head or around the neck, I wondered aloud for the first time what the war had come to. I turned and looked at Lieutenant Bates, who rolled his eyes and commented aloofly, "Fighting the 'War on Terror' . . . from the safety of Kuwait."

Our roller-coaster ride into Iraq came to a screeching halt at Camp Virginia, and the team settled into dusty tents crammed with military cots, boxes of bottled water, and little else. For three days we sat waiting for a flight into Iraq, growing more impatient by the hour. The Marines longed to get away from the rear-echelon characters that inhabited the camp, all the while marveling at the luxuries offered to the troops. MacDonald's, Subway, and Kentucky Fried Chicken were available for troops unhappy with the full-service dining hall staffed by workers from Kellogg Brown & Root, and an overstocked post exchange operated night and day, prepared to sell soldiers and Marines anything they needed in *or* out of a combat zone.

I was deeply troubled at the bloated rear area that Kuwait and Camp Virginia had become, but I found solace in the belief that Marine bases in Iraq would not be the same. Lieutenant Grubb, who had overheard me grousing, laughed sarcastically.

"Shit, sir, wait until we get to Iraq. It's just as bad now."

"What?" I replied, incredulous. "Even Marine bases?"

Lieutenant Bates chimed in. "Just wait, sir."

In the midst of my harping, Captain Hanna walked up and sat down on the cot across from me. Less than a week before departing the States we had lost Captain Flynn from the team, and I had fleeted up Bates into the spot as the team's operations advisor. Hanna had likewise assumed the added responsibility as my deputy, and together he and Master Sergeant Deleonguerrero had been running around seeking information about our transportation into Iraq.

"We're leaving tonight," he said. "We'll bus it to Ali Al Saleem, build pallets for our gear, then fly to TQ [Taqaddum] on a C-130."

I remembered my last harrowing flight on a C-130 and wondered if it would be the same this time around. I didn't look forward to the steep dive and violent impact of a combat landing, but I kept my thoughts to myself as the team boarded the aircraft for the flight to the air base at Taqaddum. Staff Sergeant Leek planted his massive frame on the nylon mesh seat next to mine, and as the aircraft powered up its turboprops and taxied down the runway through the dark he nudged me with his elbow and offered his can of tobacco. We settled back for the long ride, each Marine loudly proclaiming his delight at leaving Camp Virginia behind.

In the last hour before sunrise our aircraft touched down at Taqaddum. The tail ramp dropped, and we were greeted by a bitter cold that sliced through our clothing. The flight-line crew barked orders at the team, and the Marines hustled off the tarmac and lugged their bags into a desolate structure designated for transients like us. One by one the Marines jumped into the bare racks, seeking sleep as the sun began to rise. In their fatigue they voiced similar complaints.

"Man, who *were* those dudes on the flight line?" asked one Marine, shaking his head.

"What a bunch of fucking *assholes*!" growled another.

"Oh yeah?" replied Grubb, pointing to a laminated sheet of paper fixed to the back of the hatch leading outside. "Check *this* shit out." He began reading aloud with palpable disgust the myriad rules and regulations that governed life aboard Taqaddum.

"No beanie covers during the hours of daylight. No wearing the black fleece jacket as an outer garment. No sunglasses on your head. What the fuck?" he ranted, angrily. "What *can* we do around here?"

"Hey, listen," I said. "You're gonna find this everywhere we go. There are some people out there who are so fucking stupid that they only have one thing they can do. One thing they are entrusted with, and by God, they're gonna enforce the hell out of it, no matter who has to suffer."

The men grunted, shook their heads, and promptly fell asleep on the rows of bunks that lined the cabin, too exhausted to complain any more. *How much more of this rear-echelon bullshit will we have to endure?* I pondered as I drifted off to sleep. *Can it get much worse than this?* Of course it could—our trip had barely begun.

The CH-47 Chinook is a monster of a helicopter; its rotor wash is enough to knock you down if you aren't paying attention. We found ourselves on the airfield at Camp Taji, the gale created by the rotors threatening to push us down into the gravel that bordered the flight line. It was the middle of the night, half of our gear was missing, and we had no idea where the hell we were. With that discouraging start we began to wonder what else was in store for us at the Phoenix Academy.

A last-ditch effort by Multi-National Corps-Iraq (MNC-I) to train all advisors before meeting their counterpart Iraqi units in-country, the Phoenix Academy was poorly run and administered. Over the course of six days the school proved to be another in a series of disappointing, substandard training courses designed to prepare us for our mission. Largely taught by contracted personnel, the academy instructors seemed woefully uninformed on what our mission as advisors would actually entail, and more than ever we wished to get to our final destination and accomplish the task at hand. We also were introduced to the confusing hierarchy and chain of command that confounded the advisor effort in Iraq. To whom did we report? Was it ATG back in Camp Pendleton? Or was it the Iraq Assistance Group in Taji? There was also the Iraqi Security Forces (ISF) integration cell located at Camp Fallujah, as well as the entire MEF chain of command: MNF-W on down through RCT-5, ending with the Marine infantry battalion task force with whom our Iraqi battalion would be partnered. Finally, there were the transition teams themselves, embedded at the Iraqi battalion level and working all the way up the chain to the Iraqi division level. I was more confused than ever as the course ended and we moved on from Taji to Camp Fallujah.

The muddled situation at Camp Fallujah did little to clear the air for us, and I was happy once familiar faces from my earlier years in the Marine Corps began to appear throughout the camp. Disturbed by what I had witnessed aboard the camp, I posed the same question during the course of each mini reunion.

"Man, how do you live with yourselves out here?" I would ask. "I mean, come on, I saw a Marine walking out of the PX [post exchange] today with a Guitar Hero box under his arm!"

Their nonchalant replies of "Hey, it's not a bad way to spend a deployment" only heightened my distaste for what was happening, and I sought the safety and refuge offered by the men on my team. Their feelings echoed my own, and like me they wanted to get the hell out of Camp Fallujah and on to the end of the line.

One night, as I stood in line at the dining hall, a tap on my shoulder was followed by a familiar voice. I turned to see Chad Parment, now a captain, who as a lieutenant had been one of my platoon commanders during the invasion. His wife, Georgia—also a Marine—stood next to him, and I practically shouted my salutation at him.

"Hey! Holy shit, Chad, it's good to see you."

"Small world, isn't it, sir?" he replied, grinning.

"And getting smaller," I added.

The two of them joined me and several members of my team at our table, and for over an hour I caught up with Parment and his wife. My Marines eyed me suspiciously, occasionally stealing curious glances at Parment. They knew about my past, about the kind of company commander I had been, and they seemed to be waiting for a glimpse of my wretched former self to emerge as I traded stories with a living reminder of my previous life.

I eventually bade farewell to Parment and Georgia and made my way through the dimly lit streets back to the team's holding tent. So much had happened, so much had changed in the five years since I had been a company commander, and I had barely recognized it until a character from my past had come face-to-face with the characters of my present. I contemplated too the changes that had taken place in Iraq, and I shook my head at how different things were now. The future was once again a darkened passageway, and I found myself unsure of what it held for me. But as I turned the last corner and ventured toward my tent I was certain about one thing. In the preceding four months I had become more comfortable with the fourteen men on my team—and with my own role as their leader—than I had been as Delta Company's commander five years earlier while we prepared to wage war on that cheerless, godforsaken country.

I stopped before I reached the door to the tent, pausing to light a cigarette. My past was outside; it still clung to me like the bluish smoke trailing from my cigarette, fighting to break free and reveal itself. My future lay beyond the threshold, waiting to unfold once I took a step forward. *If* I took a step forward. Could I leave the past behind? Could I really change myself from the way I used to be?

I stubbed out my cigarette, opened the door, and stepped into the tent. Marines looked up from their racks and greeted me warmly. I lay down on my cot, stared at the ceiling, and suppressed a grin.

I was back with my people.

Chapter 6
COP South

Combat Outpost (COP) South is a lonely, desolate settlement positioned just fifteen kilometers from the Syrian border and the Euphrates River. Surrounded by ten-foot-high sand berms topped with spiraling concertina wire and populated with sand-filled HESCO barriers and rundown, prefabricated wooden huts built by Navy Seabees, the settlement resembles a forgotten desert concentration camp. Rickety wooden and aluminum guard towers dominate each corner of the camp, but what they are looking for or guarding against is unlikely to appear. So isolated and unassuming, the encampment seems more likely to blow away under the force of the periodic desert *aajaaz* than to come under enemy fire or attack. The team's chosen call sign—the Outlanders—is an appropriate one.

The MiTT compound aboard COP South is a HESCO- and razor-wire-enclosed camp-within-a-camp, an oasis that sustains my advisor team both operationally and logistically, while also tending to the Americans' globally shameless insistence on "quality of life." Filled with the same drab wooden Southwest Asia (SWA) huts that line the COP, the team's compound includes a combat operations center and armory, a makeshift kitchen and dining area, an outdoor gym overflowing with rusting dumbbells and decomposing weight benches, and a Morale, Welfare, and Recreation (MWR) hut complete with satellite television, refrigerators for cold drinks, and contractor-provided Internet terminals and phones.

But not all about our MiTT compound is first-rate, or even acceptable by most Americans' pampered, unrealistic standards. The living spaces are Spartan, with mostly bare plywood walls, crude furniture crafted from boxes and spare lumber, and aluminum bed racks whose weakened springs barely support tattered, soiled mattresses. Mice race through the living spaces with impunity. A thin film of fine dust blankets everything from personal equipment to computers and iPods, constantly threatening to disable anything that runs on electricity or has moving parts. Weapons appear filthy even after daily cleanings, and clothing fresh from the laundry service at Camp Al

Qa'im becomes dirty the minute it is removed from the laundry bag. I begin to classify my personal belongings into various echelons of disposability as I realize that the life span of everything I own suddenly becomes finite once exposed to the harsh, arid environment of the western Iraqi desert.

Personal hygiene too becomes an exercise in futility. The shower trailer, a rotting structure situated on the opposite end of the camp, is slaved to the Iraqi battalion's electrical system, which in turn is powered by a generator that is shut off during the midafternoon hours and again late at night to conserve precious fuel. No set times for generator shutoff are posted or adhered to by the Iraqis, and so the closer to the afternoon or the later in the evening I push my shower, the greater chance I risk of losing water pressure and electricity. Years of water damage inside the trailer and the resultant mold, mildew, and decay beneath the peeling linoleum floor have branded it with a permanent stench of raw sewage, and no amount of cleaning or bleaching will ease the assault on my olfactory system. But a shower is a shower, and I count my blessings that most days I can wash the desert off me and start fresh. Or, at least, fresh until the long walk back to the MiTT compound. More often than not, by the time I reach my hut I am once again covered in Al Qa'im's signature moon dust—a walking sugar cookie almost as dirty as I was before turning on the water.

If personal hygiene is an exercise in futility, then relieving oneself is an exercise in humility. Rather than the ubiquitous chemical toilets ("Port-a-Jons") or latrine trailers seen aboard FOBs throughout Iraq, our bathroom facilities are split between five "piss tubes" and a modified outhouse referred to as the "WAG shack." The piss tubes are nothing more than large PVC pipes rammed into the ground at forty-five-degree angles. You walk up, unbutton, and urinate into the tube. Over time the ground beneath the tubes becomes saturated with urine, making it necessary to rotate usage among the tubes. Even in the open air of the desert there is the sensation of standing in an untended gas station bathroom, and the smell of stale piss rising up from the inundated sand makes me curse my teammates who can't seem to aim straight.

The WAG shack is an empty wooden shed that contains a plastic toilet frame on legs. You line the frame with a WAG (Waste Alleviation and Gelling) bag—a thick plastic pouch lined with some chemical substance that seems half kitty litter and half lime—and then you sit down and do your business. Once finished, you tie the bag in a knot, place it in a plastic zip-lock sack included with the kit, and throw it in a bin outside the shack for later incineration by the poor bastard who draws garbage-burning duty that day. While initially there is something nauseating and seemingly uncivilized about handling my own warm feces, any fear of getting severely wounded by enemy fire and shitting in a bag for the rest of my life is assuaged after one use of the WAG bag.

If nothing else, waste disposal aboard COP South makes me realize the importance of garbage men in any society. Trash removal is performed twice a day, more often than not by LCpl. Travis Wardle, whose apparent love of fire has earned him the nickname "Trashcan Man," after a pyromaniac in a Stephen King novel. Garbage (including the sealed WAG bags) is collected and hauled to the burn pit, which is used by both the Iraqis and the Americans. For the Iraqis, it is enough to dump their waste in the pit and leave it to slowly fester in the heat. The Americans, however, insist on torching the pile during each garbage run, and twice daily a greasy black plume of smoke billows up from the pit as Trashcan Man dumps diesel all over the pile and watches the cremation with perverse satisfaction. Trashcan Man is good at his job—almost too much so—and there is the persistent worry that he will immolate himself during his daily ritual of fire. At night the heavens light up with his handiwork, and the orange glow of the burning pit pulses like a beacon visible for miles. By day the pit is a depressing sight, a sad reminder of the obscene amounts of waste generated by each side and the accompanying continued poisoning of this tortured country's environment.

COP South is my new home, yet I don't recognize it as such until one day when we are at Camp Al Qa'im. Frustrated with the rear-echelon nonsense of the camp's administrators, I turn to my team and say, "Let's pack it up and head home." By "home" I mean COP South, and then I realize that although my real home is ten time zones and thousands of miles away, home is also where you hang your hat, and that home is now COP South. The other one will have to wait.

Chapter 7
Arrival

The wind howled outside my hut, and everything I owned was covered in a fine layer of talcumlike dust. It was 3 March, and a sandstorm had blown in that afternoon while my team received a turnover brief from the outgoing transition team. When we walked outside the briefing room we had been met by blowing gusts and sand-filled skies. Eyes watered and mouths went dry. It had been a hell of a welcome to COP South and Al Qa'im.

We had boarded a CH-53 on the morning of 2 March after a night flight from Camp Fallujah to the Coalition air base at Al Asad. The team's desire to get to COP South was motivated less by a craving to get on with our job than it was a longing to put a stop to the endless "sea bag drag" from base to base across Iraq. Each leg of our journey had played itself out like a recording looping over and over: repack our bags, lug them outside to a staging point, wait for transportation, load the bags onto a truck, unload and stage bags at the designated airfield, wait for the bird, have someone yell "Hurry up!" at us as soon as the bird lands, load the bags on the bird, fly to our destination, quickly unload bags, then pray that all of our equipment made it. Somehow it did every time . . . eventually.

The team landed at COP South around noon and piled off the helicopter. The rotor wash pelted us with waves of sand and gravel, and as we unloaded our bags under the hot exhaust blasting from the aircraft we began to sweat beneath our body armor. From a distance the current MiTT team leader and his operations chief both smiled at us as we lugged the last bit of our gear off the aircraft. The helicopter's crew chief impatiently tapped his foot as we made one last scan of the cargo bay, searching for any forgotten bags or equipment. When the helicopter took off it would be as good as gone, along with anything we might have accidentally left on board. Satisfied that we had everything, I shouted my thanks to the crew chief over the din and stepped off the loading ramp.

Our helicopter and its escort lifted off the barren landing zone (LZ), once again showering us in a deluge of dust and sand. As the two aircraft drifted away toward the horizon it was suddenly quiet. The Marines began to take stock of their surroundings, and everyone immediately reached the same conclusion: we were in the middle of nowhere. The team leader and his chief both leaned casually against a tan Chevrolet pickup truck, chomping on cigars. The personal appearance of the two Marines greeting us startled me. Their hair was long, and they wore only T-shirts with no uniform tops. Their trousers were unbloused from their boots, and each man wore a sand-colored baseball cap emblazoned with their team logo across the front. The operations chief grinned broadly to the group and welcomed us aboard.

"*Marhaaba!*" he said in Arabic, chomping on his cigar. "Welcome to COP South."

Captain Hanna set his bags down, surveyed our surroundings, and turned toward the team leader.

"Sir, can you give us a quick orientation of where the hell we are?"

"Sure," the major replied, pointing off into the distance. "You've got Husaybah and Karabilah to the north, and to our immediate west is the Syrian border. That's about it."

In the desert shimmer the landmarks were visible only as tiny, wavy blips on the horizon. Everything else surrounding the outpost was uneven, hardscrabble desert.

"Jesus, not much out here, is there?" I commented.

"Yeah, we don't get a lot of visitors out this way," he replied.

We loaded our bags into the pickup bed, and the team walked across the camp to the MiTT compound. The outgoing team members had kindly vacated their living spaces to let us get settled as quickly as possible, and the Marines were indeed thankful. After more than two weeks of living like nomads, everyone was relieved to be able to finally settle down in one place for good.

Our first meeting with the major's team was no less shocking to me than when he had picked us up at the LZ. We walked into the team room to find nearly all of his Marines looking as he had. Scraggy mustaches drooped from tanned faces, and great shocks of unkempt hair stuck out from beneath baseball caps. Few bloused their boots, and most wore only T-shirts. Of those, several wore civilian shirts rather than the standard-issue olive drab skivvy shirts. The group standing before us appeared less like a Marine unit than they did a Special Forces team. It was an unexpected sight. One constant in all of the briefings our team had endured in the previous months had been a demand for us to resist the temptation to "go native" once we were in-country. The isolated nature of advisor duty was such that teams often operated on their own with little supervision or guidance from higher headquarters. There had obviously been enough of a trend among transition teams of going native that it had attracted the attention of the higher-ups, and now an example of it was staring us in the face. Clearly the major and his team had not heeded the same advice. He wasn't a bad guy, and his team members were not bad Marines. But I didn't agree with their casual mind-set, nor thankfully did my SNCOs. Neither did Captain Hanna. Not long after our arrival I learned that he had made a point of telling the lieutenants not to get too comfortable with the way the current team was running things. Hanna was sharp, and he took his duties as deputy seriously. It was obvious that he had been studying me and my personality, and he had begun to figure out how I felt about issues just by observing my body language.

That evening the team leader and I began our turnover by grilling steaks, ribs, and chicken outside the team's chow hall. The SWA hut that served as the team's kitchen housed two refrigerators and a deep-freezer, and with the added storage capacity provided by a walk-in freezer on the opposite end of the compound there appeared to be no shortage of food. As he flipped ribs and steaks on a grill fashioned from a converted fifty-five-gallon drum, the major spoke casually about the various nuances of being an advisor. I hounded him with questions.

"What's the battalion commander like?" I asked.

"He's not a bad guy," he began. "Definitely better than the last one. The last dude was into some crooked shit and got caught with his hands in the cookie jar. He's currently on the lam somewhere here in Iraq; they've been after him since he left. I'll take you over to meet Ayad tomorrow night. We'll kick off the turnover briefings tomorrow also."

Our conversation continued into the night. As I sat there eating my fill I thought, *Not a bad way to begin.* So far it seemed like one big beach party, and I thought, *Hmm, grilling out every night. I could definitely get used to that.*

The two groups began the relief in place (RIP) in earnest the next day with a series of briefs by the outgoing team. COP South was home to 3rd Battalion, 28th Brigade of the Iraqi army's 7th Division, and through a series of slide shows we learned that only the battalion's Headquarters and Service Company and 3rd and 4th companies were garrisoned in our camp. The remaining two line companies, 1st and 2nd, occupied compounds farther to the north along the Euphrates River's Jibab and Almari peninsulas. Their distance from COP South presented logistical and command-and-control challenges for the battalion, something we would come to realize more fully later.

We concentrated on the personality briefs, and as each member of the outgoing team projected onto the screen the mug shot of his respective Iraqi counterpart each Marine on my team leaned forward to pay close attention. The faces and names soon became a jumble, and I wondered how I would ever remember them all. Each Iraqi had multiple family and tribal names, but rather than being referred to by their rank and last name (as American service members would be), the Iraqis were addressed by their rank and first name. The matter was further complicated by the number of officers who had the same first name within the battalion and brigade. Scores of Muhammads and Alis and Husseins filled the ranks, and it was not uncommon for two Americans to think they were talking about the same Iraqi officer when they were, in fact, talking about two different men.

When the team leader could tell we had had about enough, he paused the briefings to take us to lunch in the Iraqi chow hall. As he escorted me, Captain Hanna, and Master Sergeant Deleonguerrero through the camp we passed by a burned-out structure surrounded by crumbling HESCO barriers. Blackened splinters of lumber and aluminum sheeting lay collapsed in piles of ash and charred wood, and in the middle of it all three Iraqi soldiers scavenged for usable material.

"That's the old chow hall," the team leader noted casually. "It burned down a couple of weeks ago."

"Where do they eat now?" Hanna asked, looking around.

"Over there, in those tents." The major pointed. "They used to have a food contract, but when the chow hall burned down the contract went away. The food's better now that the IAs make it themselves."

I shouldn't have been worried about eating with the Iraqis. I had eaten with the Jordanian and Kuwaiti armies before, and I was accustomed to Middle Eastern food. I had also lived in the jungle for six weeks with the Indian army, an experience that virtually guaranteed me the ability to eat anything that was put in front of me. But I was hesitant nonetheless, and I did my best to hide it. The food itself didn't concern me; the rice, grilled fish, and *hobas* (flat bread) were tasty. But watching the young Iraqi *jundi* serve the meal reminded me of the old saying that the surest way to lose your appetite in a restaurant is to watch your food being prepared. As the *jundi* scooped the food from the mess tins with bare, grimy hands, a bevy of black flies crawled in and out of the dishes. I looked around. There were flies everywhere—on the plastic trays, on the utensils, on the rims of drinking glasses, and on the tables. *Just do it*, I told myself, dreading the eventual results. *It's only your intestines*. I silently thanked Ashley for having hounded me continually until I had purchased several packages of probiotics before leaving the States. Encouraged by the U.S. Embassy, Ashley, Emery, and I had taken probiotics every day during our time in India, and we had left that country convinced that our gastrointestinal health had greatly benefited from consuming the pills. Sitting with the Iraqis and plowing food into my mouth, I hoped it would again stave off the shits as it had while I was in New Delhi.

The sandstorm that had begun during our afternoon round of briefings soon kicked up into a full-blown *aajaaz*, and everyone scattered to the safety of their living spaces. When I stepped out of my hut an hour later time seemed to have rolled back to 2003. I laughed crazily and took pictures, remembering the hell it had been to navigate my company in such conditions. With the passage of time and the forgetfulness that comes with it, the storm howling around me became a novelty. I didn't realize that the storms would become a frequent, unwelcome part of our life at COP South.

Chapter 8
Humvees

You make peace with your god very quickly once you go outside the wire.

Never mind the fact that the IED threat has diminished in our area of operations (AO). Never mind the fact that I am riding around in a M1114 HMMWV (high-mobility multipurpose wheeled vehicle, or Humvee) encased in heavy armor plating. And forget about the fact that I have been in this country before. That doesn't matter—this is another time, another war. For five years Americans have been getting blown up by IEDs along the roads in Iraq, and each time we leave the wire I wonder if there is one out there with my name on it.

Looking at my Humvee I know that its bulky, armored silhouette will make it the one vehicle that people most identify with this war, just as they recognize the venerable UH-1 Huey helicopter as the vessel of choice during Vietnam. My Humvee is not the same as the one Americans first got to know during Operation Desert Storm in 1991, nor is it the same as the one that participated in the invasion of Iraq and the long march to Baghdad. That thinly skinned antique is consigned to the history books; the insurgents and foreign fighters have guaranteed that with their ever-expanding and evolving arsenal of deadly roadside bombs.

The vehicle's strategically placed armored plates are not its first line of defense; they are the last. Nor is the Humvee's primary weapon the M240 medium machine gun or the M2 .50-caliber heavy machine gun, although the vehicle is still outfitted with one or the other. Instead, the Humvee's primary method of self-defense is advanced warning from the gunner. The gunner—who once stood exposed behind his machine gun in an open turret but now stands enclosed in a tall parapet of armor and ballistic glass—is the true eyes of the vehicle. He can see more than any of the occupants wedged inside the Humvee, including the driver. And it is his observation skills that will keep us from driving over a pressure strip or past a suspicious piece of garbage with wires protruding from it.

Wrapped in a flame-retardant Nomex flight suit and balaclava, and further encased in a Kevlar helmet, body armor, and small-arms protective insert (SAPI) plating, the gunner resembles a biomechanical robot scanning the horizon for threats. He sweats and swelters in his personal protective equipment (PPE) and groans under the weight of his body armor. But above all else he understands one thing: his personal comfort comes second to the safety of his crew. When I return safely from a patrol or convoy my gunner will have sweated off several pounds, and his back, feet, and knees will ache from the crushing load of the Kevlar and SAPI plates. But I will be alive because the gunner was focusing on his environment and the welfare of his teammates inside the Humvee.

One more thing protects the Humvee, and it is the vehicle's next-to-last line of defense. The job of the Chameleon electronic warfare system is simple: it jams radio frequencies used by potential bombers. We turn it on before leaving the wire, and when the distinctive buzzing from its emissions fills the earpieces of our headsets we wonder aloud if the electromagnetic radiation pulsing through our heads and our bodies will give us brain tumors or merely sterilize us. We complain about the exhaustive training we are forced to undergo to operate the system, but deep down we know that the Chameleon can see what we cannot—enemy radio waves—and by jamming them it might ensure we return to camp standing up, not in a bag.

Inside the Humvee no one is comfortable. Like the gunner, I am sandwiched between layers of Nomex, Kevlar, and ballistic acrylic, and the combination of shock-absorbing padding lining the vehicle's interior, the bank of communications equipment between the driver and vehicle commander (VC), and overflowing cans of ammunition constricts personal movement to a matter of inches. The driver crams himself behind the steering wheel, awkwardly hunched over the steering column, his bulky body armor pushing him farther forward in the seat and forcing his knees up into his chest. If you are tall, you avoid driving whenever possible.

The VC is similarly lodged in his seat to the driver's right. Height is a liability for the VC as well, and he wears pads to alleviate the constant bumping and abuse his knees take against the dashboard or the door. He alternates between reading the computerized display of the Blue Force Tracker (BFT) console to his left, monitoring radio traffic within the patrol, and peering out his half of the ballistic windshield. The IED threat is to the vehicle's front, so the VC leans as far forward as he can, his nose almost touching the windshield, straining to see the road ahead. His vision is blocked by blind spots: the massive, raised tow bar that climbs perilously from the grille, the swaying antennas that flank the hood's front, the support column between windshield and door. Knowing his visual acuity is dulled—and that the driver is experiencing similar limitations to his field of view—the VC relies on the gunner to point out anything suspicious on or alongside the road.

The experience as a "utility man" riding in the back of the Humvee is no less frustrating. Strapped in place by a seat belt like the driver and the vehicle commander, his movement is similarly restricted. Because he often cannot reach them himself, the VC counts on the utility man to manipulate his radios, changing frequency nets as required, and adjusting settings when comm (short for "communications") is bad. The utility man's perspective is the most limited of anyone in the vehicle. Unable to really see what is outside, he resigns himself to sitting in solitude in the darkened interior, waiting silently for the moment the IED goes off next to him. Or under him.

Riding in my Humvee, I put my faith in my fellow Marines, and in the workmanship and attention to detail of the men and women who built my vehicle somewhere in the United States. I trust in the fact that we have the best equipment money can buy, the best in the world, better than any army has ever employed. I hope the intelligence reports we receive are accurate, the ones that say the IED threat in our AO is minimal. I think back to the brief from the last team's intelligence officer, and the way he said, "You are in the safest place in Iraq." I hope he was right, and after each patrol or convoy, when everyone is safe inside the wire and in one piece, I hope my luck holds out the next time we venture outside the wire. Then I remember what Chuck Palahniuk's protagonist said in *Fight Club*:

"'On a long enough time line, the survival rate for everyone drops to zero.'"

I look at the calendar. Seven months can't go fast enough.

Chapter 9
Introductions

I had no idea where the expression "going outside the wire" had originated. It was a term reminiscent of Vietnam. Beyond that I could conjure no contemporary period of static, positional conflict as the war in Iraq had become. But the saying fit the situation in which we currently found ourselves. Each post I had passed through in Iraq on our way to COP South had looked the same from the air: miles upon miles of sand-filled HESCO barriers topped by spiraling bales of razor-sharp concertina wire. As time ticked by I often wondered how many miles of that wire had been strung up throughout Iraq, how many cubic feet of HESCO barriers had been stacked like building blocks. But this detritus of war wasn't limited to the endless Coalition outposts and battle positions dotting the countryside and the urban centers. Coils of concertina wire, tangled into massive, unsalvageable knots of rusting razors, lined the roads and polluted the landscape, and I wondered who would clean it all up once the Americans left the country.

I went outside the wire of COP South for the first time on 4 March. As part of our turnover, the team leader had planned a series of driving tours to cover 3rd Battalion's area of operations (AO) in and around Al Qa'im. Along with Captain Hanna, Master Sergeant Deleon, Lieutenant Bates, and 2nd Lt. Joseph Davidoski (the team's intelligence advisor), the major and several of his Marines and I piled into the team's Humvees for the daylong trip. A ground intelligence officer straight out of school, Joe Davidoski was the most junior officer—and one of the youngest Marines—on the team. A military brat from Virginia Beach, Virginia, Davidoski had at first been a mystery to me. He rarely talked about his family or his background, and initially I was not quite sure where he was from because he never listed his home of record on any paperwork. A bookish graduate of the Virginia Military Institute, he had traveled throughout portions of the Middle East and Central Asia before earning his commission as a second lieutenant. As is typical for those who are unfortunate enough to have complicated last names, he became known as "Lieutenant Ski," or simply "Ski." He was a rabid fitness enthusiast, and his addiction to the CrossFit exercise program and his proclaimed hatred of fat people led several Marines on the team to think he was a robotic health fanatic. But his enthusiasm as a young officer was contagious, and his youthful exuberance and frequent naïveté often reminded me of myself following my entry into the Marine Corps.

Our small convoy drove northeast toward the Euphrates River, pausing briefly on several occasions to navigate Iraqi Police (IP) checkpoints along our route to the Jibab and Almari peninsulas, home to 1st and 2nd companies. In reviewing our planned route for the tour I had misjudged the distance we would be traveling, and it wasn't long before I realized just how far away from the battalion the two companies were located. First Company, garrisoned at Battle Position (BP) Okinawa on the Jibab peninsula, was more than sixty road kilometers from COP South. Second Company, stationed at BP Vera Cruz on the Almari peninsula, was only twelve kilometers closer. The challenges associated with supporting the two companies were daunting. I would later learn that each company was responsible for conducting its own logistical resupply each week with the battalion headquarters at COP South, and communications between the two units and the battalion command element were spotty at best. The cell phone, rather than traditional VHF or HF radios, had become the principal mode of communication for the battalion. And it wasn't unusual for the Iraqi officers and soldiers of the two remote company outposts to feel as if they had been abandoned. Fuel supply was also a significant challenge for the two companies. It was not uncommon for them to run out of fuel before receiving their monthly resupply from the battalion, and as a result the two companies tended to rely more on foot patrols than on mounted vehicle patrols to cover their significant battlespace. It was easier for the two Iraqi company commanders to run their soldiers into the ground with grueling twelve-kilometer foot patrols over rough terrain than it was to request and receive additional fuel for their Humvees. All this I learned from the team leader as we made the monotonous road trip to the two battle positions. They were significant obstacles to the battalion's eventual success, but the major spoke of the issue as if it were no more important than deciding what was on the evening's dinner menu. It had been a long seven-month deployment for his team, and it was quickly becoming apparent to me that challenges such as fuel delivery were merely a drop in the proverbial bucket.

The distance to Almari and Jibab presented another challenge for the team: the danger of IEDs along the protracted route. Although the intelligence briefings we had received en route to COP South had indicated a minimal IED threat in our AO, the simple fact remained: on every trip we made to Vera Cruz and Okinawa, we would be on the road for a long time. Long road marches meant long periods of intense observation for each vehicle crew, and experience told me that the Marines could remain vigilant in their vehicles only for so long. Over the years the insurgents had adapted their tactics and IED-emplacing techniques, with the primary initiation device in the AO now being the pressure strip. We knew that our electronic warfare systems, which were designed to counter radio-controlled IEDs, would be ineffective against pressure strips. But the team leader and his intelligence officer alleviated some of our concerns; there had not been an IED strike in our AO south of the Euphrates River in anyone's memory. Most IED discoveries and detonations had been confined to the routes north of the Euphrates, and the last Marine to have been killed by an IED strike in the Al Qa'im AO had died in October 2007. It was a comforting fact, but we were warned to remain alert regardless. All agreed that the moment we let down our guard, the enemy was likely to hit us.

BP Okinawa was a newer outpost, and its condition and martial cleanliness made me think we were rolling into a Coalition camp. Crushed gravel blanketed the compound, tactical vehicles were parked in orderly rows along the HESCO walls, and there was a general absence of the blowing trash and garbage that seemed everywhere once we left the wire. The 1st Company commander, *Raad* (Major) Muthafer, welcomed us, and his tentative grasp of English made communication with him easier for all parties involved. We shared a meal with him and his troops, and the team left the battle position with an elevated but false sense of confidence in the two distant outposts.

Our bubble burst as we headed west and entered the entry control point (ECP) of BP Vera Cruz. The clean and professional appearance of BP Okinawa had been the opposite of what we had expected, and our arrival at Vera Cruz brought us back down to earth. The compound—which in the past had been occupied by numerous Marine units before being transferred to Iraqi army control—had since fallen into disarray and seemed to be disintegrating before our very eyes. In the preceding years BP Vera Cruz had been subject to almost daily mortar bombardment, and all of the billeting and work spaces had been reinforced with lumber and sandbags to provide some measure of overhead cover for the troops garrisoned there. One indication of the earlier violence in the AO appeared on the inside of a wooden hatch to one of the bunkers. In a display of gallows humor, some nameless Marine from 3rd Battalion, 4th Marines had recorded with scribbled drawings each time they had taken direct fire and mortar fire; each instance when they had either discovered an IED or a weapons cache; and every time they had been struck by an IED. The door's face was filled from top to bottom with crude stencils of AK-47s, mortar rounds, and circular bombs.

There was no doubt about it—the place was a shithole. Open refuse pits overflowing with garbage and plastic Aquafina bottles festered along the path leading into the compound, and a sour smell hung low over the encampment. We were overwhelmed by flies the moment we exited our vehicles, and when Marines wandered off to relieve themselves they returned quickly, gagging and cursing. A makeshift outhouse had been erected in one corner of the camp overlooking a steep wadi, which in turn ran into a valley that sloped toward the Euphrates. The outhouse overflowed from constant use, and the wadi into which it emptied similarly spilled over with human feces and thousands of empty Aquafina bottles. The stench was overpowering, and it drifted in an invisible, choking fog throughout the camp. Major Za'id, 2nd Company's commander, was the soft-spoken and diminutive leader of a troop of unmotivated and undisciplined officers and soldiers, and the challenge that faced us as the incoming mentors for such a group was an overwhelming one. The differences in abilities between Muthafer and Za'id were obvious, a fact most clearly demonstrated by the striking dissimilarities between the two camps. While it was true that Vera Cruz was significantly older than Okinawa, the disorganization and general filthiness of Vera Cruz was a direct reflection of Za'id's lack of leadership.

We returned to COP South, the trip back as uneventful as the one to the battle positions earlier that morning. Our first trip outside the wire had been no different than any of the patrols we had conducted during our predeployment training, and despite the mottled landscape you would have never guessed a war was still going on. The ordinary convoy underscored the words of the current MiTT's intelligence officer, who had told us the previous day that Al Qa'im was "the safest place in Iraq." But there was still cause for concern. There had been a rash of new IED discoveries in the AO recently (including radio-controlled devices), and the last thing we needed was to allow ourselves to become complacent just because it had been so quiet lately. After all, we had just gotten there.

That evening the team leader took me to meet the man who would become my counterpart for the next seven months. *Muqaddam Rukn* (Staff Lieutenant Colonel) Ayad, the 3rd Battalion commander, was a portly, round-faced man whose congenial appearance reminded me of a younger, jollier version of Saddam Hussein. A member of the Al Karbuli tribe from Ramadi, he had been an officer in Saddam's army, evidenced by his insistence on routinely donning the khaki service uniform of the old army. In time I would learn that Ayad was firmly entrenched in the old way of doing things. But during our first meeting he preached about the importance of empowering junior officers and NCOs. He smiled a lot, and throughout our conversation he acted genuinely happy to meet me and to have my team aboard. I fell for the act, and at the conclusion of our meeting I left thinking how fortunate I was to be working alongside someone of his caliber.

I wasn't the only one getting to know a new Iraqi counterpart. While the major and I conversed through our interpreter with Ayad, Lieutenant Bates was in the process of meeting his counterparts in the battalion's S-3 (operations) section. Bates was more fortunate than I; his counterpart, *Naqeeb* (Captain) Al'aa, was a self-taught English-speaking officer. Tall and wavy-haired, Al'aa could typically be seen sporting outsized aviator sunglasses whenever he was away from his hut, which was not often. He usually spent most of his time ensconced behind his computer monitor chatting with the love of his life, a woman in Baghdad named Nadia whom he had found online. The word on the streets was that the two had never actually met in person, but you never would have guessed it from the amount of time he spent communicating virtually with her online. A product of the new Iraqi army, Al'aa believed in exercising initiative and conducting proper planning and coordination, but he lacked the trust and confidence of Lieutenant Colonel Ayad. While at first Bates tolerated Al'aa's obsession with Nadia, eventually it became necessary for him to put his foot down. As time wore on, Bates was frequently compelled to tell Al'aa, "Say good-bye to Nadia, *sadie* [sir]. We have work to do."

Al'aa wasn't the only English-speaking officer. *Mulaazem* (Second Lieutenant) Anwar, the 3rd Company XO, was another young, intelligent officer who spent a significant amount of time hanging out in Al'aa's hut. He shared many of Al'aa's "new army" ideas about leadership and planning, yet like Lieutenant Colonel Ayad he was a veteran of the old Iraqi army. I would later learn that Anwar had fought the Marines in 2003 along Highway 1 near Ad Diwaniyah, the same stretch of road my company had rolled through during the war's launch. Once that information got out, a rumor began to circulate within the battalion that my company and I had fought against and killed Anwar's men five years earlier. Although factually incorrect, it was a rumor I wasn't inclined to quash. The existence of such stories was an unspoken reminder to the Iraqis that I had been there before under less cordial and friendly circumstances. Who among them knew whether I would unleash hell on them again if they didn't cooperate with me and my men? Power was everything in the Iraqi culture, and such stories would perhaps bestow power upon me. I needed any edge I could get, so it was folklore I was willing to keep alive.

Bates' meeting with Al'aa and Anwar was essentially no different than a group of American junior officers hanging out and shooting the shit together.

A television tuned in to an inane Iraqi channel called Smash TV blared nonstop American music videos in the background, and the group smoked cigarettes and drank glass after glass of hot, sweet chai tea. It was the way business was done, and in time it would differ little from my own meetings with Ayad. Turnover discussions with the outgoing team indicated that our working relationships with the 3rd Battalion officers and SNCOs would be formed during nightly meetings such as these, and little to nothing would ever be accomplished during the hours of daylight. When asked about the best way to cope with such a situation, one officer from the outgoing team simply replied, "Learn to stay up late." We were in *their* country, on *their* time, and they expected us to adapt to *them*, not the other way around.

It was going to be a long seven months.

Chapter 10

IAs

Although I have been in Iraq previously, my experience with the Iraqi army (IA) before becoming an advisor has been limited. There was a brief interaction with the fledgling Iraqi Civil Defense Corps in 2004, but beyond that my only view of the Iraqi army was through my weapon's sights during the war's invasion. Now my team and I live with them, and as each day passes I learn something new about them. I don't always like what I see.

The *junood* come in all shapes and sizes. Most are short, scrawny boys who look barely out of their teens. They wander around camp wide-eyed, unsure what they are supposed to be doing. Their AK-47s are monstrous in their arms, and I often wonder if they will know how to employ them when the time comes. We know that most of the soldiers have never even fired their rifles, and despite our pleas to the commanders of the battalion and brigade to authorize live-fire training we are constantly snubbed. Ammunition costs money and must be accounted for, and the senior Iraqi officers are unwilling to expend the personal energy required to properly train their men.

The soldiers wear frayed, baggy uniforms that hang on their slight frames like limp sails, billowing out when a strong wind blows through camp. Some show off equipment they have managed to scavenge over the years: U.S.-issue boots and gloves and ballistic glasses. Others wear aging, olive-drab magazine bandoliers and berets—holdovers from the old Iraqi army days. There is no uniformity to how they dress, and their mismatched uniforms and body armor reflect the inability of the Iraqi army to properly outfit its troops. The result is the appearance of a ragtag band of children playing war, not really understanding how to act or what is expected of them.

The Iraqi officers also seem to adhere to no particular uniform dress code. Most wear old American tricolor camouflage—both woodland and desert patterns—while others don British camouflage, or tan flight suits like the MiTT team. One day at a regional security meeting (RSM) I count twelve different uniforms sitting at the table, and on another occasion a senior Iraqi officer from 7th Division shows up at our camp clothed in a set of Marine Corps pixilated desert camouflage. I am angered to the point of speechlessness. The MiTT team is not authorized to allow its interpreters to wear this uniform, yet no one higher in the Coalition chain of command does anything to stop this senior Iraqi officer from wearing it. Apparently some standards are flexible for our Iraqi counterparts.

Red berets are the norm, and almost every officer wears parachute jump wings on his left breast even though it is commonly known that few—if any—of them have actually been to jump school. I know that there is nothing we can do about the uniforms. Perhaps one day the Iraqi army will get its act together and standardize what its troops wear, but in the meantime it will remain low on the priority list. There are bigger fish to fry.

When the *junood* aren't going on patrol or standing guard duty they are talking on cell phones. As each day winds to a close and the sun dips toward the horizon, the berm that encloses the camp fills with the squatting silhouettes of soldiers calling friends and loved ones on their cells. They don't always wait until the day is over. From our team's COC we watch the tower guards through our observation camera. Few actually stand guard. Instead, they chat on their phones, sit, squat, or sleep. When we alert the battalion's Sergeant of the Guard and show him these transgressions on the video monitor he becomes furious and storms out to the guard towers. He collects the offenders, shaves their heads, and throws them in *jundi* jail, a makeshift camp prison that is nothing more than an empty, guarded hut with no air-conditioning. With the installation of the camera we are constantly able to identify soldiers shirking their duties, and on each occasion the offenders are placed in custody. After a while so many soldiers have been put in *jundi* jail that we wonder if there will be anyone left to stand guard.

The *junood* also spend their free time playing soccer. Although they frequently mope around camp and sluggishly perform their duties with no vigor or motivation, as soon as they hit the soccer field they become energized. They dart back and forth across the field, shouting, kicking the ball to each other, knocking down their opponents, and releasing their pent-up frustrations. One day they challenge the MiTT team to a soccer match, and it isn't long before they are wiping our asses all over the playing field. The Marines are in top physical shape, yet the *junood* run circles around them and mock them. Many even play in their bare feet, negotiating rocks and divots that are strewn across the hard-packed dirt field. The soldiers know that on the battlefield the Marines are unmatched, but on the soccer field they can be defeated.

The Outlanders quickly learn that the only way to get anything done with the IAs is at night. During the day the IA officers retreat to their huts to sleep or surf the Internet. Most only work at night, and even then their work competes with blaring televisions and stereos. We sit with the officers, drinking glass after glass of steaming-hot chai tea. The tea is served in tiny glasses, and the spoons that come with the tea stand up straight in the thick silt of sugar that rests at the glass's bottom. The tea is usually served to the officers by a "chai boy," some poor bastard of an enlisted man whose only duty is to act as an officer's manservant. The officers act as if the chai boy doesn't even exist, and they forget themselves when they are talking. The chai boys say nothing but hear everything, and so anything that is discussed in the officers' huts is soon repeated throughout camp. Operational security is nonexistent. The only time the officers speak to the chai boys is when the tea is cold, or when the food is not cooked properly. The Marines cringe at the display of personal servitude.

Most of the IA officers smoke incessantly, and even when they know that a particular Marine does not smoke they still offer him cigarettes. Although I am trying to quit smoking I accept their offers when I am with them, hoping that by partaking I will gain their respect and will get more accomplished with them. Peer pressure is not just limited to high school. Other Marines refuse to smoke with the IAs, and even though I don't attempt to convince them to do so I know that one way to be successful as an advisor is to occasionally surrender your pride and judgment. Regardless, any fear the Marines may have of the dangers of secondhand smoke must be suppressed, because they know that they are in the IAs' huts, and the IAs can do whatever they want. If the Marines don't like it, they can leave. The IAs won't care.

The IAs routinely invite the Marines to eat with them, whether it is in the mess tents or the officers' quarters. The food served to the officers is superior to what the enlisted soldiers get, yet the IA officers don't feel the same guilt that the Marine officers do when they eat better than the troops. The quality of the food served to the officers is manifested by their bulging bellies. Most senior officers sport paunches that hang over their belts, and some are so grossly overweight that the buttons of their shirts strain against the load, threatening to pop off and put out someone's eye.

On special occasions we are invited to feast with the IAs, what the Marines have come to refer to as a "goat grab." The chai boys arrive with giant round platters heaped high with piles of steaming rice and mutton, and once it is all served the officers dig in with their bare hands. The Marines follow suit, tearing off chunks of lamb and mashing them together with the rice before stuffing the gooey mess into their mouths. Occasionally when the battalion commander spies a particularly good piece of meat he tears it off the bone and drops it in front of me, and as I pop it in my mouth I wonder if he washed his hands before the meal. The Iraqi officers eat before the enlisted soldiers, and in time I realize that once the platters are served we have approximately ten minutes to eat our fill before getting nudged aside by the *junood*, who attack the leftovers like starved dogs. They place the platters on the floor and squat around them in groups, picking through the bones and scattered rice, seeking hidden treasures missed by their officers. The *junood* are happy, because whenever there is a goat grab they know they will finally get a decent meal.

The *junood* suffer a miserable existence aboard COP South. Their officers live a good life, and the *junood* know it. Each day I wonder what drives the soldiers to remain in the army, to carry out orders directed by officers and a system that appear not to care about them or their welfare. Do they do it for pay? Camaraderie? The security of their country? Or do they serve because it is the only option they have available to them? I don't know. I may never know. The stories and hardships written on their faces depress me, because eventually I accept the fact that I have little chance of improving their situation. Only the Iraqi officers can change the plight of their soldiers; whether they choose to heed my advice and do so is not up to me. I am disheartened, yes, but at the same time I am enlightened, and more than anything I resolve to continue where the *junood*'s officers and their system have failed—I resolve to take better care of my own Marines in the future.

Chapter 11
Growing Pains

We were barely three days into our turnover with the outgoing team before we were wishing they would move on and let us take over operations. I knew it was important not to rush the process. Despite all of the training and briefings we had received prior to our arrival we were still in the dark and needed all the turnover and exchange of information we could get. Advisor duty is far from an exact science, and word of mouth and relaying personal experiences and techniques is always better than reading it in a book. But after three days the camp was already becoming too small for two teams, and the strains were beginning to show.

During our training at ATG I had worried aloud to Ashley that I was not cut out for the independent nature of transition team duty. An instructor and previous advisor had curtly informed us that, among other things, advisor duty requires strong organizational abilities and a capacity to thrive in an uncertain, unstructured environment. An ability, he had proclaimed, to operate "in the gray area." I, on the other hand, tended to flourish in just the opposite: structured working environments with an established daily routine and "battle rhythm." But my concerns were brushed aside by my wife, who insisted that perhaps unbeknownst to me I actually possessed such abilities. As an example, she reminded me of all the previous moves our family had made since we had married in 2001. In six years of marriage we had moved five different times, and she noted that each time we arrived at our new home the very first thing I did was throw myself into organizing our household. Her observation further reminded me of my years as the child of a career naval officer. My family had, on average, moved to a new location every two years, and—as I would later repeat in my adult life—the first thing I would do at each new house was to put my bedroom in order. In the chaotic, uncertain life of a military brat it was one small way of controlling my surroundings. That obsessive trait had carried over into my adult years, often to my wife's amusement.

Now, as a team leader, I realized I had been blessed with a group of officers and SNCOs who were perhaps as anal as I was, and they too became fixated with organizing the camp and implementing much-needed changes around our living areas. But our insistence on immediate change rankled the members of the outgoing team, and friction between the two groups of Marines began to surface early in our turnover process. At one point the team leader told me that his Marines were complaining about my team already making noticeable modifications around the camp (such as the kitchen remodeling that Marines from my team had undertaken). He implored me not to make any changes in the camp or the daily routine until the turnover process was complete and they were gone. Despite my desire to assume control of the camp and the mission I honored his request and passed it on to my Marines. "Wait for the old team to leave," I told them. "After that, it's open house."

The growing pains we seemed to be experiencing with the outgoing team made it difficult for us not to adopt a superiority complex. It was common for inbound units to get sucked into the mind-set of "The outgoing unit is all screwed up, and we are perfect." Conversely, it was just as common for outgoing units to think that the inbound unit was a bunch of idiots who would ruin all of the hard work and achievements that had been accomplished. But appearances mean a lot, as do first impressions, and our first impression of the outbound team had not been a glowing one. They were not bad guys, or bad Marines for that matter. On the contrary, many of them were genuinely intelligent and good at their jobs as officers and SNCOs. But the impression they had created upon our arrival was that they had gone native, an unforgivable sin that we had constantly been warned about in all of our predeployment training and briefs. Relaxing standards was always the commander's prerogative if he deemed it so, but even that had its limits.

And the outgoing team members complained a lot, mostly about the Marine infantry battalion to which they were attached. They claimed the battalion never supported them, but instead routinely neglected them and their logistical and operational needs. As I heard the mantra repeated over and over again, I had to wonder whether their complaints were legitimate or baseless. Was it truly as they claimed, that the Marine battalion didn't understand the nature of transition team operations? Or had the battalion over time developed the same impression of the outgoing team that we had in our short time working with them? Only time would tell.

As the team leader and I met with Lieutenant Colonel Ayad on the evening of 5 March it was obvious that the Iraqi commander was agitated about the state of the oil pipeline that ran east to west through 3rd Battalion's AO. He had visited a stretch of the pipeline earlier in the day, discovering more than thirty locations along the route where the line had been tapped by oil smugglers. As he irately pointed at photographs on his digital camera, I noted how the fissures ranged from crudely formed hammer and chisel punctures to what appeared to be square, professionally cut holes made by skilled smugglers. There were believed to be two types of oil thieves cutting into the pipeline: common Iraqis seeking crude oil to use for their own homes, and professional smugglers who may or may not have been using the profits from smuggled oil to finance terrorist and criminal activities in the region around Al Qa'im. It seemed a stretch, but nevertheless 28th Brigade had directed Ayad to step up antismuggling operations in his battalion's AO. He appeared to embrace the mission wholeheartedly, and I in turn volunteered my team's services to assist his soldiers and staff in training for observation post (what the IAs called "ambush") operations. Ayad seemed interested in what I had to offer, and I was pleased that the team soon would be gainfully employed.

As I spoke through an interpreter named Joseph, I gained my first insight into the challenges associated with working through foreign linguists. Our Arabic language instruction at ATG had been worthless, taught by an Iraqi dissident known only by his first name. Legend had it that he had been involved in high-level covert operations earlier in the war, and while he thankfully didn't make a habit of regaling us with stories of working with Special Forces, he instead spent most of his instruction time spewing profanity-laden invective about working as an interpreter in Iraq. Accordingly, our learning of Iraqi Arabic suffered, and most Marines on the team departed ATG with little more than a bastardized working knowledge of basic greetings and salutations. We were forced to rely solely on our interpreters to communicate with the Iraqis, and with that came its own set of challenges.

Joseph was a native interpreter from Basra, and he had been assigned to 3rd Battalion since its inception more than three years earlier. A tiny, wiry, bespectacled man in his forties, he had been an educator in a previous life and spoke with a crisp but often disdainful tone of voice. I had not developed an opinion of Joseph one way or another, however, until my conversation with Ayad turned to my background in South Asia. When the subject of my language capabilities was raised, I noted to Ayad that the Urdu script was derived from Arabic and Farsi, and that many of the words I knew in Urdu were the same in Arabic. At that point Joseph chose to correct what I had said, telling Ayad that I was wrong and that there was no written language the same as Arabic. I felt the color rising from beneath my collar, and

I restrained myself from correcting him. The last thing I wanted to do was engage Joseph in a semantic argument in front of Ayad and the outgoing team leader, and so rather than embarrass both him and myself I chose to keep my mouth shut. We had been taught always to keep our cool in front of the Iraqis, but we had also learned that interpreters are supposed to translate *what* we were saying, not what they *thought* we should be saying. Nor were interpreters supposed to speak off topic or offer their own opinions. Joseph had violated both tenants, and it incensed me. His actions caused me to suspect him and his abilities, and I resolved from that point forward to rely more on the three interpreters who had trained with us in the United States and accompanied us to Iraq.

The six interpreters we would inherit from the outgoing team were, like Joseph, all local nationals, and from the outset I had not been impressed with them or their abilities. Over time they had grown too comfortable with their life at COP South, and as we observed the outgoing team interact with them it often seemed as if the Marines constantly had to convince the interpreters to do their jobs. They ambled around camp dressed only in shorts, T-shirts, and sandals, and they tended to monopolize the Internet stations and phones in the MWR hut. As a whole they rarely participated in daily duties around the compound, and they never seemed to clean up after themselves anywhere they went. Upon inspection of their hut I was appalled; their living spaces were filthy, littered with old food and cigarette butts. Yet they complained that the three interpreters who had arrived with us were "too good to live with them." In general they acted as if they didn't care about their jobs or what it was the transition teams were trying to do in Iraq. Instead, the sole source of motivation for them seemed to be an almost weekly insistence that they be allowed to go home on leave.

The interpreters who had traveled with us from Camp Pendleton brought with them their own unique set of challenges. From the outset they began complaining about what they considered to be "quality-of-life" issues aboard the camp. To them everything was inadequate, whether it was the quality of food, living spaces, or the hygiene facilities. They also seemed to resent our insistence that they participate in the daily cleanup and maintenance duties around camp. As Marines we were accustomed to living in austere conditions, yet life aboard COP South could hardly be considered austere. After all, we had beds, showers, satellite television, Internet access, and phones. There was also the fact that the three of them had volunteered to deploy with the Marines—not the Army—and I had made it abundantly clear to the team prior to departing the United States what we could expect in terms of living conditions once we were in-country. None of that seemed to matter to the three interpreters, though, and in the first days and weeks following our arrival I grew exhausted with their constant repetition of the phrase "My contract says . . ."

In the end their grumblings fell on deaf ears. The Marines too had all once signed contracts, yet none of them was coming to me every day complaining that shitting in a bag was a violation of the terms of their agreement. Life is frequently hard for Marines in the field; we were used to it.

Chapter 12
Storms

The blowing *aajaaz* forms on the horizon, and I wish I could run for cover. I know the destruction and personal discomfort the sandstorm announces, and were it possible I would cocoon myself in a hermetically sealed container until the air cleared and the skies once again filled with the deep azure that has become one of the only things I admire about the desert.

The atmosphere feels electric and pressurized, almost heavy on my shoulders, and it feels as if my ears will pop as they do when aboard an airplane at altitude. The view of my immediate surroundings is unaltered, save for the horizon, which becomes shrouded in what appears an impenetrable blanket of dirty fog. The wind picks up, and soon garbage and debris flutter through the camp as if they too are seeking refuge from the gathering storm.

Knowing what is coming, I rush to protect my personal belongings and prepare my body for the physical onslaught it is about to endure. Clothing is stored in plastic ziplock bags, and towels are wedged against doorjambs to staunch the invasion of dust that the storm shepherds. Computers and other electronics are sealed in plastic or under heavy blankets in a vain attempt to preserve their inner parts. But I have been here before, and I know what happens to even the toughest laptop computers after a heavy sandstorm. The first symptom is the keypad that begins to stick and jam once depressed, turning the simple act of typing into a forceful, conscious effort. I know what comes next: slow, unresponsive operation of the machine, followed by the dull, grinding death rattle of sand and dust that has been injected into the compact disc drive and the eventually the hard drive itself. My computer's life becomes finite, and more than ever I understand the requirement to back up my data as often as I can remember to do so.

I dig through my pack and retrieve my *shemagh*, that checkered-pattern Arabic headwrap so despised by commanders for its un-uniformity but beloved by Marines for its secret ability to warm, to cool, to filter the airborne particulate matter that characterizes the *aajaaz*. Wrapping my head in the *shemagh* I resemble a uniformed terrorist, but I don't care. I grab my goggles and mount them on my forehead, prepared at a moment's notice to cinch them down tightly over my eyes. Then I watch the horizon and wait.

The wind intensifies, and soon the desert howls in our ears in a scream of tortured pain, a cry like it is being torn apart. Anything not strapped down rattles in its own attempt to escape, and the fragile wooden huts shake and moan with the echoes of the gale. My eyes water uncontrollably and sting from the needlelike sand and dust particles that infiltrate the goggles, and my mouth and nose both seal shut in a thick brown cake of grit and dried mucus and saliva.

On one occasion I am unlucky enough to be stuck in a moving convoy during a storm. My world shrinks into a tiny prism and my mind becomes as focused as the narrow field of view from within the vehicle. Visibility worsens and the road ahead of me begins to disappear from sight, being eaten alive by the storm's fury. For some bizarre reason civilian traffic continues unabated. Their inability to see our approaching convoy and their sudden, palpable fear as our vehicles emerge from the storm only feet away causes them to brake and swerve crazily, endangering themselves and our convoy. We continue our movement, common sense screaming at me to pull over and wait out the tempest. But a burning desire to get the team back inside the wire forces me forward, and I assume the risk. We have reached the point of no return, the point where it would be senseless to turn around and head back to our point of origin, and so we slow our speed to a crawl, and my vehicle commanders begin a continuous chatter that fills the air waves. The tension in their voices is evident as they too navigate their way through the din, and the radio is a chorus of warnings and acknowledgements.

"Vic One, slowing down."

"Roger, Vic One slowing down."

"Vic Two, stopping."

"Roger, Vic Two stopping."

"Vic One, moving."

"Roger, moving."

Kilometers trickle by, and what is normally a one-hour convoy becomes two or three. Time stands still, and my single point of reference becomes the slowly vanishing highway to my front.

The team returns safely to the compound, and as the day's end approaches the hidden afternoon sun begins its slow descent toward the horizon. Its dying rays electrify the sand and dust that permeate the air, and the sky glows first a blinding amber, followed by a brilliant orange, then sepia, and finally a deep blood red. The crimson skies and reddened billiard table terrain that surrounds me is not the planet of my birth, but instead a world that is both inhospitable and malevolent. Visibility drops from feet to inches, and I know that the moment the sun dips below the horizon a shroud of inky blackness will envelop us. The headlamp strapped to my forehead transforms me into a hapless miner, and I trudge my way through the void as if searching for the exit from a bottomless shaft. The neon glow of the headlamp magnifies the flying dust into charged electrons before my eyes, and my constricted vision fills with a humming, vibrating picture tube screeching a cacophony of white noise.

There is only one place to be, and that is in the safety of my hut. But the efforts to barricade my sanctuary fail, and the dust penetrates the hidden cracks and crevices, clandestine points of entry known only to the storm and the fleet of mice that creep in nightly to feast on my hidden stash of PowerBars and SweeTarts. Hazy and gray, the suspended dust cloud defeats all efforts to protect my belongings and myself. As I begin to cough and hack and choke, I eagerly await morning.

Waking comes with a convulsive coughing fit, and I reach for a tissue to evacuate the scorched, clogged sinuses that feel as if they have been filled in by a cement mixer. I blow, jagged strips of pain exiting my nostrils, and when I look at the aftermath I am disgusted by the ropy brown and green afterbirth strings of bloody discharge. Coughing consumptively, I wonder what it is like to have tuberculosis. The enamel of my teeth loses a little more luster from the storm's grit lining my mouth, and more than anything I want water. Water, and a shower.

Damage-assessment time is upon me, and I evaluate my surroundings inside the hut. The dust has settled, but a heavy film of grime plasters the walls, the floor, everything I own. I step outside into the crystal light of morning, the vacant skies divulging no trace of the previous evening's maelstrom. My teammates likewise stagger out of their hiding places, digging out from the disaster. I laugh and joke with them, pointing to their filthy faces and my own. I am relieved. The storm is gone.

Another day begins.

Chapter 13
Outside the Wire

Four days into our turnover the team leader and I reached an objective always greeted by the outgoing commander with relief and met by the incoming commander with apprehension and dread: signing over custody of all equipment on the unit's consolidated memorandum receipt (CMR). The team had already been outfitted with a host of new gear prior to leaving Camp Pendleton, everything from new body armor to night-vision goggles (NVGs). Each Marine was issued the exact same set of equipment, something I was not used to. In my earlier experiences in the fleet there had never been enough of certain items to go around, including NVGs, personal radios, and side arms. But the independent nature of the MiTT teams—the fact that we would be operating on our own and often away from each other—necessitated that each man receive the same equipment for the job.

The issued gear we brought with us made each Marine a formidable being, and the equipment we inherited at COP South only enhanced our capabilities as a team that much more. Our inventory was especially heavy on communications equipment, with an entire suite that included not only UHF and VHF radios, but also an HF satellite communications (SATCOM) set and an updated version of the Blue Force Tracker (BFT) system my company had experimented with in 2003. A host of laptop computers completed the electronics inventory, and once it was all put together it created an impressive command-and-control capability for the team. Overall, the number of serialized items on the CMR itself was not huge—nothing compared to what I had once signed for in my LAV company—but what it lacked in numbers it more than made up for in dollars. Signing for the inventory and assuming responsibility for the equipment was enough to make me break out in a cold sweat.

While I busied myself with completing the inventory, Bates, Grubb, and Davidoski set out with several Marines from the outgoing team to participate in a cordon-and-search mission in Karabilah with 3rd Company. Following a hasty brief by 3rd Battalion's S-2 (intelligence) officer, the company and the Marines sped out of the camp to the city's *souq* (market), where they searched the area for IED-making facilities. Although they never found the suspected site, 3rd Company ended up detaining four individuals (including someone who had been placed on their watch list).

Upon their return the three lieutenants briefed me on the operation, and while I was pleased that they had thrown themselves into the mix and were already taking the initiative both with missions and with the Iraqis, my lack of situational awareness about exactly what they would be doing before they left the camp gave me cause for concern. But my uneasiness was not directed at the lieutenants. Throughout the course of our training together I had become comfortable with their abilities; although Davidoski had not previously deployed to Iraq, Bates and Grubb already had plenty of experience outside the wire. I was more concerned with the hasty planning and execution demonstrated by the IAs. The debrief the officers provided me indicated that the Iraqi plan had essentially amounted to this: *We think there is a bomb-making factory somewhere around here. Let's go find it.*

Such a lack of proper mission planning could eventually lead to a catastrophe, and so for future operations I mandated mission products for each occasion team members went outside the wire. Whether it was an operation with the IAs or a simple resupply convoy to Camp Al Qa'im, the designated patrol leader would be required to generate an operations order, a mission storyboard, and a post-mission debrief and after-action report. The purpose of the products was threefold: to ensure all members of the patrol knew what was going on; to enable the team's COC to track the mission; and to guarantee that learning points from each operation could be disseminated throughout the team. The products would also serve as a historical record of the team's operations, whether it was for command chronology purposes or for command investigations if something ever went awry during a mission. It was a decision that met with some derision by several members of the team, who initially felt shackled by the premission requirements I had levied. The hurried, reckless mission planning demonstrated by the Iraqis—a trait that would come to characterize the majority of their operations—placed a heavy burden on the team to generate the required mission products in time before the IAs sped out of the camp, but I didn't care. If a combined operation with the Iraqis went to hell I didn't want it to be because the Marines hadn't done their part to ensure mission success.

The Outlanders didn't have long to complain about the new requirements I had imposed. The following day the majority of the team left the wire on its first solo mission. It was a simple logistical convoy to Camp Al Qa'im, but since every trip outside the wire counted as a mission the Marines prepared for it as such. Although I ached to accompany them I still had turnover work to do, and so I cut the apron strings early and let them do their jobs the way they had trained to do them. I rose early to observe Staff Sergeant Leek brief the patrol, and as the Humvees rolled past me and out of the compound I made eye contact with each gunner, pointed to my eyes, and mouthed the words "Keep your eyes open." There wasn't much more to do or say. I was nervous watching them exit friendly lines on their own; simple convoy or not, a trip outside the wire is a trip outside the wire. After all, plenty of other Marines had bought the farm while on simple convoys. For some bizarre reason I felt the way my own parents must have felt the first time I pulled out of the driveway after I received my driver's license. But at the same time I knew that together my Marines were in good hands. They had trained hard, had practiced their immediate-action drills and standing operating procedures (SOPs), and had learned each others' capabilities and limitations. They were more than ready. And, sure enough, several hours later they rolled back through friendly lines safe and sound. It was an uneventful mission, they told me. I was glad, and pleased to have them back.

Late on the afternoon of 6 March the outgoing team leader, Lieutenant Colonel Ayad, and I hopped aboard a UH-1N Huey for an aerial reconnaissance flight around 3rd Battalion's AO. The helicopter soared north to the Euphrates River, and as we traced the steep, curving banks of the waterway I thought back to the last time I had ridden on a Huey. It had been a similar recon flight, but along the banks of the Tigris River as my battalion secured Tikrit. Now as we flew over the Euphrates its electric greens and blues mesmerized me, and my thoughts again drifted to five years earlier and the first time I had traversed the river. My company had crossed in a dead area of marshland nearly devoid of vegetation, and the river itself had barely amounted to more than a muddy, silted trickle. Five years later and two hundred miles upstream, however, the river was wide and aqua blue, and its cultivated banks teemed with human and animal life.

Our flight continued east past the Almari and Jibab peninsulas, and then south over the Coalition base, Camp Al Qa'im, and a nearby oil-pumping station designated on the map as T-1. Camp Al Qa'im—known among the Marines simply as "AQ"—was the major American outpost in western Al Anbar, and was home to the Marine battalion task force responsible for the Al Qa'im region. A sprawling camp built around an old Iraqi railroad station and maintenance hub, AQ was a maze of converging railroad tracks, abandoned railcars, and massive warehouses capable of storing and maintaining railcars, locomotives, and other heavy equipment. The facility was further crowded by hundreds of stacked shipping containers,

SWA huts, tents, generators, and containerized living spaces called "cans." The standard amenities common to all FOBs were present at AQ: a contracted chow hall, an air-conditioned gym and movie room, an Internet café, a post office, a laundry facility, and a post exchange (PX). There was even a small shop run by local Iraqis—called the "hajji store"—where Marines could purchase bootleg DVD copies of newly released movies. AQ was our team's mother ship, and in time it would become a routine convoy destination for us so we could tend to administrative and logistical matters. But, like all other FOBs, AQ was also subject to the trappings of rear-echelon standard-bearers, and despite our frequent need to be there we tended to avoid it whenever possible.

As the Huey circled the region its escort, an AH-1W Super Cobra gunship, shadowed us, banking in wide S turns and occasionally firing off flares that trailed fiery streamers in its wake. The bright cobalt skies above us seemed to illuminate the landscape, painting it into a portrait completely different from the one I had seen half a decade earlier. I thought back to a conversation I had had with Abu Fayehdi, the Iraqi role player at Mojave Viper. He had told me that the situation now facing us was Iraq's last chance, its final curtain call. If the Iraqi nation didn't succeed now, with the Americans' assistance, it never would. From my seat high above in the helicopter the placid scenery below me seemed devoid of the violence and chaos I had witnessed in the past, and in my bliss I began to convince myself that the country still had a fighting chance.

We returned to the isolation of COP South, and later that evening my predecessor and I again called on Lieutenant Colonel Ayad. After a few minutes of formalities the major turned over the conversation to me, essentially handing me the reins as senior advisor. Although the team leader attended the rest of the meeting, he remained in the wings, speaking only to offer parting advice and seek clarification on issues I had neglected to mention. I had no illusions about achieving any major accomplishments during that initial meeting with Ayad. A relationship had to be built first, and it was only once that foundation had been laid could I hope that Ayad would listen to me and heed my advice. As I clumsily navigated my way through the conversation I slowly realized that I had no idea what the hell I was doing. The Marine Corps can train you for many things—how to fire a weapon, how to give an operations order, how to call in supporting arms—but, as I was quickly discovering, there are some things for which you just cannot prepare. Building a personal relationship and advising a foreign military commander is one of them. One thing was certain: I had my work cut out for me.

Up to that point in my marriage I had not made a habit of being absent on my wife's birthday. As near as I could remember I had only missed it once, and that had been while I was in Kuwait preparing for the invasion. It was ironic that I was missing it this time because I was once again deployed to Iraq. All throughout the day of 8 March I mulled over not being around for Ashley's birthday, and my frustrations were compounded by my inability to communicate with her. The day was spent in long, droning meetings at Camp Al Qa'im and getting acquainted with the various personalities who worked with the Marine infantry battalion task force there. The one bright spot was getting the chance to sit down with and meet the Army Special Forces detachment detailed to the camp. They were unlike any group of servicemen I had ever met. They resembled less a military unit than they did a group of backpackers and hikers, but their professionalism was obvious. The outgoing team had worked with the detachment in the past, and as we talked with them I grew to like them. Low-key but personable, they were a good bunch of guys. Their team leader, a short, mustachioed captain known only as "Pete," welcomed us back any time.

The team returned to COP South that night, and several hours later Lieutenant Ski called me to the COC with news. The battalion's S-2 shop had planned another cordon-and-search mission in Karabilah and was asking for our support on the operation that evening. I thought about the skimpy plan that had just been briefed to me and looked at Ski.

"That's all they have? A hunch that something's there?"

"Yes, sir," he replied. "They're ready to go right now."

I thought about the team, most of whom were still cleaning their equipment and winding down from the day's business at Camp Al Qa'im. There was no doubt that they would willingly put their gear right back on and head out with the IAs if I directed it, but suddenly I wasn't so sure it was such a good idea. A lot of things needed to happen in a short period. Patrol members needed to be assigned, briefs and orders had to be completed, and vehicles and gear had to be prepared. As I considered the requirements, Lieutenant Grubb jumped in.

"Sir, our weapons aren't zeroed yet," he pointed out. "After the banging up they took on the trip here we can't be sure they are still holding their BZOs [battle-sight zeros]."

Captain Hanna, who until that moment had stood in the corner without commenting, finally spoke up.

"I recommend we pass, sir. Grubb has a good point, and I don't think we can meet their timeline with everything we have to do."

I turned back to Ski and Bates.

"All right, canc [cancel] it. Ski, let the S-2 know. Bates, let Captain

Al'aa also know that we can't support it. Tell them we'll get them next time around, provided they give us a better plan."

A pattern had begun, one in which the IAs would come to us at the last minute and expect us to jump through hoops to meet their compressed time line. I was no stranger to hastily planned and executed missions. During the invasion the majority of the mission briefings I had given my company staff had consisted of little more than "Here's our current location. This is where we're going. Here's our mission. We're leaving in five minutes." But that had been the nature of Marine Corps operations at the time: swift, violent, and with a hazy intelligence picture of the battlefield. At the time we also had the full force of our battalion and the 1st Marine Division to back us up if we got into a fix. But now the MiTT team couldn't be given the same guarantee of support if we got into trouble while on a mission with the Iraqis. Additionally, the rules of engagement had been much more permissive back in 2003. They were less so now.

And while I understood the necessity for rapid planning, preparation, and execution of "time-sensitive" missions in a counterinsurgency environment, what the Iraqis were calling hasty planning and preparation hardly fit the definition. The Marine battalions in Iraq were filled with officers and enlisted men who had undergone extensive training in planning for such missions. The IAs were not yet to that level. Instead, their mission planning tended to be more reactive in nature, and the soldiers who were expected to carry out the missions generally had no idea what they were getting themselves into or what was expected of them. It was a recipe for disaster. Until we could get a better feel for how 3rd Battalion planned its missions, and until we could inject ourselves into the Iraqis' planning and preparation cycle, I wasn't willing to risk my Marines' lives for such shoestring operations. My decision at the time, and later ones like it, undoubtedly cost me and my team some *wasta* (influence or clout) with the battalion, but I didn't care. My Marines were my first concern; the Iraqis came second.

Chapter 14
Matters of Importance

The furor within 3rd Battalion surrounding the accidental shooting on 9 March was over as quickly as it happened. I followed up on the issue with Lieutenant Colonel Ayad each evening for several nights after the incident, and each time the subject was raised I received the same response: "We have a committee investigating it." It was a common answer. The IAs seemed to appoint a committee for everything, whether it was a command investigation or accounting for the unit's payroll. It was a rare occasion indeed when the commander took resolute action and simply directed that something happen. It was the way the IAs did things—an attempt to limit graft, corruption, and perhaps nepotism—and the mere mention that a committee had been assigned to any given occurrence was enervating. But I was particularly distressed over the shooting. The soldier who had pulled the trigger had been placed in *jundi* jail to await the outcome of the investigation, as well as for his own protection, but the attitude that Ayad had adopted concerning the incident was that it was merely an unfortunate accident. The Iraqi army didn't attach the same degree of gravity to negligent discharges as we did in the Marine Corps. In our system there was no such thing as an "accidental" shooting. We followed strict weapons-handling rules, and only a violation of two or more of those rules could lead to a weapon discharging. But the Iraqis believed in accidents, and in this case such an accident had taken the life of a young *jundi*. My recommendation to Ayad for my team to conduct weapons-handling and safety classes for 3rd Battalion soldiers was discarded. But as aggravated as I was to have my offer snubbed, I knew it wouldn't be the last time my counterpart refused to heed my advice. After all, the deployment had just begun.

An operation scheduled for 12 March was canceled due to a command visit to COP South by the new commander of 28th Brigade, *Aqeed* (Colonel) Ra'ed. A squat, wide-eyed officer, Ra'ed closely resembled a burlap sack of potatoes wrapped in woodland camouflage material. His undersized legs tended to dangle above the floor when he sat, and the nickname assigned to him by the Americans—"Stumpy"—was a fitting one. He waddled everywhere he went, and his overstuffed appearance epitomized the commonly accepted fact that Iraqi officers were better fed than their enlisted soldiers.

After arriving at COP South Ra'ed and his entourage toured the area in a whirlwind inspection of the camp while I hung back in the formation with Lt. Col. Ron Gridley. A wiry, angular infantry officer who shared with me a common background in the LAV community, Gridley was the leader of 28th Brigade's advisor team. He and his Marines had been assigned to the brigade since August 2007, and while he was not yet my boss (but would eventually assume that role later in the deployment), I knew it would be foolish to discard his guidance when it came to dealing with the IAs. As the advisor to the brigade commander he was routinely privy to the brigade's plans and operations, and he would be there to assist me if and when I ran into roadblocks when dealing with my own counterpart. He was atypical of most lieutenant colonels I had met, and he understood the unconventional nature of advisor team operations. During our first meeting his guidance had been simple: "Follow your counterpart around, make your recommendations to him and his staff, and don't get butt-hurt when he doesn't take your advice." "It can be a frustrating job," he had told me. "And all you can do is make sure you and your team laugh a lot, and wake up each morning and go to bed each night with a smile on your face."

His experience thus far as an advisor had told him that being directive in nature when it came to the Iraqis—or when dealing with the MiTT team members—tended not to work. And I understood exactly what he was saying. It was one thing to tell a subordinate Marine to accomplish a task. It was something else entirely to tell the Iraqis to do something. It was similarly fruitless to order a subordinate on the team to make his Iraqi counterpart do something. I knew I couldn't make Ayad do something he didn't want to do; accordingly, I couldn't expect my team members to make their counterparts do something *they* didn't want to do. And so, in time, I began to phrase my taskings to the Outlanders in these terms: "Try to convince your counterpart to do this or that . . ." That was all I could do. Whether the Iraqis did the right thing in the end was an entirely different matter. Such a lack of authority—an inability to demand compliance—was thus one of the most maddening aspects of being an advisor. Marines are action-oriented creatures. They receive tasks, they make plans, they execute missions, and they demand results. Advisors do the first three, yet the fourth—tangible results—frequently evades them.

The inspection moved swiftly throughout the camp, and as the group shuffled from building to building we were closely flanked on all sides by the armed personal security detachments (PSDs) of both Colonel Ra'ed and Lieutenant Colonel Ayad. Neither officer went anywhere without his PSD, even within the safety of his own camp. Ayad even had an armed guard standing post outside his hut at all times. It made me wonder what the real purpose for all the security was. Was it a genuine concern by the commanders for their own personal safety? Or was it merely for appearances—the fact that the commander was so important that he rated his own bodyguards everywhere he went? American commanders often traveled with their own PSDs as well, but there seemed something almost sinister about the ever-present AK-47-wielding *junood* shadowing the Iraqi commanders.

Ra'ed was impressed with the camp, commenting frequently on the cleanliness of the facilities and the tight ship that Ayad ran. The train retired to Ayad's hut, half of which had been converted into his office. Every time I sat in Ayad's office I laughed to myself at the interior decoration. Plush rugs covered the floor, a tall television cabinet stood next to the door, and big, comfortable couches and chairs lined the walls. The furniture was a gaudy explosion of golds, browns, and oranges. Cracked glass-topped coffee tables were permanently stained with rings from tea saucers and bottles. Day-Glo pink tapestries had been fitted into a makeshift drop-ceiling for the office, and the clash of loud colors screeched like an optical banshee. To top it off, the lavish, professional atmosphere of the room was offset further by the baby-blue wallpaper covering the office's walls. Outlandish cartoon monkeys blowing pink bubbles adorned the paper, the announcement "Don't burst my bubble!" imprinted under each gum-chewing primate. Other officers' huts were similarly decorated, often with brightly colored or flowered wallpaper, and plastic flowers were familiar decor throughout the living areas. It was a far cry from the dusty, bare, simple huts the Marines occupied. The only way we could explain the disparity was that the Marine advisor teams occupied COP South for a mere seven months at a time before returning to the United States. The officers and soldiers of 3rd Battalion were there for the long haul. It was only natural that they made the place as much like home as possible. I wondered if Ayad's real home in Ramadi was as garish and exaggerated as his office at COP South.

As we all sat down for chai I witnessed an interesting Iraqi military custom. Upon entering the office the brigade commander sat at Ayad's desk, and Ayad placed himself on the couch next to Ra'ed. I began to notice the same tradition each time a senior Iraqi officer visited a camp, whether it was the brigade or division commander visiting COP South or the battalion commander visiting one of his company battle positions. Each time the senior officer would assume the position behind the desk, as if he had taken command of the unit, and the on-scene commander would subordinate himself in a seat off to the side. It was a peculiar custom, as I had never seen a Marine commander do the same to a subordinate leader. It screamed, *I'm in charge here*! but it didn't seem to bother the IAs. They had their way, and we had ours. Who the hell was I to judge?

The group sat around for close to two hours, drinking chai and smoking cigarettes, socializing about nearly everything but work. What business-related discussion there was centered on topics that seemed minor compared to the larger issues confronting the Iraqi army at the time. Ra'ed offered his wisdom on such critical subjects as the correct way to run a chow hall and how to more efficiently speed the soldiers through the serving line. Issues such as fuel and spare-parts shortages were ignored. Instead, Ra'ed entertained his audience with an epic tale describing the fate of the old Iraqi army's 9th Division, which supposedly had been annihilated during the Iran-Iraq war. As the officers present vigorously nodded their heads in agreement, Colonel Ra'ed made a casual comment that piqued my interest.

"We need to go back to the old days of discipline," he said, pointing to the officers surrounding him. "Only then will we be able to continue forward."

It was the first time I had heard an Iraqi officer make such a proclamation, but it wouldn't be the last. We had defeated the Iraqi army in battle, yes, but remnants of the old regime still existed in the officer corps. I began to wonder if perhaps they were merely waiting out the Americans, waiting for us to rearm them, waiting for us to leave so they could return to the old ways. Such talk made me uneasy. Surely they would eventually see the light . . . wouldn't they?

Throughout his visit Colonel Ra'ed frequently suggested a visit to BPs Okinawa and Vera Cruz to inspect 1st and 2nd companies. Knowing how fast the Iraqis tended to pick up and move—and not wanting to get caught unprepared—I radioed Lieutenant Bates on my Motorola and directed him to prep two vehicle crews in case we needed to head out quickly with the brigade's convoy. As the socializing continued throughout the afternoon the chances of visiting the two companies seemed to get smaller and smaller, but just as I prepared to cancel the convoy planning Colonel Ra'ed put down his tea glass and loudly announced, "Let's go visit First and Second companies!"

The entourage walked briskly to a line of waiting Ford F-350 pickup trucks mounted with armed soldiers and heavy machine guns, and I scrambled back to the MiTT compound to grab my gear and jump into the back seat of a waiting Humvee. Our departure was so rushed—and I had so little time to prepare myself—that I left the wire missing half of my gear. As we rolled past a spray-painted sign at the camp's exit that asked, "Got your rifle?" I suddenly patted myself down and realized my error. I had no identification, no NVGs. I didn't even have my rifle and magazines. I was a bag of shit, and I felt naked and stupid. The long line of vehicles rolled out of the ECP, and I keyed my headset and sheepishly spoke to Staff Sergeant Leek in the vehicle commander's seat.

"Hey, Staff Sergeant, I'm all fucked up here."

"What?" he replied, turning back to look at me. "What are you talking about, sir?"

"We got out of there so quickly, I forgot all my shit." I motioned to my body armor and its empty ammunition pouches, and then held up my empty hands. "I guess I have to rely on you guys to protect me if the shit hits the fan."

"Don't worry, sir," he replied, laughing. "We got your back."

I was mortified, and throughout the long trip to the company battle positions I mulled over my grievous blunder. *Boy*, I thought. *That'll look great if we get hit while I'm out here with nothing. Really leading from the front now.*

The trip ended with a brief visit to the site of the new brigade compound that was under construction near the Al Qa'im phosphate plant. Both the brigade headquarters and 3rd Battalion were scheduled to eventually relocate to the new facility, but in the meantime it was unfinished. Again Colonel Ra'ed and Lieutenant Colonel Ayad stood around, pontificating about specifics of the facility that to me seemed superficial. The hot topic of discussion centered on how to properly divide the chow hall between brigade and 3rd Battalion personnel. As Lieutenant Colonel Gridley and I stood back and examined the exposed wiring, leaking pipes, and crumbling plaster, I wondered aloud if perhaps the two Iraqi commanders weren't focused on the wrong things.

The long convoy of vehicles returned to Camp Phoenix, the Iraqi brigade headquarters camp colocated with Camp Al Qa'im. Our two Humvees broke away from the convoy to refuel before the trip back to COP South, but by the time we returned to link up with Ayad's convoy they had left without us. I was pissed off. Coalition convoys were not authorized to go outside the wire in groups of fewer than three vehicles (unless they were partnered with IA vehicles). The sun had set more than an hour earlier, and as darkness shrouded the desert I faced a dilemma: Did I keep my Marines at Camp Phoenix overnight, or did I violate orders and set out on our own, alone and unafraid in the dark? I chose the latter. I knew it perhaps wasn't the safest thing to do, but by leaving us Ayad had placed me in a difficult position. As we exited Camp Phoenix I remembered something the previous team had once told us: *Don't be surprised when the Iraqis leave without you.* It didn't do a lot to boost my confidence in our newfound counterparts.

As we made our way back through the night our tiny convoy slowed to a stop. The Wadi al Battikah was a deep, dry streambed that cut through the middle of our route, and previously established SOPs dictated that it be cleared on foot for pressure strips or command wires before any vehicles traversed it. Leek stepped out of the Humvee, and, grabbing the vehicle gunner's carbine, I hopped out and followed him down into the wadi. We split up, Leek moving off to the right side of the trail while I took the left. Deep cuts lined the trail's banks, forcing me to hop from ledge to ledge every ten feet or so. Stumbling along in the dark, the path to my front illuminated only by the glow of my flashlight, I lost my footing and tumbled down into a ditch that bordered the trail. I went crashing down into the dirt, the full weight of my body and equipment coming down hard on my ankle. My foot on fire inside its boot, I abandoned the craggy border of the trail and instead limped along the trail itself, continuing to scan the powdery earth for pressure strips and booby traps. The pain in my ankle and my irritation at the Iraqis over abandoning us eclipsed my concern about getting blown up as I walked along in the dark, and when we finally reached the other side and paused for the Humvees to pick us up Leek looked at me.

"Damn, sir," he muttered, shaking his head. "You're crazy walking in the trail like that."

"Fuck it," I said. "Just . . . fuck it. Come on, let's get back to camp."

I was too tired, mad, and sore to care much. It had been a long day, and it was time to go home.

Chapter 15
Backing the Wrong Horse

On 14 March I sat down with the battalion commander of the Marine task force and his company commander who originally had been "partnered" with 3rd Battalion. As transition teams became the norm in Iraq the original concept had called for Marine infantry companies to partner with Iraqi battalions, in effect becoming company-sized MiTTs. Experience had shown that when the partnered companies worked closely with the advisor teams notable results were achieved. Prior to my team's arrival, however, the circumstances in 3rd Battalion had changed after a squad of embedded Marines from the partnered company got drunk one night from a bottle of liquor mailed by one man's wife. The Marines had been permanently recalled to their company headquarters, leaving the previous advisor team alone to work with 3rd Battalion at COP South. My predecessor and I had both agreed on the necessity of having an additional squad of Marines with us to assist in our job with the IAs, but we found ourselves alone in our mutual agreement.

After voicing my concern to the company commander over the removal of the rifle squad my exchanges with him escalated into a significant disagreement about how he and his company should partner with 3rd Battalion. The company commander was convinced that his squads could accomplish the mission by merely linking up with the IA companies and conducting operations once or twice a week. I, on the other hand, argued that by embedding a rifle squad with each IA company the Marines would be able to build relationships by living, eating, and training with the *junood* like my own team was doing. But I was fighting a losing battle, and eventually the battalion commander made his thoughts on the matter clear to me. The time for sitting around the campfire with the IAs and singing "Kumbaya" was over, he told me. The mission of partnering with the Iraqi army could now be accomplished by the company's squads commuting to work on a periodic basis.

had agreed to meet each week regularly, and I felt as though one small step toward progress had just been made.

As time wore on I began to learn that mutual dislike was not confined to Sa'id and Ghassan. The IA and the IP units stationed around the Al Qa'im region did not trust each other as a whole. Both Sa'id and Ayad staunchly claimed that the police force was a corrupt, unprofessional, and untrained gang. The perception was that because the IPs were mostly neighborhood boys, they knew and had grown up with all of the local criminals. Such an association, as well as the tribal ties that bound them, made the IPs hesitant to crack down on the criminals. No policeman, Ayad had reasoned, would arrest someone whom he had known and played with as a boy. The police, on the other hand, disliked the perceived preferential treatment the IA had received from the Americans, and they complained of a lack of intelligence sharing by the IAs.

Third Battalion had been accustomed to operating in the urban areas around Karabilah and Husaybah, what was now considered the urban security zone (USZ), and that was where they still preferred to be. It had been 3rd Battalion—working with the Americans—that had been responsible for chasing out the majority of the insurgents and Al Qaeda operatives in Karabilah and Husaybah in the previous years, and it was now a tough sell for us to convince them to stay out of the towns and focus more on the desert region to the south. The persistent lack of enemy activity in the desert made our task that much more challenging. As far as Ayad and his staff were concerned, the recent surge in IED activity in and around Karabilah and Husaybah was justification itself to continue operating in the USZ.

As my meetings with Sa'id progressed he began opening up, and soon our nightly discussions turned toward his concern about the performance of the battalion's intelligence section. The right people weren't running the shop, he confided to me, and *junood* working in the shop weren't properly trained. His concerns seemed justified late on the evening of 18 March when Lieutenant Ski called me to the COC. In his hand he clutched a piece of paper, and he had a perplexed look on his face. He handed me both the document and a translated version.

"Hamood just gave this to me, and we got it translated," he began. "It's from the brigade G-2. They're directing Third Battalion to roll up three suspects in Karabilah who're suspected of planting IEDs."

I examined the letter, and then handed it back to Ski.

"So? What's the big deal?"

"Well, the battalion S-2 also said that they don't intend to inform the XO until midnight, right before they plan to execute the mission."

I raised my eyebrow, suddenly a bit perplexed myself.

"What the hell? No one else in the battalion knows about this?"

"No, sir. Oh, and they also want us to go with them."

"Do they have a plan?"

"Not really."

"Hey," I said, turning to Lieutenant Bates. "This is bullshit. The S-2 doesn't have the authority to go do this on their own. Go talk to the S-3 and see what the hell is going on."

Bates returned thirty minutes later, shaking his head.

"Man, Al'aa's pissed, sir," he said. "He didn't know a damn thing about it."

As I thought about it, Captain Hanna spoke.

"Sir, do you think you should go talk to the XO about it? If he doesn't know about it he's probably going to get pissed off as well."

I pondered the issue. There was something wrong if the S-2 didn't want the battalion XO or the S-3 to know about an operation. It was something I didn't want to get caught in the middle of, and I tabled it.

"No. Let them continue with their plan. If they want to piss all over each other, let them. I'll talk to Sa'id about it tomorrow and get to the bottom of it. Regardless, we're not going with them. This is sketchy enough as it is." I turned to both Ski and Bates. "If they want us to participate in their bullshit ops, they better start putting more effort into their plans. This 'hip-shoot' shit has got to stop."

Captain Hanna's prediction had been correct. Upon hearing the news Sa'id had indeed been infuriated. As we discussed what had occurred, Sa'id grew more and more agitated while he relayed the chain of events. He had actually approved the mission concept several nights earlier, but when Hamood informed him late the previous evening Sa'id had decided that more planning was required. Disregarding the XO's directive, Hamood and his soldiers initiated the mission anyway and detained two of the three targeted personnel.

As Sa'id conveyed to me his concerns about the battalion's intelligence section, I heard what Lieutenant Ski had already been reporting to me after his nightly meetings with the S-2: Hamood was a loose cannon. A swarthy warrant officer with a bushy mustache and deeply set eyes, Hamood somehow had his hands in everything within the battalion. He had strong ties to the Abu Mahal—the dominant tribe in the Al Qa'im region—and he was also currently under investigation by the Iraqi Ministry of Defense (MOD) for charges of corruption. Hamood was a legend within 3rd Battalion. He apparently had been there forever, and whenever anyone needed anything he could get it. Did the battalion run out of food? Hamood would feed the soldiers. Has the generator broken down? Hamood would find mechanics to fix it. I likened him to the indispensable gunnery sergeant that every Marine infantry battalion always seems to have—the go-to guy about whom no one really knows what he does on a daily basis, but can always "get stuff." The only catch is that no one will ever dare to ask the indispensable gunny where he gets stuff or how he gets things done. Also, no one is ever willing to piss him off for fear that his acts of goodwill might suddenly dry up. Hamood was that guy in 3rd Battalion, but he was also the principal human intelligence (HUMINT) source manager within the battalion. He seemed to know everyone and everything that went on outside the wire of COP South, and he represented the battalion's only real intelligence link to the Al Qa'im region.

Hamood's mere presence in the battalion riled the XO, and Sa'id made it clear that he wanted the warrant officer removed from the unit. But Sa'id was also no idiot. He understood the local politics, and he was fearful of tribal retribution (which had nearly cost him his job under the previous battalion commander). It was a unique concern at all levels that seemed to work its way into every major decision made in the region. It was Sa'id's hope that my team would conduct an evaluation of the S-2 shop and present it to the battalion commander. Such an assessment would build a case for Hamood's dismissal or reassignment, as well as the reorganization of the entire S-2 section.

I wasn't worried about evaluating the S-2; we had already planned to conduct such a review of all the battalion's staff sections. My concern was that Sa'id might pay the price if we ended up submitting a negative evaluation up the chain of command. If it backfired it would not be the first time in history that an Iraqi officer woke up with his throat cut for crossing the tribal boundaries the wrong way. Sa'id was a member of the Al Khalidi tribe, and with the Abu Mahal as the region's prevailing tribe he was running scared. The Abu Mahal was the tribe that had been behind the Awakening movement in Al Anbar province, and they dominated local political control. But I also knew that Ayad was an Al Karbuli who claimed some influence in the area. I hoped he might be able to provide some measure of top cover for Sa'id if anything went south. I would just have to wait.

I didn't have to wait long. Days later I learned that Sa'id had been "reassigned"; no further information was offered. I ran to his hut to get to the bottom of it, but I found his door padlocked. In a matter of hours he had been dismissed and had packed up and left the battalion. I was nearly apoplectic, and I wondered if someone had complained up the chain to have him removed. All the progress that had been made in forging a relationship during my nights in his office had walked right out the door with him.

That night Lieutenant Colonel Ayad returned from leave, and during my visit with him I expressed my concern and disappointment over Sa'id's removal. He limply agreed with me, saying that he had opposed the reassignment, but he left it at that. There was no indication that Ayad would attempt to resolve the situation, and I left his office chafed and wondering what the real story was.

Later I sat down with Mason, the interpreter whom I had adopted as my principal linguist when dealing with Ayad. A Jordanian by birth, Mason was an American citizen who had completed a previous interpreter tour with the U.S. Army several years earlier. A restaurant chain manager in a former life, he claimed to have had experience in nearly every facet of society. As the deployment wore on the two of us spent so much time together that I would frequently seek him out for assistance in solving the endless cultural puzzles in which I frequently found myself. As the two of us discussed my conversation with Ayad, Mason suggested that perhaps Ayad might have disagreed verbally with Sa'id's removal but in fact may have been secretly happy that the XO was gone. Over time Sa'id had ruffled a lot of feathers among the local tribes, and his removal meant that Ayad would be free to be the hero and smooth things over with the tribal leaders. In effect, Ayad appeared to have sacrificed Sa'id to improve the battalion's relationship with the town elders of Husaybah and Karabilah.

But that wasn't all. Several days later I raised the issue with Lieutenant Colonel Gridley when I met with him at Camp Phoenix.

"Lieutenant Colonel Sa'id was reassigned," I told him matter-of-factly, not hiding the disappointment in my voice. "He just up and disappeared a couple of days ago."

"Doesn't surprise me," Gridley answered nonchalantly. "He was hip deep in the theft ring in Third Battalion last fall. No big loss for the battalion."

Gridley's comments left me speechless, and once it dawned on me that Sa'id had duped me I was furious with myself. How would I ever manage to figure out the Iraqis if I continued to eat their bullshit with no questions asked? The experience became a warning for me. In building relationships with the IAs it was imperative that I learn to trust them, yes, but I would also have to apply a mantra my father had repeated to me over and over again throughout the years: Trust, but verify.

Chapter 16
Al Gab'aa

Lieutenant Bates announces to the team that 3rd Battalion has planned an "intelligence-gathering" mission for 16 March, and as he explains their half-baked plan to conduct a cordon and search I am thankful that the IAs are finally conducting a deliberate operation. A plantation known as Al Gab'aa sits astride the main road in our AO approximately twenty-five kilometers southwest of our camp, and the battalion commander thinks the site is a possible cache point for transient insurgents, terrorists, or smugglers in our area. No credible reporting on Al Gab'aa exists, and the commander's decision to send a patrol to investigate is based more on a hunch than anything else. I am surprised at the decision to execute the mission because the IAs are always hesitant to conduct an operation unless they have rock-solid intelligence. They don't want to waste fuel if they aren't going to find something.

The operation is led by Captain Hassan and 3rd Company, but it isn't really a company-level operation. With 3rd Battalion's diminished personnel and vehicle numbers it is more like a platoon-level mission, and we augment the force with two Humvee crews. My team and I go along as advisors and observers—not as trigger pullers—but we bring firepower and communications assets to the operation that the IAs don't have. We are loaded for bear, each Humvee packed with belts of machine-gun ammunition and each Marine stacked with rifle and pistol magazines. Throughout the team we spread-load personal radios, satellite phones, cell phones, and the team's SATCOM system. If the mission runs into trouble we can leverage Coalition firepower, and if the Iraqi soldiers take casualties we can call helicopters for casualty evacuation (CASEVAC).

We travel south in a column along the deserted highway, the team's Humvees interspersed throughout the Iraqi patrol. It is the IA's convoy, but the invisible bubble of our Chameleons protects the Iraqis from radio-controlled IEDs (RCIEDs), and so they keep their vehicles close to ours. We concentrate on the route in front of us and the garbage strewn along the roadsides, and even though no one ever talks about the IEDs we know they are out there somewhere. Instead, the Marines chat back and forth over the vehicle intercom system. It is better than sitting in silence, alone with your thoughts.

Eventually we approach the plantation; from a distance it is an oasis in the middle of the barren desert. From high above it looks like a grid, and it is apparent that somehow someone managed to break the code on desert irrigation. The cultivated area was a deliberate project at some point in history, its neatly lined rows of trees parallel and even. But it is overgrown now, untended and wild. The rows of shaggy, unpruned olive trees crowd the paths and block any view of the plantation's center. The battalion commander and his staff are correct: Al Gab'aa is a perfect place for the enemy to hide—either himself or his weapons.

Several of the IA vehicles break off from the column and occupy blocking positions at the plantation's corners. We follow suit and set our two Humvees in the shadow of a small bridge near the southeastern entrance to the tree line. SSgt. Clarence Wolf, the team's communications chief, unpacks the SATCOM radio and assembles its antenna array. He is from Wisconsin, and he has completed a previous tour as a Marine recruiter. He has a smooth, shaved head, and his soft-spoken demeanor and youthful features are deceiving. He is capable of transitioning to a direct, hands-on leadership style, and the business and people skills he has learned during recruiting duty help to balance out the rigid drill field mentality possessed by Staff Sergeant Leek. He tends to begin his answer to every question I ask him with "Honestly, sir?" as if I might want him to bullshit me rather than telling me the hard truth. Soon Wolf is talking to the team's COC back at COP South, and once that link is established my comfort level increases. The rest of the Outlanders now know where we are and what we are doing.

The *junood* move into the tree line, and Sgt. Theo Bowers, Lieutenant Bates, Mason, Big Mo (another interpreter), and I follow them, trailing behind far enough to let the Iraqi soldiers do their job but close enough to observe them and assist them if necessary. Once past the initial barrier of trees we find a series of small houses within the plantation. The homes are tiny and rundown with age, and none appears to have electricity or running water. Chickens and unkempt, scabby dogs wander back and forth through the courtyards. Small children peer out at us from behind tattered curtains. The difference between the Marines and the *junood* is striking. The *junood* carry little more than their uniforms and rifles, while the Marines stand in the shadows weighted down by their menacing, oversized body armor and helmets. The locals who venture outside their homes eye us with no small degree of suspicion and wonder. But eventually they accept our presence and seem to forget we are even there.

The locals are compliant with the Iraqi soldiers, patiently answering questions and even offering information. When the IAs find an unregistered AK-47 with one family they question an old woman who claims ownership of the rusted weapon. The soldiers determine that the rifle is used only for home defense, and since each family is authorized to have one AK-47 they record the serial number, take her name, and hand the weapon back to her. We are unconcerned; the rifle is so worn out and rusted that we doubt it will even fire.

We follow behind the *junood* as they patrol down the plantation's long, tilled fields. The ground is soft, and it is indeed an ideal location for a cache site. What the soldiers really need for the job are metal detectors to sweep the rows of soft, plowed earth. But despite our prodding the battalion staff has failed to properly request the metal detectors in a timely manner. After more than an hour of searching through the vegetation the soldiers find nothing and call it a day. As they remount their Humvees we call for our vehicles to shut down the SATCOM relay and come retrieve us. We fall back in with the IA convoy for the return to COP South with nothing to show for our efforts.

In the end all we can do is designate Al Gab'aa as a named area of interest (NAI) and continue to monitor it. After the operation is complete we remind the battalion staff of the requirement to properly plan each operation. If we do it for them—if we request the metal detectors on our own—the battalion staff will never learn from their mistakes. They will keep relying on the Americans to pull them along. It is their country, their army. They must take ownership of both if they want to succeed.

Chapter 17
Mistakes and Mistrust

My billet as the team leader put me in a unique position, one I had never been afforded during my roles as a platoon commander and company commander. Because the Outlanders comprised so many talented young leaders I was able to float from position to position within the team, whether we were inside the wire aboard COP South or out conducting a patrol or convoy. I didn't feel compelled to lead every convoy or mission; in fact, it was much the opposite. I deliberately opted out of the mission-leader billet during nearly all convoys and patrols, choosing instead to ride behind the driver in the comm seat and manage the radios. I knew my choice was probably atypical of most type A infantry officers, but my reasons were legitimate. Above all else I wanted all of the Marines on the team to be completely cross-trained in every aspect of mounted operations in Humvees. Driving, gunning, manning the radios, or actually leading the patrols—all were important facets of the mission, and I wanted each team member equally comfortable in any role. Although we eventually developed assigned vehicle crews, no one was given a permanent position in a vehicle. Everyone took turns rotating through jobs, and by the deployment's end each Marine had led numerous patrols and had manned every station in the Humvee more times than he could count.

I had my own reasons for not constantly taking charge of each patrol. After all, I had nothing to prove. The team members knew my background, and they knew it was best not to challenge my operational credibility. Though they may not have realized it at the time, I tended to take the backseat so I could evaluate the Marines as they briefed and executed each mission. Most of the time I was a silent observer, but occasionally during a mission the vehicle commander or driver would hear me in his headset providing a gentle correction. While several members of the team had extensive experience operating in Humvees in Iraq, others did not. It became my intent to ensure all Marines on the team returned to their parent units better-trained than they had been when they left. I was more than willing to sacrifice my position in the vehicle commander's seat to ensure my team members received the training and operational experience they needed.

But not all Marines on the team understood my intent in that regard, and many began giving me hell for always sitting in the back of the Humvee during convoys and patrols. One afternoon, Lieutenant Bates sauntered into the MWR hut minutes before the daily team meeting. A convoy to Camp Al Qa'im had been scheduled for the following day.

"Hey, sir, you planning on going to AQ with us tomorrow?"

"Yeah," I replied. "Throw me in on the convoy."

"Do you want to VC one of the vics [vehicles]?"

"Naw," I answered, thinking nothing of it. "Go ahead and put me in the comm seat."

Bates paused, and then smirked.

"Sir, some of the Marines were talking shit about you always sitting in the back," he offered.

I shook my head, laughing wryly.

"Bates, I won't even dignify that with an answer. I have more time on the *shitter* than most of those Marines have commanding a vehicle or a patrol."

He recoiled at my reply and jumped to defuse the situation.

"I think they were just joking around, sir. I don't think they were serious."

"Yeah, roger," I said sarcastically.

Regardless, I couldn't help taking the bait. Later at the team meeting I directed my attention to Sgt. Theo Bowers, the team's intelligence NCO. Currently serving his fourth tour in Iraq, Bowers claimed to hail from California. But the ever-present wad of tobacco tucked into his lip, the battered old blue and white pickup he always drove, and the casual drawl of his voice screamed Texan. He had been designated as the convoy commander for the following day and was in the process of assigning vehicle billets for the movement.

"Hey, Sergeant Bowers," I said. "Put me in as your driver."

He tilted his head quizzically, as if he didn't understand me.

"Roger, sir," he replied, making a note. I turned my attention to the rest of the team.

"As for the rest of you, I heard you've been talking smack about me sitting in the back of the Humvee all the time. In case you care, the reason I do that is because I want you all to get the experience you need running the show. I've had more than enough hours and days in the VC's seat, and I'll be happy to sit down with anyone on the team and discuss in ass-bleeding detail exactly how much time I have."

I tried not to make a habit of jamming my résumé down my team's throats, choosing instead to offer object lessons from my past when appropriate. And in this case the situation warranted it. It was important to me that the Marines understood that I wouldn't ask them to do anything that I wouldn't do myself. I didn't limit that to operations outside the wire. Whenever possible I jumped in with whatever the team was doing, whether it was vehicle maintenance, camp police call, or standing COC duty as the team watch officer. The team's small size required it; everyone had to work and pull his weight. As far as I was concerned, rank was not an excuse for not doing the daily grunt work.

But my insistence on fully participating in all aspects of the team's operations also resulted in me making visible mistakes in front of the Marines on a regular basis, such as forgetting my equipment during the brigade convoy on 12 March. The convoy on 22 March was no different. It was my first time driving a Humvee while towing a trailer, and I had noticeable difficulty controlling the vehicle, especially when going in reverse. It gave me a whole new appreciation for big-rig truck drivers who routinely haul oversized loads in trailers.

My series of public errors continued later in the day as the team mounted up for the return to COP South. It had been a long day, and in what was becoming the norm we got stuck at Camp Al Qa'im when a dust storm rolled in and restricted vehicle movement outside the camp. By the time the skies cleared it was after 2200, and the team was in a hurry to get home. The convoy through the darkness wasn't without its own set of internally generated friction, including a disjointed and confusing movement through the Wadi al Battikah.

In the end we returned safely to COP South, but as I was conducting the required postoperation maintenance on my Humvee I realized with some horror that I had not activated a critical electronic system within the vehicle before leaving the wire of Camp Al Qa'im. No one had been the wiser, and my error would have gone unnoticed had I not announced my screwup during the team's post-op debrief. As I declared my mistake publicly my vehicle crew glared at me, the looks on their tired faces saying, *Nice going, asshole. You could have killed us.* I could have omitted my error from the debrief and they would have never known. But it was important to me that my Marines knew that even *I* jacked things up occasionally, and that they should learn from my mistake. But I also knew that my openness and honesty was a double-edged sword. Such frankness in admitting blunders could potentially backfire, and I hoped they saw it for what it was rather than simply thinking their team leader was just an incompetent moron.

Still reeling from my misjudgment about Lieutenant Colonel Sa'id, I refocused my efforts with Lieutenant Colonel Ayad now that he was back from *mujaas*. Waving a piece of paper back and forth, Ayad began ranting on and on, and I had a feeling I knew what he was saying even without Mason there to translate for me. On the evening of 21 March 3rd Battalion's S-2 had produced a handbill that had been found posted throughout Husaybah. The flyer directly addressed 28th Brigade, and its message was simple: Cease flying the new Iraqi flag or suffer the consequences.

The new Iraqi flag had been adopted recently by parliament, and with its unveiling had come no small degree of protest within Al Anbar province. The old flag—with its red, white, and black field, three stars, and the words *Allahu akbar* (God is great) scrawled in Arabic across the center—had remained unchanged as the country's national symbol since 1991 at the end of the first Gulf War. At first glance the new flag seemed no different than the old one. Further scrutiny revealed that subtle changes had indeed been made. The three black stars—said to represent the Baath Party—had been removed, and the Arabic script's style had been changed to a modern, almost stilted font. It was widely believed that the original script had been a replica of Saddam Hussein's own handwriting, and to a slice of Al Anbar's Sunni population the two changes together represented a deliberate attempt by the Shiites in Iraq's government to erase part of the country's heritage.

In some respects the complaints seemed legitimate, especially when, during the course of a conversation on the matter, one team member commented, "Try taking away the stars on *our* flag and see what would happen." But the new flag was the law of the land, and the Iraqi army was supposed to be flying it. Ironically, the team had already seen the handbill during a resupply trip into Husaybah earlier in the week. It had been posted throughout the *souq*. But, oblivious at the time to what it said, the Marines had ignored it.

Hours before my meeting with the battalion commander we learned that someone had placed a copy of the same flyer on the windshield of Ayad's vehicle in COP South, in effect threatening him directly with retaliation if he continued to fly the new flag. He was furious, uncertain what to do about the transgression. Captain Hanna and I had discussed the issue earlier, and our mutual solution was simple: isolate all of the battalion's personnel and toss the barracks. I urged Ayad to do so immediately, lest the anonymous bill poster rid himself of any remaining evidence. Ayad agreed to the snap inspection, but he postponed it until the next day. I knew he would find nothing. Word traveled fast in the battalion, and surely by the time the inspection was conducted any remaining flyers would be gone.

Regardless, Ayad was already certain he knew who the culprit was, even if he couldn't attach a name to the perpetrator. He believed some of his officers were involved, and he was adamant that the local police were behind the bill postings in Husaybah. It was a wild accusation, one with no tangible proof to back it up. And it was one more manifestation of Ayad's mistrust in both his own people and the Iraqi Police.

The posting of the enemy propaganda in Husaybah, in conjunction with a vehicle-borne improvised explosive device (VBIED) that detonated at the IP district headquarters (DHQ) in Husaybah the previous night and the recent spike in IEDs and weapons cache finds throughout the AO, was alarming. The 28th Brigade MiTT intelligence advisor, a grizzled prior-enlisted bear of a man named Jeff Simpson, was certain something was brewing in the Al Qa'im region. A twenty-year veteran of the infantry and intelligence community, Major Simpson possessed analytical skills that were unmatched throughout the AO. He had cautioned me the previous night about my team's trips outside the wire. In a cryptic warning he merely said, "Keep your eyes and ears open, and travel with the IA as much as possible." It was unclear whether Coalition forces would be primary targets, but we weren't going to take any chances. In light of the recent events and my discussion with Simpson I conveyed my concern to the team, echoing his guidance for increased scrutiny of trips outside the wire, as well as emphasizing again proper mission planning and execution. My parting guidance to the team was simple: our job was to advise the Iraqis and not get blown up in the process.

As time wore on the Marines gradually assumed their natural roles within the team, and despite their different backgrounds and specialties they continued to gel and increase their collective proficiency. Our progress with the 3rd Battalion staff, however, was frequently like taking one step forward and two steps back. I had been pushing Ayad to conduct regular staff meetings with his officers in an effort to increase coordination among them. Individually the staff officers tended to get by to an acceptable degree, but synchronization between the staff sections was virtually nonexistent. No big fan of staff meetings myself, I nevertheless understood the utility in conducting them, and I urged my team principals to convince their counterparts to meet regularly. It was a constant battle, akin to forcing water to travel uphill.

After much digging we eventually discovered that the Iraqi officers did in fact conduct battalion staff meetings, and on 25 March we attended for the first time. Much to our surprise the meeting was conducted professionally, even including an overreliance and general abuse of PowerPoint slides that rivaled most Coalition staff briefings. The greatest difference was Ayad's comments at the meeting's close. Rather than focus on what would routinely be big-picture issues or give broad guidance like most American commanders would, he instead read from an exhaustive list all the little things that had been pissing him off.

The discrepancies he noted were issues normally reserved for the battalion XO or sergeant major to address, but Ayad refused to employ either in that capacity. His acting XO, a monstrous, potbellied major named Jawaad, was known throughout the battalion as "Silverback," and he had a reputation for manhandling misbehaving *junood* when they failed to bend to his will. Although more than capable of running the battalion for Ayad, Jawaad was usually relegated to dealing with personnel and life-support issues throughout the camp. The battalion sergeant major filled a similar function, completing logistical and administrative duties that were more characteristic of a company gunnery sergeant than a sergeant major.

Ayad's mistrust of his officers was apparent as he rattled off his list to the staff. Such a lack of faith in his subordinates was evident in his micro-management of even the tiniest aspects of the battalion, and the frustration of the officers present at the staff meeting was written on their faces. As during the visit by Colonel Ra'ed earlier in the month, I marveled at the commander's obsession with the little things, particularly when there were so many greater issues on which to focus.

Yet Ayad's ravings weren't exactly without merit. If the petty things he described were true, then his staff was indeed letting him down, not supervising when they should have been. The issue of trust—or, in 3rd Battalion's case, the lack thereof—was a significant obstacle that polarized Ayad and his staff. For whatever reason he didn't trust them to make what would appear to be even the most basic decisions, and so every issue had to be brought to him for approval before any action could be taken. The officers and staff were generally unwilling to approach Ayad with questions or to seek guidance or clarification, and the result was an organizational paralysis throughout the battalion.

When it came to leadership and initiative, a gulf existed between what Ayad practiced and what he preached. He had told me many times that he placed great emphasis on the importance of junior leaders—the NCOs, lieutenants, and captains—but his words became merely lip service once I realized that he wouldn't give his subordinates the freedom to exercise initiative and responsibility. Despite his weak attempts at advocating modern military concepts such as the importance of junior leadership on the battlefield, Ayad was very much rooted in the customs and traditions of the old Iraqi army. His actions and decisions indicated a belief in strong, centralized leadership, and I soon realized that no amount of persuasion on my part could ever convince him to change his tune. The problem was compounded by the handbill that had been posted on his vehicle. Such incidents only heightened Ayad's sense of mistrust in his officers and caused him to tighten the reins within the battalion even further.

Setting aside the battalion's leadership challenges, I instead began to grapple with a larger issue. After having observed the battalion for nearly a month I wondered exactly what it was that was holding back the Iraqis from declaring complete independence from the MiTT team. Each month we submitted an operational readiness assessment (ORA) to our higher headquarters, and by the time the old team had departed 3rd Battalion had achieved ORA Level 2. Achieving Level 1—the point at which transition teams would no longer be required—meant that the battalion would be "capable of independent operations and sustainment."

While there were indeed leadership concerns at all levels in the battalion, the unit's Achilles' heel had actually been its weak logistical capability. But in general that weakness stemmed from a much higher level. Fuel, spare parts, ammunition—everything required to keep the battalion running—were in short supply, and neither 28th Brigade nor 7th Division could seem to provide them on a regular basis. And once I understood that I suddenly had an epiphany. Until the Iraqi Ministry of Defense was able to properly supply, equip, and maintain 7th Division, and the division could do the same for 28th Brigade, and the brigade could do the same for 3rd Battalion, Ayad's unit would not be able to achieve Level 1. We were hamstrung by the logjam further upstream, and until the MOD got its act together MiTTs would be required at the brigade and battalion levels. Until that time we could only continue to observe, offer assistance, and make recommendations when necessary. Whether the Iraqis acted on our suggestions was another matter entirely.

Chapter 18
Eye-opening Reality

The threat posed by IEDs—which until our arrival in the Al Qa'im region seemed to be on the path to extinction—had again resumed a slow, steady climb. The incidents continued to be isolated mostly to a winding stretch of road north of the Euphrates River, well out of 3rd Battalion's area of responsibility, but we followed the reports with interest and concern nonetheless. IEDs had also been found in and around Husaybah and Karabilah, and while those areas were technically the responsibility of the Iraqi Police, they were ones in which we frequently traveled. But no Coalition forces had been killed in the region since the Outlanders had been there, and I hoped our luck would continue to hold out.

Although the business of dealing with the IED threat was a deadly serious one, incidents occurred that were laced with black humor. On one occasion a patrol from the Marine task force discovered the site of an IED detonation during the course of a routine patrol. The earth was blackened and pockmarked where the bomb had exploded, and as the Marines conducted a postblast analysis of the site they discovered the disassociated remains of the person who had been emplacing it. During the arming process the device had detonated prematurely, blowing the perpetrator to kingdom come. The Marines saw it for what it was: one less jackass to deal with. On another occasion a patrol discovered the remains of a civilian truck that had triggered an IED along the side of a road. The truck had been ferrying a load of sheep, and the subsequent blast had littered the road with the singed, blackened husks of the animals. The driver was nowhere to be found, and the Marines assumed he had beat feet once he saw his livelihood get blown sky-high.

The honeymoon of no Marine casualties ended abruptly on 30 March when our COC received a report that a police transition team (PTT) had been hit by an IED in Fallujah. Although Fallujah was in a different AO far to our east, we followed the details with dread. Casualties had been reported, including one that had been classified as "urgent-surgical." Hard experience had taught me what that meant, but since no names were released it became just another faceless casualty somewhere in Iraq.

Or so we thought. Several days later Ashley forwarded me an e-mail from the Key Volunteer Network (KVN) in Camp Pendleton announcing that Maj. William Hall had been killed in action. He and his team had attended the Phoenix Academy with us, and we were stunned to hear of his death. It was a sober reminder for the team that our operating environment was not yet secure, despite all indications to the contrary. It gave us cause to review our SOPs and remind each other to wear our PPE whenever we were outside the wire. Beyond that it was a matter of luck.

One day as Captain Hanna and I sat around the MWR hut he turned to me and spoke.

"Sir, I've got an idea."

"Oh shit," I said, rolling my eyes. "Here it comes."

He knew I was joking. In a short period of time Hanna had earned my admiration and complete trust. Captain Flynn had been my operations officer and deputy during our predeployment training, and it had been clear that Hanna routinely subordinated himself and deferred to Flynn's advice and control of the team. But with Flynn gone—the result of a last-minute inability to deploy with us—Hanna had embraced his role not only as my principal logistician but also as the team's second-in-command. His maturity and ingenuity astounded me. He understood the balancing act a deputy must walk: how to carry out the team leader's intent without overstepping his boundaries. He continued.

"We've been trying to convince the IAs to have staff meetings," he began. "Why don't we show them what one of *our* staff meetings looks like? We can use the upcoming move to the new facility as an opportunity to demonstrate our planning and staff coordination process."

It was a brilliant suggestion, and in the week building up to 3 April the team focused on preparing a brief to be presented to me in front of the 3rd Battalion staff and Lieutenant Colonel Ayad. During the meeting each of the team's staff principals would brief me on courses of action that laid out different plans to move the team from COP South to the new brigade facility next to the phosphate plant. They would describe potential friction points and suggest ways to avoid them. They would also provide staff estimates for such considerations as force protection, command and control, and the amount of containers and rolling stock necessary to transport the team and its equipment. In the end I would decide which course of action to implement, and the plan would be set in motion.

But we had more planned than a simple staff brief. We rehearsed it the day prior, injecting a certain degree of theater. After identifying the areas in which the battalion staff was weak, we created scenarios we hoped would be a model for the Iraqis and that would inspire them to emulate our techniques. With the drama rehearsed beforehand the show we put on was entertaining. As the brief progressed I focused on staff coordination and engagement with higher headquarters.

"Sir," Lieutenant Grubb said as he briefed the security plan. "We have a couple of concerns about force protection. We are unsure what plan to implement based on a lack of knowledge of current enemy tactics."

"Well, have you gotten with the S-2 to match your plan with current enemy TTPs [tactics, techniques, and procedures]?" I answered.

"No, sir," he answered, faking sheepishness. "Not yet."

"Then do it," I said, pretending to chide him. "You guys have got to start coordinating and talking with each other."

Captain Hanna continued the act.

"Sir, we are getting a lot of push-back from the task force about transportation and lift," he began. "They won't commit to the numbers and types we need."

"Look," I said, feigning irritation. "You tell them it's their responsibility as a higher headquarters to support us. If they keep stonewalling you, let me know and I'll address it with their commander."

It was all a charade, but Lieutenant Colonel Ayad was impressed at the work my staff had presented to me. I hoped the rest of the Iraqi staff had bought our performance. More important, I hoped the 3rd Battalion officers would adopt some of our team's "best practices" and implement them into their own staff work. The IAs tended to imitate our actions, whether it was the way we wore our gear or carried ourselves and our weapons. Why should it be any different with our staff techniques?

But the initial high of the team's performance soon gave way to the reality of 3rd Battalion's situation. Despite the detailed briefing we had provided, the IA staff took no action to plan the upcoming move. No official order to move had been issued by 28th Brigade. Before that happened the battalion staff was content to do nothing until they were compelled to do so. The lack of initiative demonstrated by the IA staff was unsettling. Even scarier, 3rd Battalion was supposedly the best unit in the brigade. Ayad knew it, and he seemed concerned only with maintaining that image even at the risk of everything else. Privately the IA officers grumbled that Ayad had probably earned his appointment only through his political and tribal ties, and some feared that Ayad would systematically replace everyone on his staff with officers who would be nothing more than yes-men totally dedicated to him. It was not an unfounded fear. In my dealings with Ayad I learned that, to him, disagreement meant that a subordinate was either incompetent or could not be trusted. It violated what a battalion commander of mine had once told his staff: "It's okay to disagree, but it's not okay to be disagreeable." But that was an American notion, and I was not with an American military unit. I had to keep reminding myself of that reality.

The regional security meeting (RSM) was a bimonthly roundtable discussion that rotated from location to location. Attended by the district leadership of Al Qa'im, the meeting was headed by Al Qa'im's mayor, and the principals at each gathering included the Marine task force commander, the 28th Brigade commander, all of the brigade's battalion commanders, the district Iraqi Police chief, the local head of the Department of Border Enforcement (DBE), and other cats and dogs. The attendance by the military, police, and border transition teams, along with the bloated PSD detachments for the Iraqi leaders, made each meeting a crowded affair. The most anticipated aspect of every security meeting was the lavish meal provided at the end.

On 7 April the MiTT team accompanied Ayad to the RSM at the Ramanah IP station just north of the Euphrates River. The landscape around Ramanah was a stark contrast to what we were used to at COP South. The featureless desert that characterized our region south of the river was replaced by lush green crops and indigenous vegetation as soon as we crossed the sloping, girdered bridge that spanned the river. The area around Ramanah was more heavily populated than that around our camp, and we were not accustomed to the numerous buildings and throngs of Iraqis walking the streets. The locals stared; some waved. Children chased after our Humvees, holding out their hands and yelling, "Mistah, mistah! Give me one pen!" No matter how often it occurred, I could never understand the Iraqi children's obsession with writing implements.

In classic Iraqi fashion the meeting itself quickly devolved into an endless parade of self-platitudes and lip service to the need to cooperate. The long conference table brimmed with senior Iraqi officers, each staring suspiciously at the others while anticipating his turn to speak. Each officer's comments—mostly centered on his own curriculum vitae—mirrored the others: *The security situation is getting better. We must work together. We must continue to coordinate with each other.* They were saying what they were expected to say, but by the meeting's close they were no closer to resolutions regarding how to coordinate than they had been when they walked through the door.

The picture painted of the Al Qa'im region during the assembly seemed a rosy one, yet listening to Ayad each evening I began to assume the complete opposite. He didn't trust the police force, insisting to me that they were corrupt, inept, and more than likely behind most of the criminal activity occurring in and around Karabilah and Husaybah. He believed that the locals also didn't trust the IPs, and his conclusions about the efficacy of the IPs led him to insist that his battalion should resume operating in the cities and restore order.

The IPs in fact *were* inexperienced, and corruption and criminal activity were rampant within their organization. But we also knew that if 3rd Battalion continued to shoehorn itself into the cities and do the police force's job, the IPs would never rise to the occasion. The Iraqi soldiers knew the cities best and the open desert the least. They were more comfortable operating in the city, and because that was where all the enemy activity was occurring, that was where they wanted to be. It was the exact opposite of the direction given by the 7th Division and 28th Brigade commanders, but Ayad and his S-2 continued to plan operations in the cities regardless. My recommendations to the contrary were summarily disregarded, and I saw dark clouds forming on the horizon. A continued IA presence in the cities could eventually lead to a turf war between the army and the police, and it would only be a matter of time before some sort of showdown erupted.

For the Outlanders the regional security meeting was not without an upside. We had been cautioned about the kids who lived in Ramanah. Among the task force Marines they were known as the "Children of the Corn" (a moniker taken from a Stephen King story). Disregarding the warning, we packed candy and toys that had been sent from home, and once the meeting concluded the team members braced themselves against our Humvees for the onslaught. The children came first in ones and twos, curious, testing us and our reaction to their presence. Then suddenly they came out of the woodwork, and before we knew it we were surrounded. Once the Marines began handing out the gifts the children mobbed each other for every last bit they could grab. The scene depressed me and seemed to give me some sort of hope at the same time. They were impoverished, their ratty clothes hanging from withered frames as they reached out to us with rail-thin arms and open hands. But they trusted us enough to walk right up to us, and I thought, *If we can make them happy with just candy and toys, maybe there is hope for our mission here.* I continued to ponder this as we made the long convoy back to COP South, wondering if their amity toward us would last. Perhaps this generation of Iraqis would not grow up hating the Americans like the previous one did.

Despite my constant efforts at relationship building with Ayad, he continued to hold me at arm's length when it came to information sharing. On the evening of 8 April the two of us had discussed conducting a small community-relations project on the Jibab peninsula in 1st Company's AO. A local widow and her children needed basic supplies, and Ayad wanted to visit the family and help out. It was a fantastic idea. Such a mission would increase the army's standing among the locals. And there was always the hope that they would in turn offer valuable tips or information that 3rd Battalion could use in the area. My team was alerted, and Lieutenant Bates led the planning effort for the convoy to the peninsula the following day. The Marines were awake bright and early on 9 April, ready to head out with Ayad and his team. But after several hours of waiting around in confusion we received word that Ayad had inexplicably canceled the mission.

It was just one more concrete example of Ayad's lack of planning and general hot-and-cold style of doing things, and already I had grown exhausted with it. I was further irritated when I learned that he had met with the local police chief later in the day without telling me or inviting me to attend. My feelings of aggravation peaked when Mason told me that Ayad had mentioned a plan to investigate the site of a suspected weapons cache the following day. It infuriated me that Ayad had told his plans to an interpreter and not me.

"Why the hell is he telling *you* this shit and not me?" I grilled Mason.

He attempted to downplay the situation.

"He just told me because I ran into him walking around the camp," he answered, trying to calm me down before we went to see Ayad. Mason held in his arms two cases of Rip It—a heavily caffeinated soft drink the team kept around its camp that were highly sought after by the IAs—and I motioned to them.

"What are you doing with those?" I asked.

Mason shrugged his shoulders awkwardly.

"I promised Ayad I would bring him some of these."

"Goddammit, Mason," I growled. "Why the hell are you giving him shit when he won't even tell me what the hell is going on around here?"

"Sir, you have to understand this culture," he began. "It's all about give-and-take. If we give these to him, he'll warm up eventually."

"Where does it end, Mason?" I asked. "What's next? Televisions? Stereos? Computers? I don't care if that's their culture . . . I don't roll like that."

To a certain extent Mason had a point. We had only been there just over a month, and if two cases of soft drinks meant Ayad would open up to me, then I figured it to be a fair trade. But it didn't lessen my ire at the situation as a whole, and so when we delivered the drinks that night I was in a foul mood. I tried to hide my feelings, but I failed miserably. During our meeting I didn't talk much, and I when I did my questions were direct and business oriented. There were none of the perfunctory questions I was used to asking, inquiries such as how he and his family were doing. Uncomfortable with the tension in the room that my sullen mood was creating, Ayad began fidgeting in his chair, and he quickly told me about his planned operation the following day.

Over time his lack of trust and confidence in the battalion's S-2 section had led Ayad to develop and maintain his own personal network of human intelligence sources, the identities of whom only he knew. He claimed his sources were investigating a suspected cache of rocket launchers somewhere on the Jibab peninsula, and if the information turned out to be accurate he wanted to go check it out for himself as part of our scheduled trip to 1st and 2nd companies the following day. Armed with that information I excused myself to plan the MiTT's portion of the mission. It was not how I was accustomed to writing operations orders. Normally there was a significant amount of information from higher headquarters to process and translate into the order, but with such a lack of information offered by Ayad I was forced to improvise. It became what one of my lieutenants in Delta Company had once referred to as a "five-paragraph suggestion."

We were quickly learning that this was the way we had to do things as advisors. When it came to operating with the Iraqis, we would never be able to count on having enough information to make an educated decision. In many cases we would simply have to wing it.

Chapter 19
Jibab Peninsula

We sit around Major Muthafer's office at 1st Company, drinking chai, smoking cigarettes, and shooting the shit for over an hour. I begin to get restless when suddenly Lieutenant Colonel Ayad's S-2 scouts stride into the office. They are dressed in civilian attire—"under cover"—but with their pistols hanging from leather shoulder holsters they look more like self-important thugs than scouts. They tell the battalion commander that they are confirming the location of the weapons cache, and thirty minutes later Ayad's cell phone rings. He turns to me and says through my interpreter, "They found it," before moving swiftly out of the office and into his waiting Ford F-350. His three-vehicle PSD speeds off across the Jibab peninsula, leaving us in the dust. It takes the Marines longer to don our gear, fire up the vehicles and radios, and charge our weapons, and so we quickly fall behind the battalion commander's convoy. *Ayad is crazy*, I think. *Speeding off cross-country like that in his pickup trucks. They won't last a second if he hits an IED.*

Our movement on the peninsula's trails is further hampered by the load my Humvee is towing. We have left BP Okinawa in such a hurry that we forget to unhook the trailer, and it bounces around the trails crazily, threatening to break free and strike out on its own. Before long our two vehicles are lost along the tree-lined banks of the Euphrates, and Ayad's trucks are nowhere to be found. The locals stare at us, knowing we are lost, and suddenly things don't look good. When they know you're lost, they know they can hit you. Just as I make the decision to return to Okinawa we spot the three IA vehicles in the distance and move quickly to link up with them.

We slowly drive down the length of a narrow earthen trail along the riverbank, trying desperately not to dump our vehicles into the Euphrates. The IA scouts are on foot, and once Bates and Ski and I dismount and join them they lead us toward the cache site. One scout tells us there is also a possible IED farther up the trail past the site. Bates and Ski look at each other warily, and then they look at me. I shrug, and the three of us follow our Iraqi guides farther up the trail.

The scouts first show us an empty hole at the river's edge. It has been excavated, and its sides are flat and smooth, cut by someone with a shovel and a purpose. But there is no indication of what has been in it, and so we proceed farther up the trail. As we near the actual cache site, Ayad's three trucks come tearing down the trail toward us. The vehicles stop once Ayad sees me, and he nervously tells me he has received a call from the brigade commander. "Colonel Ra'ed wants me to meet him in Karabilah," he tells me through my interpreter. "I have to go now."

I am incredulous, unable to believe he has taken me all the way out here and is now going to leave just like that. I look at him disbelievingly.

"Okay, *sadie*," I say without attempting to hide the sarcasm and disdain in my voice. "I'm going to go check out this weapons cache and that possible IED. You go right ahead and go see the brigade commander."

He smiles his toothy grin and says, "Okay, very good," then speeds away with his PSD. Sarcasm doesn't translate well.

The cache of suspected rocket launchers turns out to be nothing more than a dozen ancient artillery rounds dug out of a cut in the riverbank. The shells are old and rusted, and we can't tell if the corrosion is from age or the dampness and humidity that permeate the area around the river.

"This doesn't add up," Bates says to me. "It looks like it's been planted."

I agree. "This stinks," I say, looking around suspiciously.

Ski walks up to me with an update. The scouts say they were alerted by a young boy who found the rounds. Ski interviews the boy as he sits in the cab of a small pickup truck. We can't tell if the boy is telling the truth. He speaks softly, and we are unsure what is making him nervous—the Marines clad in their bulky body armor or the Iraqi soldiers crowded around him.

The *junood* load the shells into their Humvee, and on the return trip we find more artillery rounds in a ditch alongside the trail. Like the shells on the riverbank they are old, but most have been cut into, the explosives harvested. A local farmer hands us a coil of new copper wire he has found concealed in a burlap sack next to the drainage ditch.

We return to BP Okinawa and dine with Major Muthafer, making small talk about the operation. Once we walk outside we find that the *junood* have placed all of the confiscated ordnance next to the company commander's hut. Bates and Ski catalog the rounds, determining which are live and which are spent. Some of the *junood* take this opportunity to turn in all the unexploded ordnance they have found on previous patrols and have been storing throughout the camp. Soon they are dropping off all kinds of ammunition—mortars, artillery rounds, even a primed rocket-propelled grenade (RPG) round. One soldier walks up with a sandbag full of highly volatile grains of jet-black artillery propellant. He is smoking a cigarette, and one of the Marines yells at him to drop the bag and get away before we are all blown up. We report the pile of armaments to higher headquarters and arrange for the explosive ordnance disposal (EOD) team to come out the following morning to dispose of it all.

The operation is over, and the team makes the protracted drive back to COP South. Alone with my thoughts, I reflect on the long day and the underlying suspicions we have about the cache. *Was it a dog-and-pony show?* I ponder. I don't know if the cache has been staged or not, but it seems like the entire episode has been put on for the battalion commander. And perhaps for him it has been a chance to showcase his scouts to me, a chance to say, *See, we* are *gathering intel and acting on it, and we are achieving results.*

It makes me uncomfortable thinking about it. If my counterpart can't be truthful about what is going on, if he has to stage events to prove his battalion's worth, how can I trust him to do the right thing when the time comes, after the Marines have left Iraq? Despite his protests to the contrary, I know he doesn't want us here, and I begin to think he is just biding his time until we leave. It doesn't bode well for my team for the next five months.

Chapter 20

Personalities and Paradigms

On 11 April more details about the artillery cache discovery surfaced, and it became apparent that, more than likely, the ordnance had not been planted. The battalion S-2 officer showed Lieutenant Ski video of the *junood* unearthing the rounds from the riverbank.

"We're both on there too," Ski commented to me later, referring to the tape. "I'm sure our photos will be on Al Jazeera tonight."

Regardless, it still seemed somewhat underhanded, and I continued to believe the entire episode had been staged as some sort of showcase. Whether it was for the benefit of the battalion commander or me, I didn't know. Little doubt existed that it was an old cache, and we estimated that it probably dated back as far as Operation Steel Curtain in 2005. Nonetheless, Ayad still wanted to plan a cache-sweep operation for an island that was directly north of the site, and that evening he told me he needed boats to conduct the mission. The U.S. Navy had a riverine operations detachment stationed at Camp Al Qa'im, and while I knew the sailors from the riverine squadron would be ready and willing to undertake such a task, I also knew that I didn't need to be doing Ayad's job for him.

"Request them through Brigade, *sadie*," I told him through Mason. "Seventh Division has boats you can use . . . you just need to ask for them."

"Division will never give them to us," he replied, shaking his head in disappointment.

"How do you know that?" I asked.

"No one at Brigade or Division will ever do anything to help us," he replied.

"But you won't know that unless and until you ask them," I said, frustration rising in my voice. "Look, request the boats through the brigade. We will look into how the Coalition might be able to support the operation if you don't get any results from your higher headquarters. But you need to ask your chain of command first."

Convincing 3rd Battalion's staff to engage the brigade headquarters was routinely an exercise in futility. The notion of higher headquarters acting as a supporting effort for its subordinates was lost on the Iraqis, and both Ayad and his staff patently refused to enlighten their counterparts at 28th Brigade with that concept. Whether asking for support was perceived as a sign of weakness or poor stewardship of his battalion, Ayad continued to avoid raising support issues with Colonel Ra'ed. We were there to help find Iraqi solutions to Iraqi problems, but the IA officers seldom seemed willing to try to help themselves. They preferred that the MiTT did the work for them, and that was a habit I committed myself and my team to changing. If we ever wanted to get out of Iraq the IA would have to learn to deal with problems on its own. It was turning out that, for the IA, fighting the insurgency was the easy part. The difficult part would be tackling organizational and cultural roadblocks that had plagued the army even before the Americans invaded in 2003.

At my urging Ayad planned an inspection of 2nd Company on 12 April, and as we accompanied him we hoped he would see firsthand the unsatisfactory conditions at BP Vera Cruz. It was intended to be a surprise visit, but the soldiers got wind of it and prepared the battle position accordingly. We were met by Captain Majid, 2nd Company's lumbering XO, and he began walking Ayad through the camp. An ineffectual officer at best, Majid constantly had a stunned look on his face. His uniform was tightly wrapped around a swollen belly, and he was forever making excuses about everything. It was exactly the kind of leadership that the soldiers of 2nd Company did *not* need, and the unit's discipline suffered accordingly.

With the advance warning of the battalion commander's visit the soldiers had scoured the camp from top to bottom, and as a result the general cleanliness was much better than the last time the MiTT had visited it unannounced. Majid escorted Ayad through the company's spaces, making sure he saw what Majid wanted to show him, not what Ayad really needed to see. Following his inspection Ayad gathered the company's soldiers to speak with them, and the Marines took the opportunity to inspect the area the soldiers used to relieve themselves. There had been no change since our previous visits, and as Ayad spoke to the soldiers he remained blissfully unaware of the continuing sanitation problem.

"Sir," Doc Rabor said to me, exasperated. "They've got to clean this up."

"I know, Doc," I replied. "It's fucking nasty."

HN1 Emiliano Rabor, our Navy corpsman, was originally from the Philippines and was perhaps the most sensitive member of the team. He had extensive training in combat trauma management, and his experience included operations with Special Forces in the Philippines and emergency-room duty in Los Angeles. Though often the butt of jokes and constant ribbing by the team, he was a wellspring of knowledge when it came to preventive medicine and trauma care—so much so that the Marines often avoided his care for fear that he might perform unnecessary field surgery on them. But he took his job seriously, and he often became fixated on medical issues with the Iraqis. The situation with 2nd Company's sanitation was no different.

"It's unhealthy, sir," he continued, pressing the issue. "It's near where they make their food. They're gonna get sick."

"I got it, Doc," I said. "I'll press the issue with Ayad. You just work on getting Second Company's medic up to snuff."

The convoy departed Vera Cruz and moved east to a small village on the Jibab peninsula to conduct the previously canceled community-relations visit Ayad had discussed with me several nights earlier. He had not told me of his plans to continue with the project, so the visit came as a surprise to the team. The Marines became aggravated. The team had recently received stacks of boxes from home containing candy and personal items, but without knowing about the project beforehand it had all been left behind at COP South. Throngs of local children crowded around us, asking once again for candy and pens. But the Marines could do nothing but shake their hands and pose for pictures as the IAs distributed food and money.

The impression, whether intended or not, was that the IA soldiers could provide humanitarian assistance while the Marines were just along for the ride. We didn't necessarily want credit for the operation. We were there, after all, to facilitate Iraqi operations, not the other way around. Yet while it was important that the locals see the IA as a caring force that was not just there to wreak havoc, I was nonetheless annoyed by Ayad's refusal to tell me his plans beforehand.

As we discussed the visit later that night, he asked me for a roll of power cable to help the two families we had visited slave electricity from a nearby generator. It would, he told me, help put a Marine face on the next visit.

"We could have done that today," I informed him, trying to mask the displeasure in my voice. "If you had told me last night that you planned to go out there. We could have brought a whole bunch of stuff for those people, *sadie*."

He was unfazed by my comments. "Well, you can just give us the cable and we can take it out to them tomorrow for you," he offered.

I balked at his suggestion. Given his current track record there was no way he would give credit to the Marines for the power cable.

"Tell you what," I countered. "How about we just take it out there the next time we go, okay?"

"Okay, very good," Ayad answered.

The return visit never occurred. It was an opportunity lost, but it wouldn't be the last time. Disappointment was becoming a daily sentiment among the team members.

My evening meeting with Ayad turned toward the day's visit to 2nd Company, and I suggested that perhaps he wasn't seeing the entire picture. Commenting on Majid's apparent lack of supervision, I opined that perhaps the captain's poor leadership was responsible for Vera Cruz being such a shithole when the battalion commander was not around. As I explained the sanitation issues and the associated health risk, I recommended that his next visit be unannounced so that he could see Vera Cruz as it really was. My pointing out 2nd Company's glaring deficiencies—when he had been so impressed with what Majid had showed him during the tour—embarrassed Ayad, and suddenly he changed his tune.

"Yes," he added. "I also noticed some things wrong there. *Naqeeb* Majid is on notice. I expect immediate improvement from him."

Unsure if Ayad was just telling me what he thought I wanted to hear, I pressed the issue deeper.

"Well, what have you done to put him on notice?"

He wouldn't give me a solid answer, and I knew he was trying to cover his tracks. I didn't expect him to solve the problem right then and there, but I hoped he would take to heart what I had said about Majid and the camp's condition. Performance counseling was an alien concept with the IAs. We had observed little in the way of mentoring and guidance to subordinates among the battalion's officers, and I once again had to caution myself about projecting American ideas and values on the Iraqis. We weren't supposed to be looking for the Marine Corps solution. If the Iraqi solution worked, that would have to suffice even if it didn't meet our own high standards.

As the realization sunk in that the Outlanders were unlikely to engage in direct combat operations while we were with 3rd Battalion, Lieutenant Grubb began to push for sustainment training for the Marines. The combat marksmanship course we had undergone in Camp Pendleton had made a significant impression on Grubb, and whenever possible he pushed to include such training in our schedule. Alone with the IAs in the middle of nowhere, we had more autonomy to train with our rifles and pistols, and the freedom to design whatever course of fire we wanted invigorated Grubb. On 14 April he and Staff Sergeant Leek set up a shooting course for the Marines on the small-arms range just outside the berm at COP South, and I decided to ask Ayad if he wanted to come out and shoot with us.

My motives were not entirely altruistic. I hoped that once he saw us firing our weapons it would motivate him to authorize live-fire small-arms training for his own soldiers. The *junood* had not fired their AK-47s in many months, and the bureaucratic obstacles within the IA system made it next to impossible to do so. Although 3rd Battalion possessed 134 percent of its ammunition allocation, I could not convince Ayad to request permission from 28th Brigade to receive authorization to shoot. Because the request process was so complicated, and because he assumed he would not receive approval, he continued to disregard my pleas to conduct the training. Even when I reminded him that he possessed 34 percent more than he was allotted—theoretically enabling him to expend ammunition without requesting approval—he discounted my suggestion. *What if an emergency arises and I need the extra ammunition?* he would ask. It was the same thought process he applied to fuel allocation among his three camps, a mentality that was a holdover from the old Iraqi army. Never knowing when—or if—the next shipment of supplies would come, the natural thing to do was hoard what was currently on hand. The subsequent result was a battalion that claimed it never had enough fuel to run its vehicles and generators, and soldiers who lacked the confidence and skill required to accurately and effectively employ their weapons systems.

Ammunition, fuel, spare parts—all were commodities the Marines had grown accustomed to. Although we often complained about a lack of them, we never feared that our supplies would simply dry up. The Marine Corps supply system, for all its faults, always managed to deliver, especially when Marines were in bad situations. It was not so with the IA's supply and logistics systems, and learning to navigate it was a constant challenge for us. Convincing the IAs to make their system work for them was difficult when the system hardly worked at all.

Upon receiving my invitation to our training, Ayad suited up in his body armor and Kevlar helmet and joined us on the range. My intent was for him to first observe our shooting procedures and techniques, and then let him fire both the M9 pistol and the M4 carbine. Standing off to the side with his bodyguard, he studiously watched me and the line of Marines complete the first string of fire with our pistols. But when I returned to his position on the observation line he suddenly informed me that the brigade commander had just called him and that he needed to go.

As I watched Ayad hastily move off the range and return to his office, Mason walked over to me.

"What was that all about?" I asked.

"Do you know what just happened?" he asked.

"No."

"Once you started shooting, Ayad walked up to his bodyguard and told him to go around the back of the berm and come back five minutes later and say the brigade commander was on the phone for him."

"Are you shitting me?" I asked incredulously.

"No," he insisted. "He told me that he hasn't fired his pistol since he was a lieutenant."

"Jesus," I said, shaking my head.

Unwilling to embarrass himself in front of the Marines, Ayad had instead taken the easy way out and excused himself from the training. Apparently pride and appearance meant more in the Iraqi officer corps than good training.

Ayad's questionable behavior in front of the Marines wasn't the only episode that day that shed more light on the battalion's officers. Lieutenant Bates later recounted how, upon entering the S-3 hut for his daily meeting, he found a weeping Captain Al'aa. The officer had been barely able to even speak, and Bates left him alone. Bates later heard that Al'aa had collapsed and had been taken to the hospital. Eventually we learned that Al'aa's Internet girlfriend, Nadia, had fallen ill—supposedly it was cancer—and Al'aa had experienced some sort of emotional breakdown over it.

"But he's never even *met* her!" I exclaimed, rolling my eyes.

"I know, sir," replied Bates. "Weird, huh? They sent him out on *mujaas*."

"Well, when will he be back?" I asked.

"Who knows? He hasn't been on leave in over a year."

I marveled at the situation. If something similar had occurred with a Marine officer—an emotional collapse over a faceless Internet love—he would have been laughed out of the service. If someone whom Al'aa had never even met face-to-face had been able to affect his work and personal state of mind that much, just how effective would he really be when he returned to the battalion—*if* he returned to the battalion? But Al'aa's situation was not unique. Officers within the battalion routinely departed on "personal leave" for a variety of reasons. Whatever the reason—family crises, pay problems, illness—the IA officers typically left work at the drop of a hat. It was a luxury few Iraqi soldiers were afforded, and for us it demonstrated once more the gulf between Iraqi officers and soldiers and how differently they were treated. Whether it was personal liberties and entitlements, quality of food, personal allocations of water, or constant air-conditioning, the IA officers lived a better life than the soldiers, and the soldiers knew it. It was detrimental to their morale, and I wondered if my team and I—through our own personal example—would ever be able to convince the Iraqi officers to change their paradigm.

Chapter 21
Terps and Tensions

The relationship between the Iraqi army and the police force—which had already been tenuous—took a turn for the worse on 16 April. During a routine convoy the 28th Brigade commander, Colonel Ra'ed, stopped off at an IP substation south of Ubaydi peninsula. Acting on a tip, Ra'ed and his PSD found a cache of RPG launchers and rockets, weapons that were illegal for the IPs to possess. Ra'ed and his men confiscated the ordnance and continued on their way. An angry, heated phone conversation between Ra'ed and Colonel Jamaal, the district IP chief, followed, during which Ra'ed attempted to smooth over the situation. His apologies were instead furiously rebuffed by Jamaal, and in an instant tension between the IAs and the IPs around Al Qa'im escalated. Lieutenant Colonel Gridley warned me about the potential consequences.

"Keep your eyes and ears open about what is going on right now," he cautioned. "After Colonel Jamaal motherfucked Ra'ed like that there's no telling how the IAs will respond."

"We've been trying to keep Third Battalion out of the cities," I replied. "But I don't know how much success we're going to have with that. Ayad is pretty determined to keep operating there."

"Just look out. Things could potentially get out of hand pretty quickly between the IA and IP."

Ra'ed's actions had needlessly exacerbated the army's lack of trust in the IPs, and I imagined our effort with 3rd Battalion taking another very large step backward. Unless Ra'ed and Jamaal met face-to-face and somehow managed to cool their newfound animosity toward each other, their attitudes were bound to trickle down their respective chains of command. As I had worried previously, it could climax with a shoot-out between the IAs and IPs. The results would be disastrous.

The regional security meeting that took place at Mayor Farhan's residence in Husaybah several days later was a tense affair. Colonel Jamaal did not show up, and his absence clearly insulted both the mayor and the IA officers present. Although the Marine task force commander attempted to gloss over the issue, Jamaal's nonattendance hung like an uncomfortable shroud over the entire meeting. It did not bode well for the ongoing drama unfolding between the local army and police forces.

Life around COP South was not solely focused on advising the Iraqis. Because of our isolation and distance from supporting units we spent a substantial portion of our time conducting camp maintenance and other life-support activities. A large part of our time was dedicated to running convoys to Camp Al Qa'im, where we tended to logistical and administrative matters. Around COP South there was always maintenance and area improvement work to be done, and it was always a team effort.

On 18 April, as the team worked in small groups on minor maintenance projects around the compound, Staff Sergeant Leek and I tackled a digging project that we had put off for too long. A communications cable running from the COC and across the camp's throughway to our satellite relay needed to be buried to keep it from getting cut by the IA trucks and Humvees that constantly sped through the compound. Soon after we began our work Lieutenant Grubb joined us, and for close to two hours the three of us took turns hacking away at the rock-hard ground with a pickax. Choking dust and rock chips flew everywhere, and before long we were dripping in sweat and caked with chalky powder and debris. During the middle of our efforts Ayad drove through the camp with his PSD, and when he spied me swinging away with the ax a puzzled look filled his face. As he drove away he continued to gaze at me as if I was a life-form from another planet. I turned to Leek.

"Jesus," I said, wiping the dust from my eyes. "He looks like he's never seen someone digging a fucking trench before."

"He's probably pissed that the *junood* are seeing you do actual work," Leek grunted, shaking his head. "Makes him look bad. The *jundis* know that *their* fucking officers don't do any work at all."

"Well, we aren't gonna change *that*," I said, my aggravation bleeding through. "The only physical work they ever do is lifting a fucking glass of chai to their mouths ten times a day."

The inclusion of interpreters in our team and learning how to utilize them was something entirely new to me when we deployed to Iraq. Two interpreters—Muhammad and Muhammad, both hired through a Department of Defense (DOD) contract—had joined us at the start of our training at ATG, and the intent had been for them to train and deploy with us to Al Qa'im. A third interpreter had been unable to deploy with us at the last minute, and so Mason had been assigned to the team. Involving the interpreters early in the training had been a good idea. It gave the Marines a chance to find out how to employ them and learn about the culture and language before actually setting foot in Iraq.

But our time with our three interpreters prior to departing the United States was not without friction. I had made my intent clear to the team and our interpreters early in our training. To the Marines I had simply said, "The terps are part of our team. Welcome them aboard and include them in everything we do." Similarly, to the interpreters I had said, "Welcome to the team. We are happy to have you aboard with us. You are with a Marine team; I expect you to act accordingly and participate in everything the Marines do."

The friction began soon after. Of the two Muhammads on the team, Little Mo—so named because of his slender frame, as opposed to Big Mo, who was much heftier—tended to pick and choose when to become involved. When the Marines were taking turns jamming nose hoses into each others' nostrils during our predeployment medical training he refused to participate. When there was heavy lifting to be done, he was often conveniently absent. When the team spent a freezing two weeks at Mojave Viper, he passed the majority of his time curled up in the warmth of his sleeping bag. He ostracized himself, and the situation initially came to a head during the team's after-action review at the close of Mojave Viper. When his turn to speak came, he addressed the Marines sitting around the table.

"You all have to remember that I'm just an interpreter. I'm not a Marine," he had said, slight contempt coating his voice. "If I can help out, I will. I would take a bullet for some of you guys. But you can't talk to me like a Marine. You can't treat me like a Marine."

The Marines' ears had perked up. Some *of us*, I had thought. A warning beacon had just been flashed to me, but I refused to heed its alarm.

Similar behavior continued, and as we transitioned from Camp Pendleton through the different waypoints in Iraq Little Mo's behavior became more and more unacceptable. At one point he refused to attend classes at the Phoenix Academy, choosing instead to sit in his room and pout like a small child.

His inability to mesh with the team continued after we arrived at COP South, and toward the end of March Captain Hanna pulled him aside and laid down the law. Hanna, who struck me as perhaps the most polished, levelheaded, and professional officer I had ever encountered, counseled Little Mo the way he would have a young Marine. Mo, who at age twenty-one seemed in the midst of a rebellious phase, was less than receptive to Hanna's approach, and we soon learned that he planned to request reassignment to another team.

Hearing all this from Hanna and Master Sergeant Deleonguerrero, I thought for a moment, and then turned to Deleon.

"Well, Top, what do you think?"

Deleon didn't hesitate.

"Shit-can his trash," he said, flashing me the rock band sign for emphasis.

I looked at Hanna and Lieutenant Ski, who as the team's "terp manager" had been responsible for Little Mo's routine performance counselings. Both officers nodded in agreement.

"Concur," I said. "I'm sick of his shit, and I'm not going to let him leave on his own terms. Get him on the first bird out of here. Bring him to me the night before his flight and I'll take care of it."

When Little Mo appeared at my door several days later, Deleon and I were waiting for him. I didn't mince words or waste time.

"Muhammad, it's not working out with you here, and I'm having you reassigned."

He looked shocked; clearly he hadn't been expecting it.

"Do you mind if I ask why?" he asked contemptuously.

"Sure," I replied. "You're lazy, immature, and generally not a team player. Quite frankly, Muhammad, you are a drain on the team, and your presence is disrupting for everyone."

"Well," he answered aloofly, rolling his eyes. "If that's what you want."

"You're right, Muhammad. It *is* what I want. Pack your bags. A flight will be here for you tomorrow."

I was taking a gamble. Little Mo and Big Mo had grown up together, and both had signed on together as a package deal. The possibility existed that Big Mo would make his exit with his friend, but I was willing to take that chance. Little Mo's departure would be the best thing for the team in the long run. Ultimately, Big Mo didn't quit, but he was angry about his friend's release for weeks afterward.

Big Mo's agitation wasn't the only problem we had once Little Mo had left the team. Several weeks later Hanna alerted me that the interpreters were feeling isolated by the Marines and left out of the loop. In an attempt to remedy the situation, I reiterated to the men that they needed to treat the interpreters as vital team members. After all, without them we would be unable to do our jobs with the Iraqis. I adjusted my guidance by telling the Marines that while certain cultural differences existed that we needed to respect, the terps would still be expected to participate in all team duties.

That included policing the camp and other routine duties the Marines themselves were required to perform on a daily basis. The same information was passed to the interpreters, and all seemed to be right with the world again.

But the next day, 19 April, everything blew up. As the Marines prepared to leave the wire for the regional security meeting in Husaybah, I walked back to my hut to retrieve my backpack. While I was away Shawn, one of the local-hire interpreters, wandered up to the assembled Marines, more than thirty minutes late for the team's convoy brief. Captain Hanna pulled him aside.

"Listen, Shawn," he said firmly. "You need to be on time for these briefings."

"Why do I have to be on time?" Shawn asked indignantly.

"Look, you need to be here because you were fucking told to be here," Hanna countered, his anger rising. "Period."

"I was in the toilet."

"I don't care!" Hanna said, raising his voice. "You were told to be here at zero-eight. I'm fucking tired of you always being late and always having excuses. Let me be clear: When you are told to be somewhere at a specific time, you are expected to follow through."

Shawn stepped closer to Hanna and began yelling.

"No one talks to me that way! I don't understand why it's so fucking important that I be on time!"

"I don't know who the fuck you think you are talking to, Shawn, but you will not yell at me, give me excuses, or tell me that you don't have to be on time."

As the exchange between the two began to spiral, Mason stepped in, attempting to calm Shawn down. But Shawn would have nothing of it, and he stormed away from the Marines.

"This is fucking bullshit!" he yelled to no one in particular. "Fuck you guys! I quit! I'm out of here! Someone take me to AQ right now!"

As I returned to the vehicles I heard several Marines and interpreters yelling for Shawn to come back. I rounded the bend just in time to see him storming off across the compound, shaking his head furiously and mumbling to himself. I walked up to Hanna.

"What's going on?" I asked.

Hanna, who rarely expressed anger in front of the Marines, irately shook his head.

"Shawn was thirty minutes late to the convoy brief," he began. "We just got into a pissing match." Hanna continued to relay the story to me.

"Damn, I'm sorry I missed that," I said.

"What do you want to do?" Hanna asked, calming down.

"Can't do much about it now," I replied. "Come on, we're late. Let him stew in his own juices, and we'll deal with it when we get back from the meeting. He's done, regardless."

The decision about what to do with Shawn was an easy one. He wanted to go, and I wanted him gone. By mouthing off to Hanna in front of all the Marines and then refusing to go on the convoy, Shawn had sealed his own fate. We arranged for his reassignment immediately, and once more a terp was removed from the team. Although I didn't regret firing either interpreter—or a third whom we later had reassigned for a near inability to properly translate even the simplest dialogue—I wondered if I had set in motion a pattern that would eventually result in all of our interpreters leaving the team. The standards we had set for them had not been unreasonable. They were not expected to stand duty, nor were they expected to do things above and beyond that which was expected of the Marines. Yet as much as we tried to bring the interpreters into the fold and include them as part of the team, there would always be differences that made doing so that much more difficult. Little Mo had been correct: they were not Marines. But somehow we had to figure out a way to get along. Without them we were sunk.

Following the regional security meeting Lieutenant Colonel Ayad began discussing the island cache-sweep operation he had first mentioned to me the previous week. As I sat in his office, a glass of chai in front of me, he told me he wanted to conduct the operation within forty-eight hours.

"Were you able to get the boats that I asked you for?" he asked.

"*Sadie*, you need to request them from Brigade before my team can do anything about it," I answered, not liking where the conversation was headed.

"They won't give them to us."

"Did you request them?" I asked. Conversations such as this were becoming commonplace, repeating like a broken record.

"No," he answered. "They won't give them to us anyway."

"Jesus," I muttered to myself. "This is going nowhere." I decided to try a different approach.

"Well," I continued, "if you want to conduct the mission in less than two days, then perhaps you should contract some boats from the local fishermen."

Ayad thought for moment, and then nodded his head.

"Yes, that is what we'll do since the MiTT was unable to get us the boats."

His comment took me by surprise, and I snapped back at him.

"Whoa, wait a minute, *sadie*," I said, stabbing my finger against the glass top of the coffee table for emphasis. It was time for a conversation that was long past due. "That's not how it works. We don't just 'get stuff' for you. You are supposed to request all support through your higher headquarters, and then you are supposed to follow the request through to completion."

He stared at me blankly, and I continued to lecture him.

"If your request goes all the way up the chain of command and back down with no results, only then will my team and I leverage Coalition support."

"It's useless to request anything from our higher headquarters," he protested, once again repeating his tired song. "They'll never answer our request. They don't have anything, and if they do they won't give it to us."

The conversation was pointless; I felt like I was talking to a wall. I attempted yet another approach.

"Look, *sadie*," I began. "You need to make your higher headquarters work for you. That's their job. Make them do it. You have to at least make the effort before my team can step in, otherwise the situation will never get better."

I continued, attempting to explain how the squeaky wheel gets the grease, but he still shook his head.

"Look," I finally said, exasperated. "Have you talked to the brigade commander about any of this?"

"No."

"Well, if you identify something as being high priority and you feel the brigade staff isn't giving your battalion the support it needs, then you need to engage Colonel Ra'ed on the matter."

I closed the conversation by reminding him once more that my MiTT team wasn't there to give them things or do their job for them. We were there merely to train, coach, mentor, and advise. It had been our least pleasant chat to date, and I left his office deeply distressed. Clearly the previous teams had given much more than perhaps they should have, and in doing so had created unreasonable expectations on the part of Ayad and his staff.

But I couldn't leave the conversation where it had ended, so I returned the following evening to continue the dialogue. After our routine formalities I launched right into the points I had prepared.

"You know, there's a good chance that the Coalition will be gone in little more than a year," I began, citing a series of news articles I had recently read. "We've got to set the conditions to prepare for that eventuality. Explain to me what your battalion's working relationship was with the previous MiTT team."

The Outlanders team photo. Back row, left to right: Sgt. Olanza Frazier, Cpl. Daniel Fry, LCpl. Travis Wardle, Sgt. Mark Hoffmier. Front row, left to right: SSgt. Clarence Wolf, Sgt. Theo Bowers, 1st Lt. Joseph Davidoski, Capt. Jason Rehm, MSgt. Norvin Deleonguerrero, Maj. Seth Folsom, Capt. Todd Hanna, 1st Lt. Matt Bates, 1st Lt. Andrew Grubb, SSgt. Shaun Leek, HN1 Emiliano

Captain Hassan (left) from 3rd Company briefs First Lieutenant Bates (2nd from right) and Big Mo during the cordon-and-search operation at Al Gab'aa.

Lieutenant Colonel Ayad (center) briefs officers and soldiers from 3rd Battalion, 28th Brigade at COP South. (Photo courtesy of Joe Davidoski)

First Lieutenant Davidoski (center) discusses cache-site discoveries with soldiers from 1st Company during a sweep of Jibab peninsula.

First Lieutenant Grubb (center, standing) supervises 3rd Battalion soldiers during a long-awaited machine-gun shoot.

Captain Hanna greets local children during a community-relations visit by 3rd Battalion to Jibab peninsula.

Outlander Marines observe while 3rd Battalion soldiers conduct a local security operation in the desert south of Al Qa'im.

Lieutenant Colonel Ayad and Major Folsom pause for a picture in downtown Husaybah.

Sergeant Hoffmier relaxes with a friend. (Photo courtesy of Theo Bowers)

Local leaders from Al Qa'im meet during a regional security meeting conducted at Border Fort 5.

He paused, fondly staring off into space, as if remembering a distant dream.

"We worked hand-in-hand with the old MiTT team," he said. "Whenever they had difficulties—whenever *we* had difficulties—we solved each other's problems. We didn't involve the brigade; we solved our problems ourselves."

"Give me an example."

"Whenever we needed spare parts for our Humvees, the MiTT would get them for us," he told me. "We planned operations together. The MiTT wasn't concerned about the IPs. Whenever there was a mission, the MiTT would get in their Humvees and go with us."

In other words, I thought sarcastically, *you are used to getting what you want from the Americans*. Armed with the information he had offered—and being careful not to be critical of the last MiTT team—I reiterated what I had said the previous night.

"My team's focus is not on conducting routine operations with your *junood*," I told him matter-of-factly. "We are past that. Your companies are capable of conducting routine patrols and operations without us. Instead, my focus is to assist and guide you and your staff in leveraging Iraqi army support for your operations." I remembered what Donald Rumsfeld had once said, and although it had provoked nearly the entire U.S. Army when he had said it, I paraphrased his words to Ayad. "It's important that Third Battalion learn how to fight and sustain itself with the army it has, not the army it wishes it had." Then I remembered a fitting line from the movie *Jerry Maguire*. "You've got to help *me* to help *you*," I said.

Once I had listed my main points I made sure to apply the appropriate degree of ego stroking and professional compliments. Although we had engaged in a cordial discussion, Ayad's demeanor had changed by the end, and I left his office unsure of how he felt or whether he would take my advice and counsel for how it was meant: as constructive criticism aimed at making him a better commander and his battalion a better unit. No matter how he felt, however, I was confident in my decision to finally drop the boom on him. It had been a long time coming, and it was time that someone brought him back to reality.

As Mason and I walked back across the camp to our compound and discussed the meeting with Ayad, he stopped in his tracks and turned to me.

"Ah, it's all becoming clear to me now," he said, as if a light had suddenly come on in his head. "You know what the IAs are saying about you, right?"

"No, Mason. I don't speak Arabic, remember?"

"They have a nickname for your team," he said, lowering his voice and looking around cautiously. "They call you 'pussies' because you don't go out on daily patrols with them. They don't think you all are as aggressive as the last team was."

"Whatever, Mason," I said, waving it away with my hand. "That's not our job. Besides, I don't have anything to prove to those motherfuckers. Neither does any of my team. Running outside the wire with the *junood* on some half-baked plan based on questionable or nonexistent intel isn't my idea of good headwork. It's more like suicide. I'm not gonna risk my Marines' lives just because the *junood* don't think we're aggressive enough."

I walked into the MWR hut and sat down next to several Marines watching a movie. As usual, they asked me their nightly question.

"How's Ayad?"

I relayed Mason's revelation to those around me.

"Well, apparently the IAs don't think we're aggressive enough," I said sarcastically. "Their nickname for us is 'pussies.'"

"What?" they all shouted.

"What a bunch of fucking bullshit," someone commented.

"Yeah, whatever," I said. "Who cares *what* they think."

"Pussies, huh?" Captain Hanna commented dryly, his deadpan humor breaking the tension. "What does it say about you when you're too afraid to shoot a pistol in front of the Marines?"

The Marines all laughed, but one thing was certain: the honeymoon between 3rd Battalion and the Outlanders was over. Despite the fact that I had the moral support of Gridley and his staff, I anticipated a shift in my team's relationship with the staff of 3rd Battalion. They now knew that the Marines weren't there to give them a free lunch. Whether they took our advice and applied it would remain to be seen.

I remembered something my wife—herself a professional consultant who specialized in organizational change management—had told me one night after I groused to her over the Internet about my predicament: The MiTT team was really nothing more than a military consulting team. We could advise and recommend changes until we were blue in the face, but unless there was buy-in or sponsorship from higher headquarters nothing would ever change. And yet, like consultants, one other thing was true: In the end it didn't matter if the Iraqis took our advice or not. We got paid either way.

Chapter 22
Uglat il Bushab

Captain Hussein is the ineffectual intelligence officer for 3rd Battalion, but he becomes the acting S-3 officer while Captain Al'aa is gone on leave. Hussein has been planning an operation in the battalion's southern battlespace for several days, and after several weather delays he decides finally to launch the mission. The MiTT forms two vehicle crews, plans its portion of the mission, and prepares its equipment for the coming operation. The day the mission is supposed to launch the Marines wait for the IAs at the rendezvous point for more than an hour. The Iraqis' lethargy starts the operation on a sour note—I have been awake all night on duty and am not impressed.

The IAs have planned for two companies to conduct a search-and-clear operation in two areas: Uglat il Bushab to the southeast and Um Tinah to the south. Hussein tells us that once they have picked up their source we will travel to Camp Al Qa'im and then head southeast to Uglat il Bushab. Once the first objective has been cleared we will move on to Um Tinah. He claims that they have received intelligence reports that insurgents are outfitting a truck to be used as a VBIED. We know that it is not really intelligence; it is merely a tip, but we hold our tongues. Everything is relative here.

As the convoy nears Camp Al Qa'im the IAs turn south prematurely and the long line of trucks and Humvees begins paralleling an abandoned rail line. We continue on this course for ten kilometers, then the lead vehicle turns off the road and leads the convoy out into the open desert along an old goat trail. The column weaves back and forth for several hours, venturing deeper and deeper into the southern desert, stopping only when the smaller trucks become mired in the powdery dust blanketing the route. My Humvee brings up the rear, and because our Blue Force Tracker is not working properly Capt. Jason Rehm manipulates a Global Positioning System (GPS) in the turret. He calls out grid coordinates every five minutes, keeping us abreast of our location on the map. At one point Rehm rattles off a grid and Doc Rabor and I check our maps.

"Tell me that grid again," I say to Rehm through my headset.

He repeats the numbers, and Doc taps me on my shoulder

"Um, sir?" Doc says, confused. He has just realized the same thing I have.

"What the hell," I say, thinking aloud. "We've run all the way off our map sheet." We are in no-man's-land, and I hope the second MiTT vehicle's BFT is still working.

The column finally rolls to a halt, and from atop a bluff on which Hussein has positioned us he dispatches 3rd and 4th companies to a small hamlet in the valley below.

Our team's plan is to colocate ourselves with Hussein so we can observe his mobile COC in the field and observe how he battle-tracks the operation while it is under way. But the minute Hussein deploys the companies to the village the notion of a COC as we know it goes out the window. Hussein yells to the two companies on his Motorola radio, and the radio net explodes into chaos. Officers scream orders back and forth to each other in the valley, and Hussein shouts and gesticulates from his position on the bluff. After a few minutes he orders the two companies to displace to another village farther south.

As Hussein prepares to move his own Humvee and travel with the companies I assess the situation into which we have gotten ourselves. We are off the map—both literally and figuratively—and we have already burned a quarter tank of fuel just getting here. Hussein has no coherent plan, and his "source" has taken us much farther into the frontier than originally briefed. If something goes wrong I doubt we will be able to get Coalition support in a timely manner, and with Hussein's vague mission statement I have no idea what we will roll into if we accompany him farther south. I tell Hussein my team will wait on the bluff, hoping he will take the hint and change his plan. Instead, he makes no argument and speeds off to find his companies. My confidence in Hussein's abilities disintegrates, and the team remains in place for three hours while we monitor the pandemonium on the radio net and casually watch the Iraqi vehicles spin around the basin in confused circles like a lost circus procession.

When the IAs complete their operation down south they drive past the Outlanders without stopping, as if they have forgotten about us. The Marines curse as they quickly disassemble the SATCOM relay, and we jump in our vehicles to catch up to the IA convoy.

The aimless driving through the desert continues, and we eventually learn that Hussein still plans to conduct the second half of the operation at Um Tinah. Unsure how long our fuel and patience can both hold out, I make the call for the MiTT team to split away from the IA convoy and return to COP South through the wasteland on our own. I know we will get grief from the IAs once we eventually see them again, and we are likely to lose face for not completing the mission with them. I don't care. Hussein has not put the appropriate degree of work into his planning, and the mission has become a complete waste of time.

The Marines are all frustrated because we have been prodding the IA to focus less on the cities and more on the southern desert. They have finally taken our advice, but their poor mission planning and execution yields nothing. For them it becomes an opportunity to say to us, *See, we told you there is nothing going on down there!* Regardless, we resolve to insist on more detailed planning and premission briefing for future operations to avoid the same carnival-like demonstration again.

If this is how they plan all of their operations, I think, *it's a wonder they haven't been completely wiped off the map by the enemy by now.* And again I remember that we are not seeking the Marine Corps solution, only a solution that works for the Iraqis. But even in that regard they still have a long way to go. And as I review the operation during our dusty trek back through the desert I realize that we too have a long way to go before we will succeed in our mission as advisors.

Chapter 23
Fear and Paranoia

In the last weeks of April the Iraqi army offensive against the Shiite militias in Basra weighed heavily on everyone's mind. I read with interest reports about Marine MiTT teams—including some officers I had known for years—in the fight with their counterpart battalions from 26th Brigade and the Iraqi 1st Quick Reaction Force (QRF) Division, and it was a daily challenge for me to hide my disappointment from my Marines.

When I left Iraq in 2003 I had grown tired of war in a very short time, and I wanted nothing further to do with it. But now, half a decade later, I had pushed the horrible realities of combat into the recesses of my mind, and the old spark of longing had fully ignited my desire to return to action, however foolish and irresponsible such cravings were.

The Outlanders felt it too, and keeping them motivated and focused on their jobs as advisors was a challenge for me. While more than half of the team members had deployed to Iraq before, only a handful of the Marines had actually experienced combat. To the uninitiated among the team, the offensive in Basra seemed a cruel joke, one that reminded them each day of the stagnation and inaction 3rd Battalion was suffering. When a call went out from the 7th IA Division MiTT team requiring personnel augmentation for 26th Brigade's advisor force in Basra, hands went up all over COP South. I couldn't blame the men for their enthusiasm, and after I had made the decision to submit the names of LCpl. Travis Wardle and Cpl. Daniel Fry as volunteers for the reassignment, I summoned both Marines to my hut to speak to them in private.

Wardle and Fry, the team's two most junior Marines, came from very different backgrounds. Wardle, a towheaded, angel-faced youth from Utah, was the epitome of squeaky-clean. He was an atypical lance corporal, always observing everything and measuring his words carefully before speaking. He had earned the nickname "Trashcan Man" for his frequent trips to the burn pit and his love of fire. Corporal Fry, on the other hand, hailed from Georgia, and he was known for his deep, leisurely southern drawl and bizarre sense of humor. He bore a striking resemblance to a character named McLovin from a movie called *Superbad*, and once everyone on the team had seen it the name stuck.

Both men were exactly the kind of junior Marines I had hoped for when the team initially formed, and I selfishly didn't want to give them up for the mission in Basra. But they wanted their chance to see the elephant of combat for themselves, and I knew there was nothing I could do to extinguish that yearning. I had been in their shoes at one point in my life, wanting my chance to experience combat and prove my worth. And so, rather than attempt to dissuade them, I simply made sure both Marines knew what they were getting themselves into. They were unfazed by my warnings, and in the end I agreed to support and endorse their request to redeploy to Basra. As luck would have it they were not needed; the personnel requirement was filled by Marines from the brigade MiTT team. I broke the news to both Wardle and Fry, and the disappointment on their faces was palpable.

"Don't worry," I said, paraphrasing my father's words from years earlier. "Stay in long enough and you'll get your chance to get shot at one day."

On 24 April the battalion's *mujaas* cycle—which had been delayed because of the events in Basra—resumed, and Iraqi soldiers and officers excitedly ran back and forth throughout the camp, waiting for the leave convoy that would take them home. I visited Lieutenant Colonel Ayad one last time before he departed for his own leave, and I was surprised to find Lieutenant Colonel Sabah, the 28th Brigade logistics officer, hanging out in his brown *dishdasha* in Ayad's office. I hated it whenever Sabah came to COP South. An angry man, Sabah was a rabble-rouser who constantly planted seeds of discord that got Ayad spun up every time the two men were together. He had been a colonel or a brigadier general in the old regime, and when he joined the new Iraqi army he was demoted to major (probably because of his affiliation with the Baath Party and the old regime). The demotion had embittered him, and his stump speech always included a litany of justifications about why he should still be a full colonel. He hated the government in Baghdad, and on more than one occasion I had listened to him opine that the members of Prime Minister Nouri al-Maliki's cabinet should all be "removed" or deported to Iran. In several instances, upon leaving a meeting at which Sabah had been present, I wondered to myself, *Did he just openly suggest that a military coup is the best solution to Iraq's political problems?*

I found Ayad sitting there with Sabah, chain-smoking cigarettes and clearly agitated. Ayad only smoked on two occasions: when he was stressed out, and when Sabah was around. As soon as I joined the two officers Ayad immediately launched into a tirade about the IPs. Earlier in the day an IP patrol car had collided with an IA vehicle in Husaybah, and during the ensuing argument the IP officers had drawn their weapons on the IA soldiers. Fortunately the incident didn't escalate any further, but it became fuel for Ayad to vent his spleen once more about the police force.

"They're nothing more than gangs with uniforms!" he spit out, dragging heavily on his cigarette. "Or worse, militia. They are unprofessional. They are inept. They are affiliated with criminals, and they are a danger to the security situation in Al Qa'im."

"Well, Jesus, *sadie*," I said, hoping for solutions to the problem rather than just complaints. "What do you think should be done?"

"The solution is simple," he said. "Disband the *sherta* [police] leadership and completely retrain the IP force."

It was an impossible solution, but he was convinced there was no other way. Ayad wouldn't be satisfied until the IP was either dissolved or subordinated to the army, and the IA was back and operating in the cities permanently. I left the meeting deeply troubled, relieved that I wouldn't have to deal with Ayad and his skewed reality for ten days.

The next evening, however, I actually wished Ayad had been around. As I joined several members of the team in the MWR hut to watch a movie my radio crackled to life with the voice of Capt. Jason Rehm. The team's personnel advisor, Rehm was an F/A-18 Hornet fighter pilot from Connecticut and a graduate of North Carolina State. A late-join to the MiTT, he had replaced the hole left by Captain Flynn's departure and had arrived at COP South several weeks earlier. Burly, yet unexcitable, he had quickly found his place among the Marines.

"COC, this is One," he radioed from somewhere on the compound. "Did you just hear shots being fired?"

"What the . . . ?" I said to no one in particular.

Captain Hanna stood and poked his head outside the MWR hut, and just as he did so a second staccato burst of AK-47 fire echoed from the camp's north. We jumped to our feet and walked quickly across the compound to the northern ECP, each Marine chambering a round in his pistol in unison. I keyed my radio.

"Nine, this is Six," I said, summoning Doc Rabor. "Prep your med bag. We don't know what's happening out here."

"Roger, sir," he replied. "I'm Oscar-Mike [on the move]."

I rekeyed my radio. "COC, tell everyone to grab their rifles from the armory and stand by until we know what the hell's going on."

We arrived to confusion at the ECP, where a dozen *junood* stood around jabbering back and forth and pointing to the north. I turned to Mason.

"Hey, find out what the hell's going on."

After a moment of talking with the soldiers Mason spoke.

"The *jundi* who was on guard said he noticed something moving around about three hundred meters outside the wire," he said, pointing north. "They say it was a car, and when it turned on its headlights it lit up two other cars near it. The *jundi* started firing warning shots at them, and the cars sped off."

It didn't make any sense. The northern ECP was an unmanned post. What was the soldier doing there in the first place? And why had he fired warning shots? As we asked ourselves those questions Lieutenant Grubb appeared with his night-vision goggles and knelt down on the berm next to us.

"I can't see shit out there," he said, the optic pressed to his eye. "There isn't enough illum outside right now."

He handed the goggles to me, but he had been correct. There wasn't enough ambient illumination in the night sky to get a clear picture through the NVGs.

"Hang on, sir," he said. "I'll get Wardle out here with the PAS."

Minutes later Wardle came running up, the bulky shape of a PAS-13 thermal viewer tucked under his arm. We continued to scan the horizon, but even the viewing power of the thermal sight couldn't locate anything to our front. Whatever had been out there—if there had even been anything at all—had long since left the area.

Once we returned to the COC and accounted for everyone, the Marines stood around and speculated about what had actually occurred. While it was possible that some locals had gotten lost in the dark and the Iraqi sentry had fired on them, it was equally feasible that the *jundi* had merely been spooked and fired off his weapon into the darkness. It wouldn't be the first time such a thing had happened.

Speculation aside, the episode revealed holes in our defensive plan for the compound as well as in our own internal security procedures for such an event. After a brief after-action review we developed a set of security posture levels for the team, codes that could be succinctly announced over our team radio net. We also resolved to force—not recommend—an adjustment to 3rd Battalion's security plan, including insisting that the battalion equip the tower guards and sentry posts with radios, NVGs, range cards, and signaling pyrotechnics. The new security procedures would include random inspections by the MiTT to ensure the *junood* were manning their posts properly. We knew our demands would be met with resistance by the battalion staff, but it was *our* security we were talking about. The team's small size made the prospect of providing our own constant, vigilant security unrealistic, and like all MiTT teams we were forced to rely on the Iraqis to safeguard us. Although we seemed to have dodged a bullet during the episode at the ECP, it was a somber reminder to all of us how isolated we were out there. Everyone knew that if the shit hit the fan we would be on our own for some time until the Marine task force's QRF could make its way to us. But it was a risk that had to be accepted; there was no other way for the MiTTs to operate.

Sometime shortly after midnight on 2 May a team of insurgents approached the Bagooz IP checkpoint in an area named Ar Rabit just north of the Euphrates River. The men were clad in American tricolor desert camouflage uniforms and, posing as a Special Forces team, they told the IPs that they wanted to conduct a combined patrol with them. The ruse lasted long enough for the insurgents to overpower the policemen at the checkpoint without firing a shot. After binding the IPs and placing them on their knees, the insurgents moved down the line of men one by one, cutting their throats from ear to ear. Several of the IPs' throats were hacked to the bone, nearly beheading them. One IP, however, who had been inexplicably cuffed with his hands to his front, managed to raise his hands to his neck at the last second and instead received a nonlethal slash to his neck and hands. Somehow managing to escape his would-be killers, the IP began to make his way to a nearby fort that overlooked the Syrian border from a cliff along the Euphrates.

The insurgents grabbed one remaining policeman and forced him to drive them in his pickup truck to the Ramanah IP station, where they then convinced the station's intelligence officer to come outside. After slaughtering him the group proceeded to the home of the Ramanah IP station chief. Kicking down the door, the team entered the home and kidnapped the IP chief and his thirteen-year-old son.

The group made their way back through the early morning darkness to the Syrian border and subsequently executed the driver they had pressed into service, the IP captain, and his son with single shots to the head. They quickly shed their uniforms and equipment and retreated across the border into Syria. The wounded IP, who earlier had escaped death, arrived at the border fort and begged the border guards to open fire on the attackers as they stole across the border. Although the border guards would later claim to have fired thousands of rounds at the withdrawing enemy, the wounded IP insisted that they did nothing to halt the getaway of the insurgents.

Suspicion and speculation abounded, and at the regional security meeting that was convened the next day at the border fort every agency of the Iraqi Security Forces (ISF) adamantly insisted on a different version of what actually happened. Charges were leveled that the wounded IP was left alive on purpose; that the border guards had been paid off to look the other way; and that the attack had been planned and orchestrated by the Syrian intelligence agency. A report even surfaced that a Syrian antiaircraft gun had fired skyward as a homing beacon to direct the attackers' movement across the border. Throughout the three-hour meeting the army, police, and border guard officers all angrily pointed fingers at one another, and the atmosphere in the crowded meeting hall seemed electrically charged. The summit ended with nothing resolved, and once more I sensed a deepening chasm of mistrust between all agencies of the ISF.

Later that night our team received a nervous call from 3rd Battalion's COC. The tower guard posted at the camp's southern ECP had reported that four vehicles resembling Humvees and MRAPs (mine-resistant, ambush-protected armored trucks) had approached the ECP, paused briefly, then turned around and made a hasty departure. We began radioing Coalition units throughout the Al Qa'im area, trying to determine if the vehicles had been friendly or not. When we kept coming up with nothing the team and the battalion went on alert until the situation could be resolved. No Coalition vehicles appeared on the BFT's digital map readout, and no unit could account for vehicles in 3rd Battalion's AO.

In the end the Marine task force finally relayed to us that one of their units had been in our sector conducting a battlespace tour with Marines from the oncoming task force. Their failure to properly coordinate their movement through our area of responsibility could have had disastrous consequences. The shock of the attack on the IPs in Ar Rabit had placed the soldiers of 3rd Battalion on a hair trigger, and the possibility had existed that they could have opened fire on the Coalition patrol. The Marines breathed a collective sigh of relief once the situation was defused.

Like the shooting incident at the northern ECP a week earlier, the episode emphasized the difficulties inherent in coordination between American and Iraqi units. Third Battalion "owned" the significant battlespace that surrounded COP South, and it was the Marine task force's responsibility and obligation to coordinate movement through it. The frequent failure to do so was a trend the team had noticed as far back as our time at Mojave Viper, when the Marine forces routinely traveled through the Iraqi unit's area without any prior coordination. Such disregard for the boundaries of the IA units was not only dangerous to the Marines traveling, it was also an insult to the IAs. It implied that the Americans did not recognize IA ownership of battlespace, and it polarized Coalition and Iraqi units. If the Marine task force and the Iraqi army could not coordinate with each other, if they could not truly conduct combined operations together, the Marines would never be able to fully hand over the responsibility for security to the ISF. This would prove to be a recurring theme, and at the risk of appearing parochial or of being apologists for the Iraqis, both my team and the brigade MiTT continued to browbeat the task force about coordination requirements.

There was no doubt about it: the executions in Ar Rabit had thrown 3rd Battalion into a deep state of paranoia. The fact that the IPs' assassins had attacked under the guise of being American forces had petrified them, and nowhere was this more prevalent than at the camps of 1st and 2nd companies. Days later, when the Outlanders made a trip to Okinawa and Vera Cruz, I was met by an agitated Major Muthafer. Third Battalion's COC had failed to inform his company that we were coming, and when our vehicles appeared at Okinawa's gate the soldiers had freaked out. Upset that we had showed up unannounced, Muthafer anxiously expressed his fear of an attack like that the one that had occurred in Ar Rabit. Despite my profuse apologies he remained on edge until I promised him that all future visits by Coalition forces would be properly coordinated. I realized that the coordination problem was not the Coalition's alone; the Iraqis too seemed to have difficulty applying the basics of battlefield tracking and deconfliction.

The fallout from the Ar Rabit massacre continued to snowball, and numerous investigations were initiated at all levels. The reporting of the incident eventually made its way up the chain to MNF-W, and a week after the attack I read with interest the commanding general's comments in his daily situation report (SITREP). Maj. Gen. John Kelly—the commander of MNF-W, who had also been the assistant division commander of 1st Marine Division and the commander of Task Force Tripoli during the invasion five years earlier—was not a man given to hyperbole, yet his words in the report were raw and emotional, betraying his feelings of deep frustration with the Iraqi government. He discussed the IP attack at length, indicating that he was considering pulling the Marine border transition teams (BTTs) from their outposts for their own personal safety. I had never read comments from a general officer that were so personal and that cut through all the bullshit, and I wondered just how much success we were really having there in Iraq. How much would we really be able to influence the Iraqi agencies to mend their infighting? It had been a confusing, frustrating week, and as my team approached the three-month mark of its deployment I realized just how little we understood about that country, and how much further we had to go.

The long week of confusion and tensions in the wake of the Ar Rabit killings culminated in the early hours of 9 May. In a haze of sleep I heard Master Sergeant Deleon's voice crackle over our team radio net.

"Three, this is Eight," he said from inside the COC. Moments later a groggy-sounding Lieutenant Bates answered.

"This is Three."

"There's something here you need to see."

I drifted off back to sleep but was awakened minutes later by Bates knocking loudly at my door.

"Uhhnn," I said, sitting up from my bed. "What's up?"

"You need to know what's going on, sir," Bates said, holding a scrap of paper in his hand. "Something's happening with Second Company."

Just before midnight three unidentified civilian vehicles had sped past 1st Company's position at BP Okinawa and continued west along the highway. The company's sentries had radioed 2nd Company about the three vehicles' approach, and the soldiers at Vera Cruz had gone on alert. The speeding vehicles eventually came to a stop at Vera Cruz's unmanned checkpoint along the road, and as they attempted to navigate around the coils of razor wire blocking their path a tower guard from the battle position began firing warning shots at them. The vehicles' occupants, startled by the small-arms fire coming at them, returned fire in Vera Cruz's direction until they could push their way through the barricade and escape to the west. The officers of 2nd Company alerted the Joint Coordination Center (JCC) and the Saffrah IP station, which lay farther west and directly in the path of the escaping automobiles. But the vehicles never arrived at Saffrah, having somehow melted into the night. A report had also filtered in that 2nd Company had launched its QRF to chase down the vehicles, but once the soldiers closed in on the IP station the policemen had opened fire on the IA vehicles with warning shots until the IAs could prove their identities. It was a miracle that none of the 2nd Company soldiers had been killed or injured in the confusion.

"The battalion's gone on high alert," Bates continued. "They've gone to 'stand-to' on all posts and the *junood* are ready to repel boarders."

But holes riddled the story, and Bates spent the rest of the evening trying to get the facts straight from the recently returned Captain Al'aa. We all knew that following any incident the first reports were usually unreliable, and this occasion was no exception. At first the IAs reported that the vehicles had been three black Opels—compact sedans common throughout Iraq—but later that report changed to one Opel and two Land Cruisers. Debate stirred about whether the policemen at Saffrah had actually fired upon the 2nd Company QRF. And some unverified witnesses had claimed that the vehicle drivers were wearing American flight suits and tricolor desert camouflage. The Ar Rabit massacre still fresh in their minds, the Iraqis latched onto this last report, fearing that they were under attack once again by insurgents posing as Americans.

When I spoke with Ayad the following evening he was highly agitated by the episode, claiming the vehicles had been filled with Americans.

"No way, *sadie*," I protested, attempting to dissuade him. "American forces would never drive around in uniform in civilian vehicles."

He waved his hand, dismissing my explanation.

"I have directed all of my guard posts that if a vehicle approaches at night and does not stop, flash its lights, and wait to be cleared by my soldiers, then they are cleared to open fire."

His orders, fueled by emotion, were potentially dangerous to Coalition forces, especially in light of the fact that there had been so much recent confusion with American units traveling around at night without coordinating their movement with the Iraqis.

"Okay, *sadie*," I told him. "I'll relay your intent to the brigade MiTT and the other Coalition forces in the AO. But it is important that your *junood* not be too quick on the trigger, or else they might shoot up a friendly vehicle."

I left Ayad's office nervous about his new orders to his battalion. A real possibility of friendly fire suddenly existed, and unless I could convince him to ease up on his orders the outcome could be catastrophic.

The next morning I received a call from the brigade MiTT's operations officer.

"Hey, you're not gonna believe this," he said. "You know those vehicles that got shot up at Vera Cruz last night? It was the SEAL team."

"What?" I exclaimed. The Navy SEAL detachment had just recently arrived at Camp Al Qa'im. "Are you fucking kidding me?"

"Nope," he replied. "It was them all right."

"Well, shit," I said, my irritation bleeding into the phone. "Now I've got to eat crow with Ayad tonight."

"Why?"

"Because if I don't tell him and he finds out later—which he will—he's gonna accuse me of covering up for the Americans."

"Have fun," he said, hanging up.

And so, swallowing my pride, I walked across camp to explain to Ayad what had happened. His answer caught me off guard.

"Yes," he said, nodding knowingly. "We knew it all along. Our sources and witnesses said from the beginning that it was Americans."

Sources? I thought. *Witnesses? It was the middle of the night in the middle of nowhere!* I doubted that Ayad's sources had actually reported anything, instead thinking that he was using the incident as some sort of leverage against me. But then I remembered him telling me the previous night that the personnel had been wearing American uniforms. It was a no-win situation for me, and I left our meeting embarrassed for the Coalition forces and unsure of Ayad's reaction. More important than my embarrassment, however, was my concern that Ayad had ordered evening training for his guard posts. They were directed to rehearse procedures for defending the compound in the event of an attack.

As I walked through the camp back to the MiTT compound, the quiet darkness was interrupted by spotlights and whistles. Soldiers spilled from their huts, sprinting to the guard towers and makeshift bunkers that dotted the camp's berm. The drill was already under way.

The entire episode had left a bad taste in my mouth about the Navy SEALs operating in our AO. They had always had a reputation for being cowboys, something Lieutenant Grubb corroborated based on his experience working with them in Ramadi the previous year. Their recklessness and failure to coordinate their movement through 3rd Battalion's AO had not only endangered their own lives and the lives of 2nd Company's soldiers, it had also threatened to disrupt relations between the Coalition and the Iraqi army. I wondered how many more incidents like that the IAs would be able to endure before they began shooting at anything that went bump in the night, and I prayed that the SEALs' error would be the last of the close calls between the Americans and the Iraqis.

Chapter 24
Gifts and Free Lunches

Weeks passed. The weather, which until recently had been pleasant, suddenly made the transition from spring to summer, and with it came the blistering winds and searing heat that radiated from a sun that boiled daily in the afternoon sky. We baked in our Kevlar gear and body armor, and the cabins of our Humvees turned into infernos. Marines returned from convoys drenched in sweat, their tan flight suits sticking to them and bleached white with salt. I thought of a variation of a line from Kipling: *Only mad dogs and Englishmen go outside during the Iraqi summer*. We surely weren't English . . . so there could only be one other explanation.

The Outlanders began to languish in the isolation of COP South, and Captain Hanna commented one day that our existence in the camp had begun to mirror the monotony of shipboard life. Between the heat and the boredom, the Marines occupied themselves by reading, exercising, and watching movies. A *lot* of movies. The days seemed to blend together, yet we continued to conduct our daily meetings both within the team and with our Iraqi counterparts. Occasionally the Marines would spin up for last-minute missions announced by the Iraqis, but more often than not the operations were either canceled or produced nothing of value. Despite COP South's size, it became cramped, and the team grew frustrated with the situation as a whole and with each other. Indifference and listlessness took hold, and it was a daily challenge to keep them motivated.

And I had just about had it with Lieutenant Colonel Ayad. On the evening of 22 May I went with Mason to visit my counterpart one last time before he left for his *mujaas* the next day. But when we arrived at his hut the sentry informed us that he had already departed. Irritated that Ayad had once again left without telling me, I stormed off back toward my hut. Issues had needed to be resolved before he left, and now I would have to wait another ten days before I could discuss them with him.

"This is fucking bullshit, Mason," I vented. "If my relationship with Ayad is ever going to progress he has *got* to start telling me more and trusting me with more information. That includes telling me when he's leaving."

Something in my words ignited a flame that had been smoldering in Mason, and he let loose a long, angry tirade about what it was we were doing there and the world as he saw it.

"What do you want to accomplish here?" he asked.

"What do you mean?" I asked.

"What exactly do you want to happen with the IAs?"

"Well," I said, "what do you think? I want them to start doing things on their own so the Americans can get the hell out of here."

"Listen," he said. "If you want to make things work with Ayad then you have to work the way they do. It's all give-and-take here."

"Yeah, it's 'give-and-take,' all right," I replied. "We give, and they take."

"Well, if you help them out, they'll help you out."

"In other words, if I want the IAs to get anything accomplished I need to give them things."

"Exactly."

"Mason, that's total bullshit," I said, gritting my teeth. "That's not my fucking job."

"Well, what *is* your job, then?"

"It's to train, coach, mentor, and advise them," I said, rattling off the only thing that anyone from higher headquarters had given me that even closely resembled a mission statement. "My mission sure as hell isn't to give them the fucking gifts they've been asking me for."

"But that's the way it's done in this culture."

"Okay, so if I want Ayad to be a better battalion commander, then I need to give him all the shit he's been asking me for the last couple of weeks? Eye-pro [eye protection; i.e., ballistic glasses or goggles]? Combat boots? Concertina wire? Bullshit! He only wants that stuff for himself; he doesn't want it for his soldiers."

"You're being too inflexible," he chided. "You are a career military officer. You can only see things in black and white. You have to be able to see the gray."

"Watch what you're saying," I warned. "Just because I've made the Marine Corps a career doesn't mean that I'm a fucking stooge. That has no bearing on how I think about this."

"Regardless, you are never going to see any results if you don't bend the rules and understand Ayad's motivations. If you can't do that, then you are better off just letting the IAs do their own thing and you do yours."

It was a disconcerting conversation, but it forced me to reflect on what we had been doing and, more important, on my own questionable abilities as an advisor. While it was true that the guidance I had received from both the Marine task force and the brigade MiTT early in our deployment was to reduce 3rd Battalion's reliance on the Coalition—to begin cutting the apron strings—my own personality and perspective had also played heavily in my performance. In the previous weeks and months I had come to understand the old Iraqi army culture—and Iraqi culture as a whole—and I had also grown to despise it. It was a culture of bribes, of mistrust, of entitlement, of "What's in it for me?"

The Americans had invaded Iraq and subsequently shattered the government and military apparatus. It was true that it had become our obligation to rebuild what we had destroyed. But as I reviewed all that the United States had accomplished in the previous five years—all that we had given the Iraqi army and done for it—I realized that the time for us to leave was fast approaching. The MiTT teams previously assigned to 3rd Battalion had done their jobs, yes, but in a way they had also set up my team for failure. When we finally reached the point that we had—the point at which it was time to cut off the Iraqi army and force it to do its own work—the IAs were instead unwilling to accept the fact that the Americans would eventually leave. They simply refused to believe that we would stop giving them things.

During our time at ATG the instructors had stressed the importance of operating "in the gray area." When Ayad departed for leave and I suddenly found myself with more time to ponder the situation, I realized that I was not cut out to be an advisor. A trainer, yes. Had Ayad and his staff been willing and eager to embrace the vast knowledge and experience my team brought to the table, then I would have excelled. But Ayad was rooted in the old ways, and he was largely uninterested in what I had to offer. If giving him gifts—if continuing to drag out 3rd Battalion's reliance on the Americans—was operating in the gray area, then I was unable to do it, and perhaps unsuited for the job. I had been trained to lead men, to take decisive action, to do the right thing. I was brought up to award achievement and effort, not laziness and complacency. As I saw it, my mission was to teach 3rd Battalion to fish so they could eat for life, not to give them a fish so they could eat for just one night. But it was becoming increasingly apparent that the officers of 3rd Battalion didn't *want* to learn to fish. They only wanted their dinner served to them each evening.

And while it was true that the battalion staff as a whole had difficulty adapting to our recommendations, the critical barrier to progress within the unit was Lieutenant Colonel Ayad himself. More and more it became evident that his leadership was the obstacle preventing the battalion from advancing further. The Marines had made notable progress with several members of the battalion staff. Lieutenant Ski had continued to develop the S-2's intelligence-collection capability, and Lieutenant Bates had likewise developed the S-3's planning and coordination skills. Perhaps most significantly, Captain Hanna had reduced the S-4's (the battalion logistics officer's) reliance on us for fuel and spare parts. But Ayad still controlled his staff with an iron fist. He made every decision within the battalion and neither encouraged nor allowed initiative among his junior officers. They despised him. And while I knew that it wasn't necessary for subordinates to like their boss, I also knew that when enmity becomes an obstacle to progress there is something seriously wrong. Command climate was not just some touchy-feely concept limited to the American military culture. If subordinate leaders in any unit feel that they cannot approach their commander with problems—or tactfully disagree—then the unit becomes paralyzed. I had known numerous commanders who had been relieved from their duties because of command-climate problems. Hell, if someone had surveyed the Marines of Delta Company before the war began *I* probably would have been relieved from my post as a company commander for the very same reason.

The 3rd Battalion staff was comprised of many young officers who had developed a different outlook and way of doing things, yet they were unable to proceed with their ideas without fear of reprisal by Ayad. He was content with his centralized command of the battalion, and because he had been told again and again that 3rd Battalion was the best in the brigade he was unwilling to do anything different that might possibly ruin his reputation. Accordingly, the battalion looked good on paper, the camp looked good, but as a whole—beneath the surface—it was dysfunctional and festering.

Lieutenant Colonel Ayad returned from leave on 2 June, and he brought with him a surprise: his eight-year-old son, Iha'ab. At first I thought the boy was only there for a brief visit—perhaps a day or so—but I quickly learned that he would be there with us at COP South for Ayad's entire twenty-day work cycle.

"Um, *why, sadie?*" I asked, perplexed.

"He wouldn't let me leave home without my bringing him along," Ayad replied, beaming.

I was somewhat annoyed. An army camp in the middle of nowhere brimming with weapons and heavy equipment didn't seem the ideal place for a young boy to be running around unsupervised. More than that, however, I was chafed because I had planned to launch a campaign of tough love with Ayad. At Mason's recommendation the team had planned to host an evening feast for the 3rd Battalion staff. We would make a trip into

Husaybah and buy all the fixings at the *souq*, then cook it all up for the IAs. According to our plan, following the meal each staff principal from the team would sit down with his IA counterpart and lay down the law, essentially telling them *Okay, we have demonstrated our hospitality and fed you; now it's time to talk business.* My intent with Ayad would be similar, to say, *Here are my goals. And now I want to hear what your goals are in the remaining three months the MiTT is with 3rd Battalion.* Every other time I had attempted to elicit an answer to that question he had snubbed me or simply changed the subject. I hoped to force his hand by feeding him and his staff. It was a long shot, but I had nothing to lose.

But Iha'ab's presence hindered my plans and made it difficult to conduct business during my evening meetings with Ayad. I had prepared a laundry list of problems that had occurred in his absence, but with his son constantly sitting there it became next to impossible to raise the subject. Ayad clearly doted on his boy, and with Iha'ab constantly in the office his father preferred to talk about his son rather than the business of his battalion. Not wanting to be deterred, I stuck to the plan and invited Ayad and his staff to the feast, and the Marines began making preparations in anticipation. By that point Ayad had fully demonstrated his flakiness to me, and so I reminded him of the event each night in the week leading up to the feast. As fate would have it, the night before the team's trip into Husaybah to buy the food Ayad received a call during our meeting. After a few minutes he hung up the phone and looked at me nervously.

"What's up, *sadie*?" I asked.

"The brigade commander just invited me to dine with the old brigade commander tomorrow night." He didn't specifically ask me to cancel the meal, but his eyes did, so I called it off.

How convenient, I thought wryly, thinking back to the "phone calls" that had resulted in him speeding away from the ordnance-cache find and removing himself from the MiTT team's marksmanship training. *I wonder if he always gets a call whenever he's nervous about something.*

One evening a week later, as I prepared to leave my meeting with Ayad, he spoke privately to Mason for several minutes. It wasn't the first time he had done it, and it typically meant that he was asking Mason to ask me for something. I had learned to ignore it. Over time Ayad had asked for a host of things for himself, the most outrageous having been a request for me to buy him a hunting rifle from America. I had balked at the suggestion.

"No, *sadie*," I had said, shaking my head. "I can't do that for you."

"But the last MiTT team bought a hunting rifle for the old battalion commander," he had protested.

This was an outright lie. The previous team had given many things to the officers of 3rd Battalion, but surely they hadn't obtained a high-powered rifle for the battalion commander.

"*Sadie*," I had said, bluntly, "sorry, but that's just plain illegal for me to do, no matter how you cut it."

As Mason and I walked back to our camp I asked him what Ayad had just requested.

"He asked me to buy him a laptop computer," he answered, nonchalantly. Ayad seemed to have learned his lesson about asking for such things from me.

"You're not gonna do it, are you?"

"Yeah," he said. "I'll help him pick one out, he'll give me the money, and I'll order it for him."

"Jesus, Mason," I said. "*Why?* We're not supposed to do that."

"He needs a new computer so he can communicate with his family in Ramadi, and he has no way to get one."

"Well, fine," I said, disapproval tingeing my voice. "I can't stop you from doing it. But I think it's the wrong thing to do."

The pressure from the battalion for us to give them things was unrelenting. But as much as I wanted to simply cut them off from *all* Coalition support—to force them to sink or swim—we still occasionally found ourselves in the position where we felt compelled to provide them mission-supporting items. In one instance, Master Sergeant Deleon procured two three-hundred-gallon fuel-storage tanks for Vera Cruz and Okinawa. The Navy Seabees at Camp Al Qa'im had been planning to discard them, and Deleon had rightly figured it was better to give them to the IAs than see them get thrown away.

In another case, Captain Hanna had managed to provide the battalion with a bevy of spare Humvee parts. He had arranged to bring two IA Humvees and their crews to Camp Al Qa'im for maintenance training with the mechanics from the Marine task force. While the *junood* pointed out all the broken components on their vehicles, the Marines taught the IAs how to repair each problem (at the same time supplying the parts). It was a loophole in the system we chose to exploit. Rather than insist that 3rd Battalion induct its Humvees into the Iraqi army maintenance cycle—a complex, protracted process that inevitably resulted in the vehicles returning with more wrong than before they were inducted—we chose to help them out with the task force's time, expertise, and copious spare parts. Hanna's initiative was a windfall for 3rd Battalion. Their Humvees were older models that required many parts that were different from those in our newer M1114s, and once the Marine mechanics had finished they offered the IAs all of their older spare parts that didn't fit the M1114s. Grinning from ear to ear, the *junood* loaded their two vehicles to the brim with the spare parts, and they were treated like returning heroes back at COP South.

It was hardly a triumph for us, but what it did was provide the Outlanders a significant degree of leverage with 3rd Battalion. As I met with Ayad that night I made sure he understood the great pains we had gone to in procuring the fuel tanks and the spare parts. It was an exaggeration, of course. But he didn't know that, and the supplies we had provided became money in the bank for us—an act we could reference if and when we needed assistance, or, more likely, if we really wanted the IAs to do something. Bribing them with deliveries of tangible items like the storage tanks and parts turned my stomach, but to a certain extent Mason had been correct: sometimes it took doing things the Iraqi way to get anything accomplished there.

I finally achieved a minor moral victory, however, on 13 June. The previous night, after my conversation with Ayad about items we had supplied his battalion, I shifted gears into a discussion about the future. The Marine task force in Al Qa'im had begun to transition into "overwatch," whereby principal responsibility for security in the region would become the responsibility of the ISF, and the task force would largely remain in reserve in case an emergency arose. The switch to overwatch would not only affect the ISF in and around Al Qa'im. The Outlanders relied on the task force for supplies and maintenance support, and the pending movement would drastically affect its ability to support us. That in turn would translate into reduced support for the IAs. As I explained all this to Ayad, I raised a difficult question.

"How will 3rd Battalion function and support itself without the Coalition to rely on?" I asked.

He nodded, contemplating my question, and although he quickly changed the subject I could see the wheels turning inside his head. He was at least as concerned about the issue as I was.

The following day the IA 7th Division's commanding officer, General Abdullah, visited 3rd Battalion with the brigade commander and both of their entourages. As the mob of officers crowded into Ayad's office and began the ritual of chai and cigarettes, Ayad spoke.

"*Sadie,*" he said, parroting to Abdullah my words from the previous evening, "the Marines are beginning to withdraw, and they will not be able to support the MiTT team or my battalion like they have been doing. I am concerned about not getting the assistance I need with my battalion."

I suppressed a grin, and for the first time I truly felt like an advisor. He was using my words, and I was pleased that he had summoned the courage to express his concerns to the general in front of the brigade commander

and all of the other officers. Despite the fact that it was my remarks coming from his mouth, this was a step forward, a determined effort to engage his higher headquarters and insist on their support.

Abdullah told Ayad that whatever he needed he would get. It was an empty promise, to be sure, but I had at least done my part in convincing Ayad to get the issue out into the open.

That afternoon, still reveling in my success in getting Ayad to speak to General Abdullah, I received a radio call from Sgt. Olanza Frazier. The team's gruff supply chief, Frazier was a barrel-chested Marine from South Carolina who looked like he had been throwing heavy things around a warehouse for years. He was as straightforward in his speech as they came, and I sometimes thought he lacked the capacity to filter appropriate and inappropriate comments before they left his mouth. But even as a sergeant he was a master of the Marine Corps supply system, and his ability to "acquire" essential equipment and supplies for our isolated outpost made him a valuable member of the team.

"Six, this is Four-one," Frazier said. "You've got a visitor at the COC."

"Who is it?" I asked.

"A *jundi* has a gift for you."

Waiting for me outside the team's operations center was Akeel, the tiny, graying warrant officer who ran 3rd Battalion's chow hall, and one of his assistants. He spoke to me through Joseph.

"Why don't you and the Marines ever eat with the *junood* anymore?" he asked.

"Akeel, I know food is pretty hard to come by around here. We don't want to be taking food out of the *junood*'s mouths."

"There is plenty for the Marines," he insisted. "It is an honor for your team to eat with us."

"Okay, okay, Akeel," I said, caving. "I promise we'll start eating with the *junood* again."

He turned to his assistant, who handed him a tray of *hobas*, chicken, and vegetables, which he then presented to me.

"This is for you," he said, grinning.

"*Shukraan* [thank you]," I said, taking the plate. Then he dropped the boom on me.

"Can I have some 'magic water'?"

I had walked right into Akeel's con. For some reason he was convinced that the bottled water the Marines drank was "magic water," and whenever possible he came around our camp and asked for some. It never occurred to him that the Aquafina that the IAs drank was probably better-quality water than the locally bottled water provided to the Coalition. But since it was American water it was magic water, and he begged us for it at every opportunity.

And so, stuck with the plate of food in my hand and no way out, I told Joseph to give Akeel a case of our magic water. I had learned the lesson once again: There are no free lunches in Iraq. In this case, literally.

Chapter 25
Abandonment Issues

It is 14 June—Flag Day—but no one knows this because the Americans are forbidden from flying the American flag anywhere in Iraq. Back in the United States people raise their flags and celebrate how patriotic they are from the safety of their own homes. The Outlanders, meanwhile, prepare for yet another patrol outside the wire.

The blast furnace of summer is upon us, and even though it is still early in the morning the Marines break a sweat loading their gear and weapons into the Humvees as they prepare for the trip. Rings of perspiration darken the material under their arms, and beads form on their foreheads. We load bags of ice into coolers we have stored in the trunks of the Humvees, and on top of the ice we place bottles of water and Gatorade. The last thing we want to happen is to get stuck somewhere in the heat without anything to drink. One of the things everyone knows but doesn't talk about is the fact that you can die very quickly in the heat of the Iraqi desert if you aren't careful.

Today the team will accompany Lieutenant Colonel Ayad and his PSD on their convoy to the regional security meeting at Border Fort 5, and for once Ayad and his soldiers are on time. Lieutenant Bates and I meet with Ayad before the convoy departs COP South, and together the three of us review the route our vehicles will take. Ayad tells us he must first go to the brigade headquarters at Camp Phoenix. He wants to travel to the security meeting with the brigade commander's convoy. This information is new to me and Bates, and we look at each other and shake our heads. It will throw off our time line, and we will be late to the regional security meeting. Again.

We insert our two Humvees into the PSD's column of three Ford pickup trucks. *Junood* from the PSD sit in the beds of the trucks, manning machine guns and AK-47s. The trucks are not armored, but Ayad prefers to ride in the comfort of air-conditioning rather than the protection afforded by one of his armored Humvees. The file of vehicles exits the ECP and moves onto the highway. The PSD picks up speed, and soon our Humvees begin to fall behind. Our vehicles are so heavy that they can't keep up. But then the soldiers in the pickup trucks realize that they are outside the protective bubble of our Chameleon jammers, and so they slow down until they are back under our invisible shield. It is the way things are here—the more the Iraqis begin to pull away from us, the quicker they return, seeking what we have.

The convoy veers onto the dirt trail that is 3rd Battalion's shortcut to Camp Phoenix, and as we approach the Wadi al Battikah, which bisects the trail, the Marines take bets on whether the *junood* from the PSD will dismount and clear the wadi by foot. They don't, and instead the PSD blows through the deep cut in the trail, oblivious to the potential danger of pressure-strip IEDs that might line the washout. As they blaze the trail we follow—if there is a pressure strip, the IAs will be the ones to trip it, not the MiTT members. *One day,* I think, shaking my head, *they're gonna get a rude awakening if they don't start clearing the wadis on foot.*

The convoy approaches the ECP that leads into Camp Al Qa'im and Camp Phoenix, and as we draw closer I radio the Marine task force.

"This is Outlander Mobile," I say into my headset. "Request permission to enter the west ECP with five vics and twenty-five pax [personnel]."

"Roger, Outlander," a faceless voice answers. "You are clear to enter at this time."

Our convoy pulls into the serpentine HESCO barrier maze that leads to the ECP's gate and the vehicles roll to a stop. The *junood* and the Marines dismount, and one by one each man begins clearing his weapons, ensuring no one enters the camp with a loaded firearm. The act itself is second nature for the Marines, and after stepping out of my Humvee I point my rifle at a sand-filled HESCO barrier. I remove the magazine of ammunition and then, rotating the weapon onto its side, I pull the charging handle to the rear and eject the round from the chamber into my outstretched palm.

As I repeat the procedure with my pistol the ear-splitting report of a gunshot echoes next to me. The proximity of the gunfire catches me by surprise, and I almost jump out of my own ass at the noise. The round thuds dustily into one of the HESCO barriers to my left, and I jerk my head toward the direction of the blast. A *jundi* manning a PKM machine gun on the pickup in front of my Humvee has negligently fired off a round into the HESCO barrier next to me, and I quickly turn back to my vehicle crew.

"Is everyone okay?" I ask.

"We're good," one of the Marines replies, shaking his head angrily.

I turn back toward the *jundi* in the truck. He is still standing behind his machine gun, a nervous half-smile twitching on his face. He knows what he has done, and he knows it will be his ass. The Marines remount the vehicle, and I key my headset.

"This is Outlander-Six," I radio to the task force once again. "Be advised, an Iraqi soldier in our convoy just had an ND [negligent discharge] at the west ECP. There are no casualties."

There is a long pause. Then the voice on the other end of the radio answers.

"Outlander, where did you say the Iraqi soldier was hit?"

"Negative," I say, correcting the radio operator. "There are no casualties. Say again, zero casualties. Will send you a report once we arrive at Camp Phoenix."

We pull into Camp Phoenix, and Lieutenant Bates summons the PSD commander and the *jundi* to get the information required for the negligent-discharge report. He goes back and forth with them, speaking through Mason. I can tell Bates is becoming angry and frustrated, and I walk over to the group.

"What's going on?" I ask.

"He left a round in the chamber," Mason says. "Sometimes it happens."

"What?" I say suspiciously.

"You didn't unload the weapon properly," Bates says again to the *jundi*.

The soldier is indignant. He doesn't think he has done anything wrong, and his PSD commander is trying to protect him.

"Sometimes you just have to discharge the weapon," says the PSD commander matter-of-factly.

"Bullshit," I say, raising my voice and pointing to the two Iraqis. "You failed to properly clear the weapon. That is a negligent discharge. Period. And you're on report."

I turn and head back to my Humvee, pissed off at the soldiers' nonchalance. Neither seems to care about what has happened, but I do. After all, I was the one closest to the round impacting in the dirt.

We wait in the dusty staging lot for Ayad to link up with Colonel Ra'ed and the brigade PSD. Ayad has disappeared into the brigade compound and we have no idea what the hell is going on. Suddenly a stream of Humvees and trucks spills out of the compound and heads toward the camp's exit. Ayad's truck is near the head of the column, trailing behind the trucks carrying the brigade commander and the division commander. In his haste to position himself near the colonel and the general, Ayad forgets about his two other PSD trucks. They fall in with us at the rear of the twenty-vehicle convoy, and soon Ayad's pickup is out of sight. He has left us and the bulk of his own PSD. I am nonplussed, but there is nothing I can do except follow the speeding circus procession through Karabilah and Husaybah.

The convoy stretches over several miles, and by the time the Outlanders get to the border fort we are twenty minutes late. The fort is a squat stone castle surrounded by a tall, razor-wire-topped berm. It looks like a picture taken directly from *Beau Geste* and the French Foreign Legion. The court-yard encircling the fort is clogged with Coalition and Iraqi vehicles. A gaggle of Iraqi border guards directs our Humvees to a remote spot behind the castle. The Marines enter the meeting hall, embarrassed once again by our counterpart's tardiness.

The gathering drags on for far too long, and once it finally ends the meeting hall empties quickly. Lieutenant Bates finds the PSD commander and tells him to wait for us, and we rush to our Humvees as the courtyard rapidly begins to empty. The Marines throw on their gear and we speed out of the fort's ECP, but it is too late. Ayad has abandoned us once more. We find ourselves again at the convoy's tail as the long procession of vehicles heads north toward Camp Gannon and Husaybah. Bates radios me.

"Six, this is Three," he says. "I don't think we're gonna be able to catch up to Ayad's PSD before we get to Husaybah."

The implication in his voice is clear: our two Humvees will soon be isolated from our Iraqi escorts. I have no other choice.

"Roger, Three," I say. "Continue to roll. We'll push through the city as fast as we can. Everyone keep your eyes open."

Soon we are driving through the slums of downtown Husaybah, once again alone and unafraid. It is a risk, but I have no alternative. As we push hard through the crowded streets I seethe with anger that Ayad is more concerned about his appearance in front of his bosses than he is about the safety of the Marines.

Because Ayad and Ra'ed are traveling with the brigade MiTT team, I am able to track Ayad's movement on the glowing electronic screen of my BFT. By the time we make it out of the city they are more than ten kilometers ahead of us. They are heading to Vera Cruz and Okinawa for a site visit to 1st and 2nd companies. I hear Bates's voice again on the radio.

"Do you want to keep going?"

"Negative," I say, unwilling to try to catch up to the Iraqi convoy far to our front. "Fuck them."

Our two vehicles split off onto the highway that will take us back to COP South.

That night I convey my irritation to Ayad about the negligent discharge and him leaving us behind twice. I remind him it is not the first time he has abandoned us. He is unrepentant and disregards my irritation about getting left behind. Instead he briefly addresses the shooting incident.

"The *jundi* has been punished," he says.

I leave his office, still gnashing my teeth. As I exit I see the *jundi* in question standing guard outside the battalion commander's hut. He hasn't been punished at all. He is, after all, one of Ayad's bodyguards.

Chapter 26
Running Out of Patience

As the Outlanders grudgingly prepared their equipment and vehicles for the trip into Husaybah the omnipresent sandstorms kicked up again, forcing us to cancel all movement outside the wire. Our second attempt to visit the *souq* for our feast with the 3rd Battalion staff was thwarted, and I wondered if perhaps it was a sign. Watching the Marines unload the Humvees and begin returning their weapons and radios to the team's armory, I pulled aside Master Sergeant Deleonguerrero.

"I don't think this storm is gonna go away anytime soon," I said, my eyes watering from the stinging airborne particles.

"Yeah," he agreed, squinting. "It's some nasty trash out here."

"What do you think, Top?" I asked, my arms crossed. "Should we postpone the feast?"

"We need to just cancel it altogether."

I thought for a moment. It was difficult to disagree with him. My heart wasn't exactly exploding with goodwill toward Ayad and his staff at that point, but I wanted to hear the master sergeant's opinion.

"Why?" I asked.

"Sir, those crazies don't rate a feast right now with all the fucked-up trash they've been doing around here lately," he explained. "The guards sleeping, the battalion commander leaving you guys yesterday, the *jundi* shooting off his machine gun. No one wants to cook for them right now."

"Yeah, you're right," I replied. "My ass is still chapped about yesterday too. All right, let's postpone it indefinitely. Maybe we'll do something for them before we leave this joint."

The decision to cancel the feast was not protested by the Marines. No one's heart was in it, and I sensed that, like me, the team's amity and sense of benevolence toward the IAs was declining rapidly. And it was no surprise. The Marines had worked hard to put aside their distaste for many of the Iraqis' cultural idiosyncrasies and instead had focused on doing whatever they could to make 3rd Battalion a better, more capable unit. Their efforts with their counterparts on the IA staff, however, were met with the same stubbornness and sense of entitlement by the Iraqi officers that I had encountered with Lieutenant Colonel Ayad. Their patience, like my own, was running out.

Shortly after midnight on 14 June a *jundi* had a negligent discharge while standing his post. The next day Corporal Fry delivered the details of the incident, and during the course of my nightly get-together with Ayad I presented the information to him. Fry and Staff Sergeant Leek had begun conducting random inspections of the camp's posts and guard towers—often at great personal risk to themselves because of the *junood*'s jitteriness and questionable weapons proficiency—and I wanted Ayad to understand what was going on with his guard force and the risk it posed to my Marines. No one on his staff had told Ayad about the incident, and he was upset that he had had to learn about it from the Americans.

"So, *sadie*," I said, "what are you going to do about it?"

"The *jundi* will be punished," he told me. "That is unacceptable."

"Well, from what I hear he's already in *jundi* jail."

Ayad nodded in approval.

"When *junood* mishandle their weapons, that is the punishment they deserve."

"You're right, *sadie*," I said sardonically. "But if that's the case, then why isn't the *jundi* from your PSD who fired off his PKM in jail?"

"He has already been punished. He has to stand extra duty and his *mujaas* has been suspended."

"That concerns me," I replied, trying unsuccessfully not to sound like I was lecturing him. "The perception I think you are creating within the battalion is that you are favoring the *junood* on your PSD, and that they are not receiving the same treatment and punishment as the rest of the soldiers who screw up."

Ayad was uninterested in my observations.

"The *jundi* from my PSD is new and inexperienced," he explained. "He made a mistake and he will receive further training. The *jundi* on post was negligent with his weapon; it wasn't a mistake."

"How do you know that?" I challenged. "You didn't even know about it until I told you. You don't know if he was negligent or if he was inexperienced like the *jundi* on your PSD."

"But I need that *jundi* on my PSD."

The conversation had begun to go in circles, and I finally realized that nothing was going to happen. Ayad had dug in his heels, and he was not going to mete out justice to the soldier from his security detachment. For me it was just another battle lost in the long war to convince my counterpart to do the right thing.

A Marine had once told me when I was a second lieutenant that I wore my heart on my sleeve. It was a character flaw I had struggled with throughout my career. Those around me always knew when I was pissed off, when I was upset, or when I was happy. It wasn't an admirable trait to have as an officer, and it routinely betrayed me during my time as an advisor. As June reached its middle, Ayad—apparently sensing my growing frustrations—invited me to lunch with him and Colonel Ra'ed one afternoon. As the three of us ate together, Ayad extended an open invitation to me to eat with him any time I wished. He also made it clear that the Marines were welcome to dine at the battalion chow hall. One of the interpreters had told him the Marines were eating out of cans inside the MiTT compound, and he was appalled.

"I don't want you to starve," he said magnanimously, reiterating the gesture the next evening after he had again invited me to dinner. "And while I am gone on *mujaas* you can even use my cook to make meals for you."

I graciously thanked him for his offer, fully intending not to take him up on it. The potential impression it could create would be catastrophic. The Outlanders would harass me about it endlessly, and, more important, the battalion's soldiers would merely think I had been corrupted by their commander. I had long known that Ayad, as the commander, received the best food in the battalion; the *junood*, in turn, received the leftovers. If I were to roll in during Ayad's absence and insist that his cooks prepare food for me from their stores the *junood* would never trust me again. The Marines and I were on shaky ground with them as it was; we didn't need to give them additional fuel for their suspicions.

As the weeks and months passed us by, Ayad seemed to be taking more and more personal leave—much more than the ten days each month the soldiers were officially authorized. Before his departure on 19 June he had told me he would be gone for fifteen days. He had to return Iha'ab to Ramadi, he told me, and he had some personal business at home. Ayad's increasing leave presented a significant barrier to progress, as he never left anyone in charge of the unit in his absence. As a result, everything always seemed to fall apart in the battalion as soon as he left. His exit on 19 June was no different. That night, only hours after Ayad had left, another soldier standing post negligently fired off his rifle. As usual the culprit's head was shaved and he was thrown in *jundi* jail.

Incidents of misbehavior and inattention to duty seemed to grow exponentially, and we soon turned to our new observation camera to assist us in policing the battalion. Originally designed to scan the area around COP South for enemy activity during both the day and the night, the camera became the team's own "nanny cam." It was perfect for monitoring the guard towers and the camp's interior, and we began to notice immediately that the tower guards were doing everything *but* guarding the outpost. They slept, they sat in the shade, they chatted on cell phones . . . the list of infractions was endless. One day Leek—who as our advisor to 3rd Battalion's Sergeant of the Guard had taken his role with deadly seriousness—dragged Warrant Officer Hameed into the COC to show him the soldiers sleeping in the towers. Seeing the infractions, Hameed stormed out of the COC and started throwing soldiers in *jundi* jail left and right. I thought once again, *At this rate there'll be no one left in the battalion to stand guard.*

A pervasive gastrointestinal illness—universally known by Marines as "the shits"—spread throughout COP South, and after evading its clutch for months I finally succumbed to it on 23 June. Yet despite my weakened condition I insisted on accompanying the team the next day on a routine convoy to Vera Cruz and Okinawa. I realized my error in joining the Marines as soon as we exited the wire, and throughout the course of the trip I was essentially useless—drained of energy, nauseous, and, above all else, cranky and difficult to be around.

And neither visit to the two companies camped out at the battle positions made me feel any better. Captain Majid, the bumbling XO at Vera Cruz, explained to me and Captain Hanna that 2nd Company was only allotted enough fuel from 3rd Battalion to run their generators about eight hours a day. In a confused, protracted discussion—during which we struggled with deciphering a series of convoluted mathematical equations through our interpreter—Majid continued his tale of misery by claiming that his *junood* each only received one bottle (1.5 liters) of water per day. A similar conversation with First Lieutenant Ali, the XO for 1st Company, revealed similar life-support woes at Okinawa. Not enough fuel and water was being distributed by the battalion headquarters to the remote company positions.

Hanna, ever the analytical, balanced logistics officer, was clearly the more rational of the two of us. I, on the other hand, feeling under the weather and—more important—completely fed up with the situation, snapped the same thing at both Iraqi officers.

"Listen," I said, exasperated. "I will only talk to your battalion commander about this if you promise to do the same."

"But he won't listen to me or Major Za'id," Majid said, equally incensed. "He only listens when you talk to him."

"Okay, look," I said finally. "The MiTT team isn't going to be here forever. What will you do when we are gone? You have to figure out a way to talk to your battalion commander without always going through me."

Majid and Ali finally agreed separately to convince their commanders to raise the issue with Ayad, but I had little confidence they would follow through and honor our deal. As always, the long ride back to COP South gave me time to reflect on my visit to the two battle positions, and I couldn't decide which troubled me more: the fact that Ayad's company commanders relied on *me* to speak to him for them, or the possibility that the two companies were getting shortchanged on fuel and water during the middle of a very long, hot, and dusty summer. Both issues were potentially symptoms of more serious problems. If the company commanders couldn't talk to their boss without my intervention, how could the battalion ever hope to succeed without the Americans' assistance? And if it was indeed true that Ayad wasn't properly allocating fuel and water to his companies, then their ability to accomplish the mission was severely hindered. A lack of fuel meant generators couldn't operate. That meant that refrigerators couldn't be run constantly. Food would be spoiled and water couldn't be cooled. Air-conditioning units couldn't be turned on. Rather than concentrate on their duties, the soldiers would turn inward and focus on their own misery in the stifling summer heat of Al Anbar province. Moreover, a lack of water for the *junood* was dangerous. They conducted multiple foot patrols each day, and while they weren't burdened with the same amount of body armor and equipment that the Marines were, a liter and a half of water just didn't cut it—in any man's army, not just the American military.

Later that afternoon I found Hanna next to one of our Humvees, quietly seething about our visit.

"You know, sir," he said, shaking his head slowly, "I've just about had it with this fuel game we're playing. I don't want to give any more fuel to 3rd Battalion for their fucking generators unless it is going to Vera Cruz or Okinawa."

"Yeah, I'm with you," I agreed. "This is total bullshit. No more daily allotment for them here at COP South."

"Well," he added, "we're already on track to have them down to zero by the beginning of August. We'll just speed it up and cut them off early."

"Sounds good," I said.

"And I recommend we redirect what's left for the next month to Vera Cruz and Okinawa. We can send out three thousand liters to supply both positions in a couple of days."

"Good to go," I said. "That should get them over the hump until I can figure out what the hell the real story is with Ayad."

I later walked into the COC to find Hanna standing in front of a dry-erase board filled with numbers and equations. He had done his homework. By calculating the monthly fuel allotment from the brigade and factoring in consumption by generators and Humvees he had determined that each company required approximately 8,000 to 9,000 liters each month to remain fully functional. The numbers he presented to me added up, and they were well within the limits of the 39,000 liters provided to 3rd Battalion each month. But that was the easy part. The trick would be to convince Ayad that it was the right thing to do, and sometimes convincing the IAs to do the right thing was like screaming in deep space.

The Outlanders had arrived at COP South expecting to find a battalion ready to conduct advanced training when it wasn't performing routine patrols and operations. Such an expectation was yet another of many bubbles that had been burst shortly after our advisor mission began. Lieutenant Grubb, who was always champing at the bit to plan and lead live-fire marksmanship training with the battalion, quickly discovered that the proficiency of the *junood* was not what we had expected. That much was clear from the number of negligent discharges that had occurred in such a short period. And, after learning two months earlier that the battalion had not fired its weapons in recent memory, figuring out a way to get them to shoot had become an obsession with us.

The two obstacles to shooting—Ayad's insistence on hoarding ammunition and a convoluted Iraqi military supply system that made it next to impossible to use live ammunition in training—finally seemed negotiable after the series of negligent discharges. Perhaps in a gesture to appease me, Ayad had promised before leaving on *mujaas* that the battalion would conduct a live-fire machine-gun shoot on 25 June. But a third obstacle to training suddenly appeared in the form of Captain Ali, the battalion's training officer and Lieutenant Grubb's counterpart. In the week leading up to Ayad's departure he had assured me each night that the battalion would shoot, even in his absence. Ali, meanwhile, had spent that last week telling Grubb that the battalion did not have the ammunition to shoot. No matter how many times I tried to get to the bottom of it before Ayad went on leave, each man stuck to his story.

"*Sadie*," I would ask, "is the shoot for next week still on schedule?"

"Yes," he would say.

Later that night I would talk to Grubb.

"Ayad told me the shoot is on."

"Sir," Grubb would counter, "Ali says there is no shoot scheduled. He says they don't have the ammo."

I would then go back to Ayad.

"*Sadie*, Captain Ali says the shoot won't happen because there isn't enough ammunition."

"No," he would answer. "The shoot will still happen on the twenty-fifth." It was dizzying, and, as with the fuel allocation issue I no longer knew whom to believe.

Ayad left on leave. The shoot didn't happen. I was pissed.

At midnight on 25 June Staff Sergeant Wolf radioed me from the COC.

"Sir, you need to come see this."

Minutes later I walked in, rubbing the sleep from my eyes.

"What's up?"

"The brigade MiTT just sent us a message," he said, pointing to the computer display in front of him. "The tower guard at AQ reported a burst of machine-gun fire from a Third Battalion convoy leaving their wire."

"What?" I said, suddenly awake.

"Oh wait, there's more, sir," Wolf said, smiling. "The IA convoy reported to brigade that it was *the tower* that fired on *them*."

"Man," I said, once again shaking my head. "What in the *fuck* . . .?"

I keyed my radio.

"Three, this is Six."

"Uhnn, this is Three," Lieutenant Bates replied, still half-asleep.

"Need you in the COC."

Moments later Bates appeared, clad only in T-shirt and shorts and trying to adjust his eyes to the light—a mirror image of me just minutes before. I explained what had happened.

"Go get with Captain Al'aa and find out what the hell really happened."

"Roger," he replied. "When the convoy arrives, if they give him the same bullshit about the tower guard firing on them I'll just tell them we'll run a GSR [gunshot residue] kit over their weapons to find out if they're telling the truth."

"I wouldn't do that if I were you," I cautioned. "You know we don't have any GSR kits. If they call your bluff, you're screwed."

"No sweat, sir," he assured me. "I'll get to the bottom of it."

Thirty minutes later Bates returned. When challenged by Captain Al'aa the IA convoy leader had admitted that one of the Iraqi soldiers had fired a negligent discharge as they departed friendly lines. My patience had finally run out. Until that point the team's advisors had merely recommended certain changes to their counterparts. Now, more than ever, our own safety was on the line; I could only tell the Marines to be careful around the *junood* carrying loaded weapons so many times. It was time to force the battalion to carry out our orders. I directed a mandatory weapons-safety stand-down the next morning. If the Iraqis couldn't teach proper weapons handling, we would do it for them until they got the picture. It wasn't the optimal way to do things, but necessity had forced us into that position. The last thing I wanted was for one of my men to go home in a bag after getting shot by an Iraqi soldier.

Chapter 27
Holding Down the Spring

Amid reports that violence was on a downward trend throughout Iraq—in particular in Al Anbar province—we received word the evening of 26 June that a tragedy of monumental proportions had occurred. Earlier that day, during a routine local leadership engagement in the town of Karmah in eastern Al Anbar, a suicide bomber dressed in an Iraqi army uniform had walked into the courtyard in which the meeting was being conducted and detonated himself. The suicide vest, packed with twenty pounds of homemade explosives (HME) and ball bearings, exploded in a massive fireball, killing the mayor, twelve local sheikhs, and others assembled for the conference. The dead included the commander of 2nd Battalion, 3rd Marines (2/3), one of his company commanders, and a young corporal. In all, more than twenty people had been killed, and a grim milestone in the Iraq War had just been met: Lt. Col. Max Galeai became the first American battalion commander to be killed in Iraq. It was yet another eye-opener for the team, and although the incident had occurred in a different AO than ours it reminded us that death could find anyone in that country. I was particularly troubled. While I hadn't known Lieutenant Colonel Galeai personally, his demise—like that of Major Hall on 30 March—made me recognize yet again that death in Iraq didn't just seek the young Marines patrolling the roads and towns. No one was immune, I realized, glancing down at the subdued metal oak leaf insignia adorning my collar. That included field-grade officers.

The three American deaths were alarming in another regard. The cultural indoctrination all Marines had been receiving as part of their predeployment training had placed special emphasis on shedding personal protective equipment (PPE—body armor, Kevlar, gloves, and eye protection) when meeting with local Iraqi leaders. The rationale was clear: a Marine commander who insisted on wearing a full complement of PPE presented a threatening, mistrustful appearance to the Iraqis. Simply put, it was not conducive to building relationships with sheikhs and senior members of the ISF, and so over time it had become standard practice for all Marines directly involved with such meetings to remove their gear and instead rely on the local security provided by the other Marines and members of the ISF. But in this case the security cordon around the meeting had failed, and the suicide bomber had taken advantage of the Marines' cultural sensitivity. In truth, it was perhaps doubtful that the three Marines would have survived the detonation even if they *had* been wearing their body armor, but it was disquieting nonetheless. The Outlanders and I routinely attended such meetings with Ayad and his officers, and I had lost track of all the times we had shed our armor and entered the assembly without a second thought. I wondered how the attack in Karmah would affect further regional security meetings in our own AO. Would the Marines still be inclined to demonstrate their trust and remove their PPE after what had happened to Galeai and his men?

On the evening of 27 June Captain Hanna knocked at my door.

"Sir, we need to talk about some of the issues going on in the battalion."

"Okay," I said, raising an eyebrow. "Shoot."

He sat down and leaned back in his chair and rolled one eye, a trait I had come to recognize as meaning he had been deep in thought and wanted to get something off his chest.

"Two of the warrant officers from the IA S-2 cornered me and started venting about the battalion commander. They want to talk to you in private about it."

"All right, fine," I replied. "Set it up for tomorrow night."

The next evening two warrant officers named Aamar and Abd-al-Nabi appeared in our camp, and after Hanna had sequestered them in an empty hut they began a long diatribe about Lieutenant Colonel Ayad. I sat and listened patiently, being careful about what I was letting happen. Giving the two men an audience for their complaints was a fine line for me to be walking. I couldn't afford to create the perception that I was playing the officers of 3rd Battalion off one another, and so I made sure they understood that I would listen to their grievances but not promise anything. They thanked me for my willingness to listen, and they continued.

"Lieutenant Colonel Ayad is out to get the S-2 shop," one insisted.

"He has been misappropriating battalion life-support funds," the other added.

The list went on. The soldiers weren't getting enough food and water. Officers were selling fuel on the black market in Husaybah. Ayad was abusing soldiers and officers alike. Major Za'id of 2nd Company had been abusing a *jundi* so badly that the man had shot himself. Most were complaints and accusations I had heard before in the preceding months, but now that

Aamar and Abd-al-Nabi had finally sought me out on the issue it was time to act. The two warrant officers were definitely no angels; a cloud of suspicion constantly hung over the battalion's entire intelligence shop, and I knew it would be a mistake to take their testimony at face value. I told the two officers only that I would investigate the issues and left it at that. I didn't expect any miracles, and it would have been senseless to falsely elevate their hopes. But I was definitely concerned. Both men had come to me at great personal risk to themselves and their careers, and they had placed substantial trust in me by complaining about their commander. The potential consequences for them could be dire. If they trusted me enough for that, I felt I had to act.

The two men left, and as Hanna and I walked back to the COC we discussed the accusations.

"I wonder what that was all about with Za'id beating up on the *jundi* and the guy shooting himself," I said. "That sounds a little crazy."

"We'll check it out," Hanna answered.

No sooner had we entered the operations center than Lieutenant Bates walked in and handed me a piece of paper with a translated report.

"What's this?" I asked, glancing at the document. Bates grinned evilly.

"A soldier from Second Company shot himself in the leg today because he wanted to go on leave," he said.

Where there's smoke, I thought sourly, *there's fire*. Our suspicion continued to climb.

I needed to see the fire for myself, and so on 2 July the team convoyed out to Vera Cruz and Okinawa to visit 1st and 2nd companies once again. Captain Hanna and I sat down with Major Za'id in the bunker of his office, and for more than an hour we discussed the complex fuel issue. Za'id stuck to the same story Captain Majid had painted for us on our previous visit: Ayad continually refused to provide 2nd Company with the fuel it desperately needed for running its generators. It was fast becoming a tired old song for us, and in Ayad's absence there was nothing I could do to effect change for any of the companies. Sensing that I needed a shift in subject, Hanna interjected.

"*Sadie*," he said, leaning forward, "we heard about the *jundi* who shot himself out here several days ago."

"Yes," Za'id replied, producing a piece of paper from a file and pointing to it. "He was a bad soldier, and he shot himself just to get out of work."

I looked at Hanna and rolled my eyes. *Sure*, I mouthed.

"Well, *sadie*," Hanna added. "I'll be honest with you. We heard that the *jundi* shot himself because he was being abused out here at Vera Cruz."

Za'id sat upright as if he had been given an electric shock, and he launched into a drawn-out explanation of what had actually happened, including an overly detailed description of how the young man had pressed the barrel of his AK-47 into the meat of his calf and pulled the trigger. Za'id vehemently denied roughing up the soldier, and in the end he explained that the soldier had been treated at the hospital.

"Well, where is he now?" I asked.

"I sent him home on medical leave," he replied.

I grimaced.

"You said he shot himself because he wanted to go on *mujaas*," I began.

"Yes."

"Well," I continued, "I hate to say it, but by sending the *jundi* home you just gave him what he wanted. And now all of your soldiers know that if they really want to go home on *mujaas* then all they have to do is shoot themselves."

"But we didn't have the facilities here to look after him," Za'id countered.

"That's not really the point," I said. "Besides, you could have transferred him to COP South. He could have been watched there. Our medic could have monitored him."

Za'id was dismissive, insisting that the soldier would be charged once he returned from leave. It was a dead-end conversation; Hanna and I both knew we wouldn't get the answers we sought, and so we dropped the subject.

As Hanna and I left the office Za'id followed us, continuing his rant about fuel. I finally turned to him.

"*Sadie*, look," I said sternly. "I already told your XO this, but I'll repeat myself. I will talk to *Muqaddam Rukn* Ayad about the fuel issue when he returns from *mujaas* only if *you* promise to talk to him as well. I'm not going to do it alone. You have to get involved and speak up to your commander."

He promised he would. I didn't believe him.

Things began to unravel around the camp in Ayad's absence. That evening, as I sat with several of the Marines watching a movie, my radio beeped.

"Six, this is Two," Lieutenant Ski said.

"Send it."

"Chow hall report for you," he said plainly. "Just got back from chow with the IAs. The food was plentiful and fit for human consumption. And a *jundi* just fired off a green-star cluster inside the chow tent."

"What?" I said.

"Roger," he replied. "The flare hit the *jundi* in the face and bounced around the tent then went through the roof."

"Is anyone hurt?" I asked.

"Negative. The *jundi*'s face is bruised and cut, but that's it. There are burn marks all over the floor, and there's a big-ass hole in the tent."

"Jesus," I said to the Marines seated next to me. "They're like a bunch of fucking children."

I rekeyed my radio.

"Three-one, this is Six."

"Three-one," Lieutenant Grubb answered.

"Did you hear Two's report?"

"Roger."

"Go collect all the flares from the guards," I told him. "They obviously can't handle them properly."

"Roger, I'm on it."

Grubb and Staff Sergeant Leek returned an hour later, arms filled with the signal flares we had issued the tower guards weeks earlier.

"Couple of them were stored already primed," Grubb said, shaking his head.

"Are you kidding me?" I asked. Staff Sergeant Leek handed me one of the green plastic tubes that were used to store the cylindrical flares.

"Here, check this out, sir," he said, pointing to the inside. A soldier had armed the flare by affixing the cap with the firing pin inside the tube's base so that the flare's primer would rest against it. Storing the flare in such a manner was akin to cocking the hammer on a pistol and carrying it around ready to fire. It had been an accident waiting to happen, and sure enough it had. It was an act of absolute stupidity on the part of the soldiers, made even more unacceptable because Grubb had already instructed them on the proper storage of the flares when they were not in use. The soldier who had fired the flare had been lucky to escape with only cuts and bruises. He just as easily could have lost an eye, or worse.

The nonsense continued. The following day, as Grubb was out running laps around the compound, a speeding convoy of IA trucks barreled down the gravel path directly at him. I watched frozen from afar, expecting the vehicles to run down the lieutenant and leave him dead by the side of the road. Instead, they barely missed him, blanketing Grubb in a choking cloud of the chalky moon dust that permeated the compound. He continued to exercise, shaking his head angrily back and forth and mouthing the word "Motherfuckers."

It wasn't the first time the IAs had sped like madmen through the camp. Whenever the battalion commander was not around the *junood* inevitably drove like idiots, especially when returning from patrols. My deep-seated fear of the Marines getting shot by a careless Iraqi and his rifle was nearly matched by my worry that one of my men would get run over by the IAs. My concerns weren't baseless. Nonbattle injuries and deaths from mishaps like vehicle accidents were a persistent danger in Iraq, and the fact that my Marines were constantly in close proximity to a bunch of Iraqi soldiers who were borderline psychotic behind the wheel was practically enough to give me the shits. On several occasions I too had nearly been hit by IA drivers speeding through camp at night, and I had finally had enough. Lieutenant Bates relayed my irritation to Captain Al'aa and convinced him to lay sandbags throughout the camp to serve as speed bumps for the reckless *junood*. But it wasn't long before the soldiers simply started driving around them. Our effort to slow their movement through the compound had produced exactly the opposite effect. The IAs now had a high-speed slalom course that they could practice swerving through as fast as possible.

The morning of 5 July dawned bright and hot, and as the team prepared to convoy to the regional security meeting in Husaybah, Hanna walked up to me.

"Sir, a report just came in," he said. "The battle position at Samsiyah just got blown up."

"What?" I said skeptically.

"Yeah, they said the BP was completely destroyed."

Samsiyah, located more than two and a half hours to our east, was in 2nd Battalion's AO. I knew the MiTT team leader for that battalion, and my concern for him and his men skyrocketed.

"Any Coalition casualties?" I asked.

"Nothing reported yet," Hanna replied.

I followed him back to the COC, where the information about the incident began to trickle in. As usual the initial reports were sketchy, but eventually it unfolded that an explosive-laden truck had sped into the ECP and detonated after one of the Iraqi guards opened fire with his machine gun. The resulting concussion and fireball tore apart the truck and flattened several buildings around the ECP. Eventually more than a dozen Iraqi casualties were reported, but thankfully no Marines were wounded. Days later photos of the scene were displayed to me. The suicide bomber's flattened, charred face and scalp had been found dozens of meters away from the point of detonation. It looked like the mask of human skin worn by Leatherface in *The Texas Chain Saw Massacre*.

Dark humor, indeed.

Lieutenant Colonel Ayad finally returned from leave on 5 July, and the next evening I went to see him. In the days leading up to his return I had organized my notes for our eventual meeting, planning to drop the hammer on him about everything that had gone haywire while he had been away. But he beat me to the punch and confessed to all that had gone to hell in his absence. At last his staff had provided him a full brief, and for nearly two hours I listened to him recount what had happened. As he listed every transgression committed I offered my views on each. Carefully acknowledging each incident, he was visibly embarrassed by all the ways in which his battalion had shown its ass. But one thing was missing from his confession: his own sense of personal responsibility for what had taken place while he was on leave.

"My officers let me down," he said angrily, beginning a message he would cling to throughout the conversation. "They let me down and did not supervise the *junood*. That's why everything went wrong."

I nodded, saying nothing and allowing him to explain his side of things.

"I will crack down on my officers," he declared. "Managing my officers is like keeping a coiled spring compressed with your hand. You must hold down the spring. If you don't, then the minute you take your hand away the spring will go crazy."

I understood what he meant, but such heavy-handed tactics would always result in chaos as soon as he wasn't around. I turned to the topic of discipline.

"*Sadie*," I said, exhaling, "I think what happened while you were gone was merely a symptom of a much greater issue. I think there is a discipline problem in Third Battalion."

He looked at me blankly. One of the benefits of working through interpreters was that in the time it took my sentences to be translated I was able to collect my thoughts and measure my words appropriately before speaking again.

"You say that discipline in your battalion is important to you, and that your *junood* are disciplined," I continued. "And that's true. The *junood* are disciplined when you are around. But the definition of true discipline is when soldiers do the right thing even in the absence of supervision. Your *junood* aren't doing the right thing in your absence."

"But look at the officers I have working for me," he replied, skirting the subject. "Captain Ali, Captain Hussein, Captain Al'aa . . . they are lazy and incompetent. They are the officers who are in charge and allow these things to happen when I am on *mujaas*."

"If they are incompetent, then you need to fire them, *sadie*," I said. "Otherwise you need to counsel them and make sure they understand what you expect of them whenever you go away."

He was noncommittal about my suggestions. Sensing that I had taken that subject to its limit, I turned to the issue of fuel and water distribution to the camps.

"Here is the perception that the soldiers from First and Second companies have," I explained. "They don't receive the same amount of fuel and water as the soldiers who live at COP South do. They know that the generators run longer at COP South. That means the air-conditioning is run longer each day at COP South. That means the refrigerators are run longer each day at COP South. They also know that the soldiers at COP South get more water each day than they do. What all that really means to those soldiers is that the men who live at COP South are better cared for and therefore more important."

"But I increased the amount of fuel for both companies from five thousand liters to six thousand liters each month," he countered.

"Do you *really* know how much fuel they need to run their generators?" I asked. "Or are you just relying on what they tell you?"

He didn't answer.

"You can't really know how much fuel First and Second companies require unless they track their fuel consumption. Otherwise they are just guessing how much they need. Or they are selling the fuel out in town."

"None of my officers would ever sell their companies' fuel out in town," he said defensively.

"Okay, but if you say you are giving them enough, and they say you aren't giving them enough, how do you really know where the fuel is going?" I asked pointedly. "How do you know how they are really using the fuel?"

"Okay," he agreed. "I will direct a fuel study by the two company commanders to find out how much they actually use and how much they actually need."

"That's a good idea," I said. I was starting to make some progress.

"But I need to keep a reserve here at COP South," he added. "What if there is an emergency and we need fuel? The brigade didn't submit the monthly fuel request, and the delivery has been delayed again."

Convincing Ayad to abandon his ingrained inclination to stockpile supplies would be difficult. But since he had just demonstrated a willingness to do the right thing and supply more fuel to the two companies, I decided to offer him a carrot.

"Okay, here's the deal," I began. "If you give a full complement of fuel to First and Second companies and you run out of fuel here at COP South, then my MiTT team will give Third Battalion thirteen hundred liters per day for your generators and Humvees until the brigade finally delivers fuel."

"Okay," he said, smiling his toothy grin. "Very good, thank you. And thank you for your advice and for being honest with me about my battalion."

I left Ayad's office more confused than ever about him and the battalion as a whole. While it seemed that I had achieved a victory in the fuel issue, a numbing sense of defeat still plagued me. In our long months at COP South I had been searching the battalion for an honest broker, someone the Marines could always trust to tell the truth and who would be the battalion's champion for organizational change. As I walked back to our compound I realized no such person had materialized. Two camps existed within the battalion: Ayad, and his officer corps. Neither camp trusted the other, and we didn't know who to believe. Everyone had his personal agenda and twisted the facts on every issue to suit his own particular situation. Our dealings with the IA staff had become one big game of "he said, she said." I knew that the truth lay somewhere in between, but no matter how hard we tried we couldn't seem to find it.

I plopped down on a dusty couch in the MWR hut, emotionally spent, and as I conveyed my frustrations to Hanna, Bates, and Ski I realized something else. Despite our confusion and skepticism, the team seemed to have finally reached a significant watershed. As the previous MiTT advisors were departing COP South they had told us it took them about four months to really figure out what was going on in the battalion, to really get to know their counterparts on a personal level, and to finally earn some measure of the battalion's trust. We had naively insisted to ourselves it wouldn't take us that long, but sitting down with my officers I realized that we had just reached that point. Now, even though there were only two months left in our deployment, we might actually be able to accomplish something.

But then it dawned on me. We would soon have to turn over the reins to a new team, and the whole process would start anew once again. I lay awake for a long time that night more discouraged than ever, wondering how any measurable progress would ever be made.

Chapter 28
Critters

I t is not long before the Outlanders realize that the Iraqi army soldiers are not the only tenants with whom we share the camp. The critters are out here, and very quickly we come to accept that it is actually *their* camp, and we are merely visitors. The critters will be here long after we are gone.

We are overfed and overstocked with food. Our kitchen bulges with boxes of peanut butter, loaves of bread, and crate after crate of processed, prepackaged food. It is the mother lode for the army of mice that burrows in the hidden recesses of our huts, and our efforts to halt their attacks on our food stores are feckless. Finding traces of mice in the kitchen is common, and when grabbing something to eat it becomes customary for the Marines to inspect their food before biting into it to ensure that a rodent has not beaten them to the punch. Food inspection techniques include the bread-bag flip, the peanut butter spin, and the potato chip bag pressure check. I take nothing for granted, because biting into food that the mice have already sampled gives me the same queasy, sick-to-my-stomach feeling as when you bite into an apple and find a wormhole.

At first we rarely see them. Just as we take time to get used to our surroundings, so too do the mice to get accustomed to our presence. It starts with one peeking out from a darkened corner, waiting to see if we will pursue it. But we are too busy watching movies or eating to give chase to a creature that is smaller and swifter than we are. Soon they scurry through the MWR hut and past our boots in broad daylight, daring us to go after them, and then one day they run *over* our feet. One evening less than three months after our arrival, as I sit on the couch and watch television, one brave bastard of a mouse pokes his head through an opening in the couch's headboard. His tiny face is right next to mine, and given our bizarre circumstances I half-expect him to crack a smile at me. And in that moment I realize that they have won. No amount of mousetraps and vermin proofing of our food and huts will stop them. Despite the Marines' occasional parading through camp of a hapless victim snared by a glue trap, we know we are fighting a losing battle.

Yet the campaign to eliminate our vermin neighbors is hindered by my own personal idiosyncrasies. I dislike snakes, and even though the best cure for a case of mouse infestation is the presence of slithering reptiles I still resolve to kill them any time I see them. We know from our multitudes of predeployment briefings that Iraq is home to a host of poisonous serpents, several of which produce venom that will kill you within hours of your being bitten. I never remember seeing a snake the last time I was in this country, and so I initially convince myself that no snakes will come near our human dwelling. But then one day Master Sergeant Deleon announces that he has found one near the COC, and despite my dread I come running with entrenching tool in hand. Soon the snake is in two pieces, and as it snaps at us and tries to rejoin its two severed halves we strain to determine what kind of snake it is. It is a baby, and although its markings resemble those of a Levantine viper we are unsure, so we play it safe anyway and burn what's left of the snake. I know that where there is one there are more, and the next day another snake is found next to the COC. The Marines kill it too, bifurcating it and tossing its remains in the burn bin. No one wants to get bitten, because everyone knows it is painful and that it is a long way to the nearest Coalition base. And no one wants to die, especially from, of all things, a snakebite.

The snakes become only a passing concern. We know that if we watch where we step and where we put our hands we will be fine, and after a while I begin to forget about them. But it is impossible to forget about the flies. They are everywhere, and while I dislike snakes, I despise flies. They swarm in black masses near our garbage cans, and they exploit every opportunity to invade our living and cooking spaces. Doc Rabor attempts to limit their breeding and gathering places by crafting heavy, wooden lids for the refuse cans that dot our camp, but his efforts are in vain, and so we hang fly traps in every room. The fly tape curls down from the ceilings in long, adhesive streamers, the corpses of flies and other small insects frozen into statues on the sticky surface. Occasionally Marines bump into the fly tape and it sticks to their faces, and as they peel it off their skin they must also peel off the blackened husks of fly cadavers that have made the migration from tape to flesh. We throw foul-smelling blue crystals of bait around areas we think to be congregation sites for the flies, but it does little to solve the problem. Nor does the clear plastic bag of water suspended from a HESCO barrier near the chow hall that Captain Hanna swears will ward off the winged insects with its ability to refract light.

I react with disgust when I see flies crawling on our food, and while it is acceptable for me to curse and shoo them away when I am in the presence of my fellow fly-hating Marines, it is perhaps not acceptable to react that way when I am eating with the Iraqis. The flies seem only a casual nuisance to them, and the Iraqis are less bothered than I am by flies alighting on the food and staking out their claim with feet that moments ago were likely frolicking in garbage and human shit. But I am unable to hide my revulsion when a fly lands in my mouth, or on my eyeball. I angrily swat at the pests, and for the thousandth time I long for a world without flies.

Winter ends, and as our brief spring quickly heats up into summer the mosquitoes arrive at our camp. At first I don't understand it; there shouldn't be mosquitoes here in the dry, arid desert. But then I think about how close we are to the Euphrates River, and I remember the heavily irrigated plantation that sits adjacent to our camp. The mosquitoes thrive in this environment, and for them COP South has become a giant restaurant with human blood as the special of the day. They come in ones and twos at first, testing our reaction to their presence, and once they determine that we have let down our defenses they move in for the kill.

I awake in my hut one evening, itching with the swollen bites of the tiny, invisible vampires, and as I turn on my headlamp I see them for the first time. They have found their way into my living quarters, and they buzz in circles over my head, waiting patiently for me to fall asleep so they can resume their feast. The Marine supply system—from which we can order refrigerators and satellite dishes and flat-screen televisions—is unable to provide us with mosquito netting, so each night I slather all exposed flesh with insect repellent and crawl into my sleeping bag and wait once again for the nightly feeding. The Outlanders suffer the same aerial assault each evening, and each morning a new Marine appears with red welts marring his face and arms. We search for mosquito coils to ward them off, but they aren't available either. The Iraqis offer us pungent incense sticks they claim will drive away the pests, but we choose to gut it out instead. The tang of burning garbage aboard the camp every day is enough, and we are tired of foul-smelling odors filling our nostrils. We brave the mosquitoes and keep applying bug juice—and wait to see what new critters will join us.

Chapter 29
A Change of Plans

Late in the evening of 10 July I was aroused from my slumber by chatter on the team's radio net. I first heard Lieutenant Bates.

"Nine, this is Three." After a moment with no response he repeated his radio call to Doc Rabor. "Nine, this is Three," he said, impatience rising in his voice. "This is Three . . . does anyone have eyes on Nine?"

A rumbling outside my hut caught my attention, and as I walked out into the darkened camp I saw a crowd of soldiers circled around an ambulance next to the motor pool. I poked my head in the COC and found Corporal Fry manning the radios.

"What the hell is going on?" I asked.

"Another *jundi* shot himself, sir," he replied emotionlessly. His bland response was indicative of how immune the Marines had become to such tragic occurrences around the battalion. The incident in which the soldier had shot his friend our first week at COP South had been shocking. Now accidents and mishaps among the soldiers bothered the Marines not at all.

By the time I made my way to the motor pool the IAs had loaded the *jundi* into the ambulance and begun racing toward the center of the camp. Catching up to Captain Hanna, Lieutenant Bates, and Doc Rabor as they briskly followed the ambulance on foot, I breathlessly called out to them.

"Hey, hold up," I said. "What the hell is going on?"

"Another ND," Bates explained. "One of the *junood* shot himself in the foot as he was coming off duty."

"Well, why the hell are they taking him deeper into the camp?" I asked. "Why aren't they taking him to the hospital?"

"It's not serious," Hanna said, referring to the soldier's injury. "They're taking him to the camp clinic first."

We arrived at the clinic to find what in India I had called a "rent-a-crowd" surrounding the ambulance. In New Delhi it seemed that any time an incident occurred—whether it was an automobile accident or some other public spectacle—there was always one rabble-rouser who would instigate

a near riot among the masses of curious onlookers, who would then immediately form into a raging crowd. The same kind of sideshow was now
developing at the clinic, where a throng of partially clad soldiers swarmed
the ambulance. The soldier who had shot himself cowered in the back of the
ambulance, terrified by his injury and the excitement generated by the mob.
I turned to Hanna.

"We need to get these fucking people away from here," I said, pointing
to the jabbering soldiers. "That dude is petrified."

Hanna nodded and grabbed our interpreter.

"Hey!" he yelled over the commotion. "Tell everyone to back the fuck
away from the ambulance!"

The sea of soldiers slowly parted, and we got a good look at the *jundi*
lying on the stretcher. He was truly freaking out, but as I looked down at
his injury I saw that Hanna's assessment had been correct. The soldier's foot
had already been bandaged, and only one small dot of blood colored the
cloth wrapping.

The ambulance accelerated into gear and raced out of the camp, and as
we returned to the team's compound we began to hear rumors that the *jundi*
had shot himself on purpose. We would later hear that it had something to
do with an upsetting call he had received from his girlfriend. Another version
of the story was simpler and, in light of recent events, more believable: the
jundi wanted to go on *mujaas*. The die had truly been cast in 3rd Battalion;
the average *jundi* now knew that shooting himself in the foot would be a
one-way ticket home for leave. But a greater concern for us grew out of the
chaos of that evening. Hanna noted that the IAs' casualty-handling process
had been so haphazard and disorganized that he wondered what would
happen if something serious actually were to occur. What would they do if
and when they eventually took casualties while they were outside the wire?

That same evening a patrol from 3rd Battalion set up a "snap" vehicle checkpoint (VCP) along the main route that ran south from Al Qa'im toward the
border town of Akashat. During the course of the surprise checkpoint the
soldiers stopped a lorry filled to the roof with smuggled cigarettes. After
being stopped by the soldiers the truck's driver dismounted and fled into
the darkness on foot. As he escaped into the night the soldiers reportedly
fired nearly a hundred rounds of ammunition from their AK-47s, PKM
medium machine guns, and DshK heavy machine guns. They then detained
the truck's second passenger and brought him and the lorry back to camp.

The next morning I was skeptical as I read the report.

"A hundred rounds?" I said, looking at Bates. "That's a little overkill,
isn't it?"

"Yeah, I'm gonna go see Al'aa and get to the bottom of it," he replied.

It wasn't long before he returned.

"You aren't gonna believe this, sir," he said, frowning.

"Probably not," I replied.

"They didn't fire their weapons at all," he said. "Al'aa tried some bullshit on me, but he finally admitted that they filed a false report so they could get extra ammo for the battalion."

"Jesus, *why*?" Hanna asked. "They won't even shoot the ammo they already *have*."

That night I asked Ayad about the patrol.

"*Sadie*, I heard you nabbed a smuggler last night."

"Yes, and we will catch more with the random checkpoints," he said proudly.

"What about all the rounds your men fired?" I asked.

"The driver escaped," he explained. "And the *junood* were trying to light up the area to see where he went."

Okay, I thought, rolling my eyes. *Now that's just stupid.*

"Well, *sadie*," I said, staring intently at him. "I heard that your soldiers didn't fire a single round."

He paused, and then continued without missing a beat. "Yes, we reported that we fired at the smuggler so that we could get additional ammunition."

"Let me get this straight," I said, unable to believe that he had just freely admitted to filing a false report. "You told them you expended ammunition even when you didn't? What happens if Brigade finds out?"

"It's okay," he explained. "Colonel Ra'ed told me it was all right."

"The brigade commander told you it was okay to file a false report?" I asked, not believing my ears.

"Yes."

I sat there speechless, not knowing what to say. I had always guessed that Ayad was involved in a certain degree of corruption, but I hadn't expected him to openly admit it, nor had I thought the brigade commander would be involved as well.

My straightforward questioning seemed to have unnerved him, and he also appeared embarrassed that I had caught him in a lie. He quickly changed the subject and asked me for my thoughts about the battalion and what my concerns were. I didn't hesitate to answer.

"I'm concerned about the individual training and discipline of the *junood*," I said. "And I'm concerned about the lack of initiative and supervision by the officers."

He nodded, and I continued.

"I'm worried about the mistrust that exists between you and your staff."

He listened intently, agreeing with everything I had to say. We talked about my observations for over two hours, and I was genuinely surprised at how receptive he was to my critique. But I knew that anyone could listen; the real test would be whether he took my observations and recommendations to heart and acted on them. To date he had largely ignored what I had offered. Why should he do any different now?

A gaggle of rumors began circulating back and forth on e-mails and message traffic that claimed our MiTT team would "decouple" from 3rd Battalion early, and that there would be no advisor team replacing us. We had first heard about the possibility months before, and although we had no hard facts to back us up we had begun laying the groundwork for terminating the mission with the 3rd Battalion staff. Each time they came to us with a problem we would remind them that our team might be the last MiTT to be partnered with their battalion. And on each occasion they dismissed our warning, insisting that the Americans would not be leaving.

But now the buzz appeared to be true, and on 12 July Lieutenant Colonel Gridley and his MiTT staff convened a meeting at Camp Al Qa'im for all of the brigade's advisor teams. Gridley confirmed that the rumors were now fact, and he announced that the Outlanders would indeed decouple from 3rd Battalion as soon as possible. The MiTT from 2nd Battalion would likewise decouple and would not be replaced by another team. My team would turn over its equipment to an incoming MiTT that would be designated as an "overwatch" transition team, and once established the overwatch team would augment the brigade team by providing general advisor support to the two battalions that were not partnered with advisors. It was a complicated plan and a heavy task for our team. I wondered how we would get it all done in time.

The battalion had been planning an operation south of our AO, and what was initially supposed to be an intelligence-based search operation evolved into planning for a combined reconnaissance mission with a company from 2nd Light Armored Reconnaissance (LAR) Battalion. But as the 3rd Battalion S-2 and S-3 sections continued to plan the operation the target area began to encroach deeper and deeper into 2nd LAR's AO. On 13 July I pulled Bates, Ski, and Hanna aside and polled them.

"What do you think?"

"I'd like us to do one last op with them," Bates said. "Especially since we have finally gotten them to do some real fucking planning. But . . ."

"But what?"

"Well, like I said, I want to do it, but it's gotten a little too complicated."

I turned to Ski.

"Agree, sir," he said. "They don't have enough intel. I think it will be another wild goose chase."

"Yep, concur," I said. "I think it's a bridge too far, especially with all the work we have to do to get out of here." I turned back to Bates. "Tell them we can't play."

It was a disappointing decision to make. As Bates had noted, we would miss our last chance to go on a mission with the battalion. More important, we had pushed 3rd Battalion hard over the preceding months to put more work and detail into their planning efforts, and now that they had finally taken our advice and done so, we ended up recommending to them that they cancel the operation. It was not a good way to end our time with the IAs.

Unconcerned about the reconnaissance mission to the south that had been canceled, Ayad was instead excited about conducting antismuggling operations in 3rd Battalion's AO. The capture of the cigarette truck had been a political victory for him among his Iraqi colleagues and had helped to dispel the rumor that 3rd Battalion had gone to ground at COP South, either unable or unwilling to venture outside the wire on operations.

When I visited Ayad on the afternoon of 13 July he was excited about a car one of his patrols had snagged early that morning. At 0400 Lieutenant Ski had awakened me and summoned me to the COC. The Marine task force had been tracking an automobile from the Syrian border as it made its way down into 3rd Battalion's AO, and an unmanned aerial vehicle (UAV) had filmed the car transferring something to another vehicle at the border.

"The border forts need to go check that out," I had said irritably. "That's *their* job."

"I know, sir," Ski had replied. "They won't do it, so the task force has asked Third Battalion to do it."

We had alerted 3rd Battalion's QRF and relayed the coordinates provided to us by the UAV, and thirty minutes later it was speeding outside the wire and into the open desert in hot pursuit of the suspicious vehicle. In the end the QRF had detained the car and driver, but all it found was two cartons of cigarettes.

But it had been a minor victory in synchronization between the task force, the MiTT, and the IAs, and Ayad was more than happy to take the credit for the arrest. I didn't bother to remind him of the role the Marines had played in coordinating the mission. Sometimes the best way to encourage success in someone is to allow him to think everything was his idea.

As we discussed the details of that morning's mission, it occurred to me that Ayad had begun sitting next to me during our daily meetings since his return from leave several days earlier. He had normally sat across the office and behind his desk. It seemed that he was growing closer to me in more ways than one. Barriers were crumbling, but I feared it was too late. Lunch was served, and I broke the news to him about the MiTT leaving 3rd Battalion. He was visibly crushed.

"I don't know what we'll do without the Americans here," he said, slowly shaking his head. "You have done a lot for us. It won't be the same without your help."

"I know, *sadie*," I said, trying to console him. "But I think Third Battalion is ready to be on its own."

"Well," he replied, "you must have lunch with me every day until you leave."

Our meal continued, but he didn't eat much. It had never occurred to me that I would have such an impact on him when it eventually came time for us to leave. But then again, I wasn't sure what it was that truly upset him. Was it the fact that I was leaving, or was it simply that there was no replacement team coming after us?

As our remaining days at COP South began to dwindle the Marines noticed a marked shift in the Iraqis' attitudes toward us. The rank-and-file *jundi* in the battalion seemed not to care. To them we were pretty much just another group of Americans who had come and would soon be gone. But the battalion staff reacted to our impending departure with a peculiar mixture of glee and dread. Dread, because they knew their lifeline was essentially getting cut. They had failed to heed our warnings, and our looming absence meant they would be on their own to succeed or fail. Glee, because they couldn't wait for us to depart our compound so that they could move in and assume control of whatever we left behind.

In preparation for our exodus my guidance to the team was clear: the most important items to account for and pack up were obviously our serialized and personal equipment. Anything that the new team could possibly use at the new brigade facility would also be packed up. And I placed special emphasis on accounting for classified material. There was to be nothing left behind that could potentially compromise Coalition operations after the team was gone.

The Iraqi officers grew bolder as each day passed, often asking the Marines what we would be abandoning. They also wanted to know what we personally planned to give them. One evening Master Sergeant Deleon commented to me on what was occurring.

"Check this out," he said glumly. "Sergeant Major Sattaar asked me point-blank last night, 'What are you going to give me before you go?'"

"Damn, that was pretty ballsy," I said.

"You know, sir," he said, shaking his head in the same crestfallen manner that had become common among the team, "it's just disappointing. All these crazies care about is what we can give them. They just want a handout."

"Well," I said, "it won't be long now before they get a rude awakening."

Regardless, the Outlanders hosted the 3rd Battalion staff at a goat grab in our compound on 15 July. Crowded around tables brimming with platters of steaming rice and lamb, the Iraqis and the Americans laughed and joked together. It was a far cry from the stilted conversations held among the same men just five months earlier, when they had been complete strangers. Something resembling camaraderie seemed present during the feast, and I silently cursed that it had taken so long for a bond such as this to develop. The cultural differences had simply been too great, and the time had simply been too short.

The meal complete, we presented each Iraqi staff member with framed photographs of the Outlanders and each team member with his Iraqi counterpart. The Iraqis seemed genuinely appreciative. As I presented my gift to Lieutenant Colonel Ayad I spoke to the assembled audience.

"*Sadie*, our experience with Third Battalion has been interesting. We have learned a lot. And our experience with you and your battalion will be one that we never forget. We learned a great deal about you and your men, and I hope you were able to learn something about us."

Because I was speaking on behalf of my Marines I had carefully chosen my words. I knew how they collectively felt about what had happened, and I didn't want to falsely represent their feelings. During our time together they had observed closely my growing estrangement from Ayad, and had I stood in front of everyone and painted a rosy picture of friendship, equanimity, and harmony between the Americans and the Iraqis I never would have heard the end of it from my men. But I also didn't want to embarrass the Iraqis. Nothing I said had been dishonest, but I wondered if they would be able to read between the lines.

The Marines began the packout of the camp in earnest on 16 July, and the following day the IAs increased their personal requests for gifts. Captain Ali and Warrant Officer Saadik arrived at our COC and presented to Lieutenant Grubb a typed, translated letter formally requesting supplies, including flash drives and a computer. The two men made a big production of it, and once they left Grubb showed the letter to me.

Name of God the Merciful
Sovereignty respected officer

I told you a few days ago I was needy to Flash 8 bytes and yucca to paper for use in the office of the securities in excess of your answer has been received so far and I hope that Karim Al-Janabi looking to you for using calculators father Tubb for use against me personally a sum of money for badly needed I hope that this matter myself to you and I should be grateful to you You know the Iraqi market expensive and I appreciate that the father bought a calculator Tubb amount Ghali and the memory of an American officer in the army served with us and we were collaborators together in various ways, for the second time I say to you that this is a secret to me Pink

Addressee
N z Sadik
Office training

Howling with laughter, I thrust the letter back at Grubb.

"Hey, 'Father Tubb,'" I said, tears running down my face. "I can't even tell what the hell they are asking for. Who translated that?"

"Who knows?" he asked with annoyance. "You believe that shit, sir?"

"Yeah, I do, man," I said, shaking my head. "I really do."

I folded the letter up and filed it away, a permanent reminder of the miscommunication and hilarity that had characterized our time as advisors to the Iraqi army.

Chapter 30
Leaving

S omething was different about Ayad, but I couldn't place it. He sat at
his desk the night of 17 July, shoulders squared, and he seemed to look
around his office with an air of confidence I had not noticed before. He
rose to greet me as I walked through the door, and he warmly embraced me
in a hug that lasted longer than normal.

Man, I thought, *he's in a good mood.*

He sat next to me, and after a minute of making our routine small talk I
noticed the shine of new cloth material on his uniform's shoulder epaulettes.
An additional star had been added to his rank insignia, and he wore the
new shoulder boards of an *aqeed* (colonel). Once he realized I had figured it
out he burst into a broad grin, and I heartily congratulated him. A promotion always brings with it a deep sense of personal accomplishment, so I
was happy for him. But I was also conflicted. The promotions for scores of
soldiers in the battalion had been held up for months, and there Ayad was,
flaunting his new rank. I also couldn't help wondering how he would leverage his newfound authority as a colonel. Would he use it to improve the lot
of his soldiers, or would he use it to elevate his own standing in the brigade?
Our imminent departure meant that I might never know.

Before my evening get-together with Ayad, Lieutenant Ski had informed
me that on the previous two nights 3rd Battalion had conducted raids into
Karabilah. As we sat drinking chai Ayad did not mention the operations
to me until I asked. He waved it off, saying there were some bad people in
Karabilah who needed to be picked up.

"Did you coordinate the raids with the IPs?" I asked.

"No," he replied. "The IPs are corrupt. They would have told the people we were coming."

His words—and the battalion's actions—let me down. We had come full
circle. In the previous months the Outlanders had gone to great efforts to
convince the IAs to stay out of the cities and let the police do their job. Now
there we were, preparing to leave, and already the Iraqis were returning to

their old tricks and habits. *I can see we've definitely left a deep impression on them*, I thought sarcastically.

The next morning the team moved quickly around the camp, dismantling and cataloging equipment. Two Marines walked into the COC.

"Man, the IAs are going nuts out there with all that stuff," one of them said.

I walked across the compound to the MWR hut. Iraqi soldiers were everywhere, carrying away crates of food, soft drinks, and supplies. It looked like a free-for-all, and I lost my cool.

"Hey!" I shouted to the Marines. "Get the IAs the hell out of here!"

Sergeant Frazier walked up to me.

"I thought we were gonna give them all our extra stuff," he said.

"Not yet we aren't," I growled. "Get these motherfuckers out of the compound. This isn't a fucking yard sale. I don't want them in here until we are gone. *Then* they can have what we leave behind."

But even after Frazier shooed away the soldiers one lone warrant officer remained, insisting to Lieutenant Bates that he be allowed to haul away everything.

"The battalion commander told me to come get everything," he said through our interpreter, Sammy.

"Negative," Bates replied. "Take what you already have in your truck and get out. You can get everything else after the MiTT is gone."

"No," the warrant officer demanded. "I have to take it all now."

Sammy then raised his voice at the man. "Look, I don't care what your commander told you!" he said, pointing his finger at the Iraqi. "The Americans just told you to get out. Now get out and come back after they are gone!"

Less than an hour later two more Iraqi NCOs found me and Captain Hanna outside the COC.

"Major Rabah told us to come pick up everything," they told Hanna. "Where is it all?"

I stepped forward.

"Listen," I said curtly. "I'm telling you this one last time. Get the hell out of here, and tell everyone not to come back until the MiTT leaves."

The two soldiers walked away, mumbling to themselves. I turned back to Hanna.

"Jesus," I said, exasperated. "They're acting like fucking vermin. They're just waiting to pick our camp clean."

Once again I felt my goodwill toward the IAs rapidly disintegrating. As much as I wanted our mission with 3rd Battalion to end on a positive note, the closer we got to leaving, the less likely that possibility became.

That afternoon the newly promoted *Ameed* (Brigadier General) Ra'ed and Lieutenant Colonel Gridley arrived at COP South for a farewell lunch hosted by 3rd Battalion. After the meal the Outlanders filed into Ayad's office, where he presented small gifts to them one by one.

"We are truly thankful for your presence and all the help you have given us," he said. "We have lived side by side, through good times and bad, and you will always remain in our hearts."

His words were touching, and in light of our frustrations with the *junood* that morning Ayad's speech was what I had hoped for: a fitting way for our time there to end. But we weren't gone yet.

By the morning of 19 July the camp was completely barren. Furniture, computers, equipment—all had been accounted for, cataloged, and packed in a row of massive shipping containers that lined the border of our compound. With nothing to do, the Marines sat around in their barren huts and shot the shit, waiting for the arrival of the trucks that would take us and our equipment to Camp Al Qa'im.

That afternoon Colonel Ayad called for me to have lunch with him one last time before the team left. As Sammy and I sat with him waiting for the food to be brought in, Ayad began listing his problems with fuel.

"Fuel is a constant problem for us," he said. "I don't have enough to run my battalion."

"You're right, *sadie*," I said. "It will continue to be a challenge for you until the MOD and Division and Brigade start giving you more."

"Yes, I don't get enough," he repeated. "And so I will have to ask you for fuel before your team leaves COP South."

I should have seen it coming. I just shook my head slowly.

"Sorry, *sadie*," I told him. "It's no longer my fuel to give. It now belongs to the Coalition."

A dejected look filled his face, and I continued.

"But I want to tell you what we *will* be leaving behind in our camp," I said, reading from my small notebook. "Rolls of concertina wire, empty HESCO barriers, six fully functioning huts with air-conditioners, bottled water, soft drinks, food, and personal hygiene items."

"Thank you," he said, smiling now. "All of the supplies will go to the *junood*, and we will use the buildings for billeting spaces, offices, and classrooms."

"I think that's a great idea, *sadie*," I said, relieved. "I'm glad you have a plan for it all."

With lunch finished, I prepared to take my leave from Ayad. I had thought long and hard about what I would say to him before leaving, and as our time together came to a close I spoke.

"*Sadie*, I've been your advisor for five months," I said. "My job has been to give you my advice and recommendations, so before I leave I will pass on to you my parting guidance."

He sat, listening intently, and I continued.

"No commander makes it to the top by himself. It is not only his skill that gets him there. He gets there because of the men he leads—"

My words were cut short by Ayad's cell phone. His cell had been the bane of my evening meetings with him; our get-togethers frequently had been interrupted by its ring. The courtesy of not answering a phone call when you have company clearly had not yet made it to Iraq. And so it was during our last meeting. He chatted with some local sheikh for ten minutes while Sammy and I stared at each other.

I had wanted to tell Ayad that leaders are made by the people that they lead, that the most important thing he could do as a commander was to take care of his soldiers. To do so would earn their trust and confidence, and they would eventually do anything for him and the battalion. I had wanted to tell him that it is the staff that makes a battalion work, and that it is the junior officers and NCOs and enlisted men who, when empowered to make decisions, accomplish the mission. I had wanted to tell him all of these things and more, but his cell had rung. In the end a phone call had been more important than what I had to offer him. When his call ended he hung up and looked at me.

"Well," I said coldly, rising to my feet. "Time for me to go, *sadie*."

I stood up and walked out of his office.

The trucks pulled into COP South, and as our shipping containers were being loaded the Iraqi soldiers lined up outside the spiraling concertina wire that circled our camp, waiting for us to leave. As the moment of our departure grew closer the *junood* brazenly began walking into the camp's perimeter, practically pushing the Marines out. The Marines stared at them.

"Look at them," I commented. "They look like a bunch of white trash lined up at the Wal-Mart entrance for a midnight sale."

"Sir," one Marine laughed, pointing to the soldiers slowly making their way into the compound. "We got gooks in the wire."

The Outlanders loaded into their vehicles, and I hopped in the team's Chevy pickup truck for the drive to Camp Al Qa'im. I had never pictured being able to ride in a truck on the roads in Iraq and still feel secure, yet there I was. It was perhaps a testament to how safe our part of the country had become.

As the long convoy of vehicles pulled away from the compound and turned toward COP South's ECP I glanced at my rearview mirror. The Iraqi soldiers were filing into our camp in droves, eagerly searching for what the Marines had left behind.

The Outlanders returned to COP South four days later as part of an AO tour we were providing for the overwatch MiTT. Eager to introduce the new team leader to the battalion commander, I escorted him across the camp to Ayad's hut. But I had timed the visit incorrectly, and we learned from Ayad's bodyguard that he was asleep. With nothing else to do, I turned to the captain at my side.

"Come on," I said. "I'll show you where our team used to live."

We walked to the MiTT compound. The entrance, which had always been blocked with a strand of razor wire strung across it, was wide open. Trash and debris casually fluttered through the ghost town the camp had become. Glancing around, I was floored by the sight that greeted me. In our absence the IAs had come in and completely wrecked the place. Huts had been ransacked, doors had been torn from their hinges, and bed frames had been broken. Inside the huts all internal wiring and fuse boxes had been stripped, and all light fixtures had been torn out. Bags of garbage had been torn open, their contents strewn across the compound. To add insult to injury, one *jundi* had even taken a shit in the empty throne of the WAG shack, yet had neglected to use a WAG bag. Another had likewise crapped in the concrete cave of the team's indirect-fire shelter.

The Marines were livid. I too wanted to feel the same rage, but instead I was merely overcome with utter and complete disappointment. I remembered King Lear's sad utterance and numbly thought to myself, *"How sharper than a serpent's tooth it is / To have a thankless child!"*

The team had turned over a fully functioning camp to the soldiers of 3rd Battalion, and they in turn had repaid us by raping it. Ayad had assured me the compound would be converted into useful spaces for the soldiers, but now the buildings were unusable. It was a final slap in the face to the team, and the Outlanders departed the camp in a dark mood, utterly disillusioned with what we had been doing.

It was perhaps the worst possible way for us to complete our time as advisors, and everyone—myself included—fought to rinse the bad taste lingering in their mouths. My confidence in 3rd Battalion's ability to succeed was shaken, and more than ever I began to question what we were doing there. Remembering software engineer Robert Glass's words about the true definition of reality, I wondered sadly if the "beautiful theory" of the advisor team mission had been murdered by "a gang of ugly facts." My Marines had done everything they could to help 3rd Battalion—more than they probably should have—but now the Iraqis truly would have to do it on their own if they wanted to succeed. It was time to throw them in the water and let them sink or swim. Our part there—my part—was done.

Chapter 31
Dogs

S ome of the inhabitants of COP South walk on four legs. But the dogs
that roam our camp are not a nuisance; instead, they are our guard-
ians. And, in time, they become our friends.

When we arrive we find four dogs that are holdovers from the previous
team, and although initially I am not pleased with their being there it is not
long before I realize the benefit their presence brings: they hate Iraqis. The
junood have mistreated the animals, throwing rocks at them and teasing
them and tying them up, and now the dogs go apeshit whenever an Iraqi
soldier comes near the American compound. They become my alarm system at night, alerting me and the team whenever a *jundi* attempts to sneak
inside the wire to steal cases of water or soda. We hope they'll warn us if
the insurgents attempt to infiltrate our compound and cut our throats in the
dark of night.

Three of the dogs have names. Snowflake, Mama, and Louie wander
in and out of our compound, seeking food and attention. The fourth dog
is referred to as "the mean one," or simply "that big, black bitch," and she
stays hidden deep inside an abandoned HESCO structure on the far edge of
camp. She has had a litter of puppies, and any attempt to get near her or her
babies brings with it the risk of losing a hand. Before long the puppies have
grown, and they too join their mother and determinedly guard their empire
on the far edge of the camp. They want nothing to do with us, and so we in
turn want nothing to do with them. Their mother disappears, and we never
hear from her again. Eventually her pups join her, wandering the wasteland
that surrounds COP South.

Mama has also gotten herself pregnant, though we are unsure who the
father is. We think it might be Louie. As the weeks pass her belly swells
and we see less and less of her as she searches for a nesting spot to deliver
her litter. When the puppies finally come she won't let us near them, but
the Marines line up anyway to catch a peek of the seven runts that have
survived the birthing process. Sure enough, several of them look like Louie.

Snowflake also appears randomly, happily taking handouts when he is not blackened and filthy from scavenging food in the charred hole of the camp's garbage pit. He prefers our leftovers, not the bags of dried dog food that one team member has convinced friends to send to us. When our convoys leave the camp, Snowflake often follows us outside the wire, bidding the Outlanders farewell when our vehicles leave the dirt trail and turn north onto the hardball.

Louie is a big, dumb puppy, and his dirty gray and black coat and raw-boned enthusiasm remind me of the stray puppy I once adopted as a child in Italy. Louie is the dog that the team loves to hate, and he is a nuisance. Piles of Louie droppings litter the area like twisted land mines, and I threaten to banish him from the camp if the Marines don't clean up after him. One morning I find three gifts Louie has left by the door to my hut. In a fit of rage I grab him by the scruff of the neck and drag him outside the concertina wire, yelling at him not to come back. But he twists his way back inside the coiled wire and moments later is vying for my attention.

I am livid, yet in my anger I remember how I handed over my Italian puppy to an uncaring master, and how the dog met his horrible end at the hands of an insidious canine illness. The last time I remember seeing the dog he was lying in a putrid swirl of his own blood, feces, and urine, and he stared up at me with big, sad eyes as if to ask me why I had abandoned him, why I had consigned him to such a hideous fate.

And then I forget my anger with Louie, and I remember that a lance corporal temporarily assigned to our team has convinced some humanitarian organization to pay $3,000 to ferry Louie back to the United States. The young Marine has tended to Louie since he was born, and he has decided that he cannot live without the mutt. One day a team of contractors shows up at the camp and whisks Louie away to America and a future rendezvous with his Marine savior. Two of the team members sink into a depression after Louie's departure. One of them, Sgt. Mark Hoffmier, abandons his gruff exterior and shifts his attention from Louie's disappearance to the new litter of puppies being reared by Mama. Hoffmier, the team's resident firearms enthusiast, is often brooding and unhappy. But beneath his acerbic exterior lies a conscientious, compassionate young man who demonstrates this by caring for the litter of puppies.

Hoffmier counts them daily, retrieving errant puppies that have wandered away from the concrete bunker in which Mama has nested them. Eventually the sergeant builds a tiny doghouse outside his hooch, and then he builds a dog run next to the hut. One by one he moves the puppies from the bunker into the dog run and the waiting doghouse, and he spends his free time watching over the mutts as if they are his own children. He picks out one puppy that closely resembles Louie, and he begins making arrangements for the dog to be spirited away to America the same way Louie was. But our premature departure from COP South means that Hoffmier will not have the time to coordinate his puppy's salvation, and he sadly accepts the fact that the dog will have to remain behind to fend for itself.

At first I am irritated at the time and attention Sergeant Hoffmier and all of the Marines have expended looking after the mangy pack of animals that roam our camp, but then I become conscious of the silent impact these dogs have had on all of us. They remind us of home, and they allow the Outlanders to be human in a place where it is easy to lose one's humanity. The Marines hate the critters, but they love the dogs, and it is only after I realize this that I finally understand how we will win this Long War. The Marines are not robots. They are not mindless. They are capable of killing, yes, but they are capable of something much more powerful. They are capable of loving—loving their country, loving each other, and, yes, even loving the pack of ratty mongrel dogs that, like us, have made COP South their home.

It is that ability to love that makes my Marines invincible. But will our Iraqi counterparts learn the same thing? Will they be able to set aside their petty squabbles, their tribal infighting, their allegiances to the past, and instead embrace each other as brothers? Will they choose the lighted path toward progress, or will they veer blindly into the darkened corridor toward regression? We don't know; all we can do is watch the dogs.

And wait.

Chapter 32
A Way Forward

In the long, sweltering weeks following our hasty exodus from COP South and 3rd Battalion the Outlanders languished at various FOBs, suffering the miserable existence of transients waiting patiently for an early flight back home to their families and their lives. As I wandered the Coalition outposts and marveled again and again at the bloated logistical footprint the Americans had imprinted in the Iraqi sands, I reflected on what my team had done there and what we had ultimately accomplished. I kept thinking that perhaps I should feel proud that 3rd Battalion was now on its own.

But I didn't feel that way. All jobs come with daily frustrations—that had certainly been true of our time as advisors. Marines by their very nature are results-oriented beings, and I had to look inward deep within myself to find any positive, tangible effects from our efforts with the Iraqis. I wondered constantly if our presence had made a difference, if we had truly made an impact on the soldiers and officers of 3rd Battalion. Ronald Reagan had once said, "Some people wonder all their lives if they've made a difference. The Marines don't have that problem." In my experience as an advisor I wasn't so sure that had been the case. Would the Iraqis in 3rd Battalion do the things we had showed them? More important, would they be able to stand on their own after we left? For the last question I knew the answer had to be yes. Somehow they would make it. It wouldn't be the solution *we* would choose, but somehow they would make it work. They had no choice. The Americans would be gone soon. It was up to them now.

The Iraqi army has a character flaw. It lives in a constant state of denial, seeking ways to blame others for their problems in life. Whether it is the junior officers blaming the army's leadership or the senior officers blaming their higher headquarters and the Iraqi government, Iraqi soldiers will never solve their internal dilemmas until they accept responsibility for themselves, their problems, and their own destiny. To a certain extent it is the same in the Marine Corps. One day the junior Marine officers and NCOs—the young men and women who have grown up in the uncertain shadow of the Long War that began on 11 September 2001—who choose to stick it out will progress through the ranks, and eventually the face of the Corps will change into something different than what it is today. So too can it be in the Iraqi army. If the young Iraqi officers stick to their guns—if they don't throw in the towel and return to civilian life—one day they will run the organization, and the challenges they face today will become a distant memory.

The Americans also have a character flaw. We are naive and shortsighted. We thought we could invade Iraq and liberate the people from tyranny, and once that was accomplished everything else would work itself out. We thought we could force change on the Iraqi military and perhaps make it into something it is not: a modern, American-style force with American ideals and determination. We now think we can pull out of the country prematurely and turn it over to the Iraqi Security Forces, and they in turn will be able to assume control of their country and their own future. But the Americans can't achieve these feats on their own. Change must come from within; it must come from the Iraqis themselves. They have to *want* it to happen.

Naive and shortsighted though we are, we also possess the ability to recognize our mistakes and seek ways to amend them. Winston Churchill once said, "Americans can always be counted on to do the right thing . . . after they have exhausted all other possibilities." So too has it been in Iraq. We made errors while planning the invasion and during the subsequent occupation. Of that there can be no doubt, and only the most stubborn and uninformed people will challenge that assertion. But gradually we realized our miscalculations and committed ourselves and our national treasure to correcting them. The cost has been extreme, and like thousands of others my thoughts frequently churn in sad, hopeless circles at the memories of my friends and other fellow Marines who sacrificed their lives serving their country. But while I often sit alone and ponder what is and what could have been in this war, I will never dishonor the memory of so many who fought and died—who fought and lost themselves—by claiming that what we did *as a whole* in Iraq was a mistake. My conscience will not permit it.

Will Iraq ever be truly free? Will it ever be stable? Will I ever be able to visit it again, not as a Marine but instead as a tourist? Whenever I think of that possibility I think about the dogs.

And wait.

Epilogue: Dream

My daughters are grown, much older now. I cross the Kuwaiti border into Iraq, and I tell them, *This is where it all began.* Years have passed for me, and sometimes I forget just how long it has been since I was an impetuous young captain, a company commander leading 130 Marines and sailors and a fleet of light armored vehicles. My daughters' journey begins, and in a way it is a new journey for me too.

They begin to ask questions, probing at first with innocent yet at the same time broad inquiries. They ask things such as *What was it like over here?* I ponder it momentarily, unsure if I will even be able to answer them, and if so, where I will begin. But time has dulled the jagged edges of memory, making it somehow easier for me, and suddenly the words come and I find myself telling them everything. With the landscape of Iraq as my backdrop I begin to tell them the story.

This is where we crossed the Euphrates, I tell them, remembering the pontoon bridge and the unfinished dirt trail that served as a road. Only now the span is an actual engineered bridge, and the dirt road is now a bustling, modern highway that stretches deep into Mesopotamia. What were once parched, alkali-saturated marshes poisoned by Saddam Hussein's campaign of drought against the Shiite Marsh Arabs now flow wet and bristle with exotic, nameless flora and fauna. My daughters casually comment on the beauty of the marshes that skirt the highway, and I say to them over and over again, *No, this wasn't here. None of it. It was nothing but mudflats, crisscrossing levees, and shallow canals.* And I explain how I couldn't take my vehicles off the road for fear of getting them stuck in the mud or rolling them over into a canal.

I explain how the artillery—both friendly and enemy—fell in sheets, and as we approach Ad Diwaniyah I point to an inconspicuous patch of earth a hundred meters off the highway. To my daughters it is just another tilled field, no different from countless others they have seen so far inside the breadbasket of Iraq sandwiched between the Tigris and the Euphrates. But I am pointing to the spot where I lost my first Marine, and my words catch in my throat as I explain how I tried to save him, and how he died. They don't understand when I tell them that it was friendly artillery that killed him, because they don't understand the nature of war. They don't understand the fog that hovers over the battlefield, the mistakes that are made, and the consequences that follow.

Farther up the highway I come to a sharp bend in the road, and I kneel in the dirt and draw them a picture of where my vehicles were along this elbow when I drove into my first ambush. The skies are a brilliant sapphire, just as they were that day, and I point to the west and describe the glorious sight of the gunship helicopters that came to my company's rescue. I describe the brilliant flash of exhaust heat on my face as the gunships fired their rockets fifty feet above our vehicles, and the way the dirt seemed to splash like towering geysers of black water as friendly artillery rounds plummeted into the enemy positions. My daughters are puzzled as I crawl in the reeds next to the Tigris River, and their eyes suddenly light up when I return, filthy and covered in tiny cuts, with spent shell casings from that day. They are not difficult to find, because my company fired so many, and it will be years before the earth swallows their rusting forms and there is no longer any trace of the exploding hell that flourished that day at the elbow. My younger daughter turns a shell casing over and over in her hands, and she announces that she is going to make a necklace out of it. *Youth*, I muse to myself. *Only kids can manage to find beauty in anything. Even war.*

Baghdad looms on the horizon, and I enter the city expecting anarchy, because that is what I bore witness to the last time I was there. But there is no chaos, no looting. No mobs fill the streets, hauling away everything they can get their hands on. A bizarre sense of order seems to reign, and as the city dwellers go about their business in the markets and shops my daughters don't believe that this city could have ever been anything but the peaceful, cosmopolitan community that it is now. *But it was*, I tell them. *There was a time when these streets ran red with the blood of Americans and Iraqis alike.* They shake their heads, unable to understand, and so we continue north.

The sun breaks on the horizon behind me as I approach Tikrit, just as it did that day. The tunnel is not difficult to find, because I remember the map northing by heart, and as I check my GPS I realize I am standing right on top of it. I take my daughters down the highway's embankment, and the darkened culvert tunnel yawns at me like a sleeping dragon. And when I realize that the dragon is about to rise from its slumber I go silent, suddenly unable to speak. My daughters know what happened to me here even without me telling them because they see it in my eyes, and it frightens them. The cold concrete walls of the tunnel magnify the thunder of gunfire, and I feel my ears ringing even though I haven't fired a weapon in years. The gunfire I hear is the memory of this fetid hole in the ground discharging in my mind. My daughters seem to understand, and then they realize that this is the place where my life changed irreparably, irreversibly.

I don't speak much as my daughters and I travel west. The radiant greens and blues of Mesopotamia fade back into the dull beige of desert as we approach Al Qa'im, and we turn south away from the Euphrates, past the crowded streets of Karabilah and Husaybah. Our trip from Tikrit has been long and uneventful, and in my stillness I think of the towns I have passed through—Ramadi, Ubaydi, Husaybah—and I remember my friends and colleagues and Marines I lost there so long ago, and I think back in quiet shame to a period when I thought the war was lost, that it was unwinnable. And when one of my daughters comments that she is tired of driving, that she is bored, I explain to her that there was once a time when driving along this road was the closest thing possible to suicide. I tell her how IEDs seemed to line the road like hidden mile markers, how thousands of Marines and soldiers—American and Iraqi—lost limbs, lost lives, lost minds to the roadside bombs that littered this country. Once again it is difficult for my daughters to comprehend such a thing, because no blackened craters scar the roads now, no blood gathers and congeals in lumpy gobs in the gutters.

In the open desert I point out the barren spot that used to be COP South, and the corners of my mouth begin to curl into a grin at the recollection that comes to mind of my time as an advisor. My daughters ask why I am smiling, and I try to explain the black humor and the sense of futility that comes with advising a foreign army—an army whose language and culture are so different from your own that nothing seems to make sense, an army in which up is down, wrong is right, and forward is backward. I explain how, in my transition team's attempt to revitalize the Iraqi army and help it bring security to this country, the only way to make it through the days was to laugh—at the Iraqis, at my fellow Outlanders, at myself.

I pause to tell my daughters stories about my teammates—who they were, where they came from, and why they were there in Iraq with me, so far away from their own families. *The Outlanders were my brothers*, I tell them. *As near and close to my heart as my own flesh and blood*. And as I describe their professionalism I remember how, in the end, they wanted the same thing I did: to accomplish the mission and go home. I think about how, faced with an impossible task, they carried out their responsibilities with the same energy and determination for which Marines are universally known. *It was an honor and a privilege to serve with them*, I tell my daughters. *I was truly blessed.*

We move on, and I scan the roads for Iraqi army checkpoints or convoys. Nothing appears, and I head toward the last place I remember. *The phosphate plant*, I remember thinking. *A peculiar place to put a brigade headquarters.* But it is still there, and the Iraqi soldiers man their posts and go about their daily routine. They look smart in their uniforms, and their weapons are clean and well maintained. They rehearse battle drills, NCOs moving back and forth, instructing the soldiers, mentoring them. Inside the buildings staff officers bustle about, filing reports and planning training exercises. There are no more patrols in the desert, no more nighttime raids into Husaybah or Karabilah. The Iraqi army is training for something, but it doesn't know what it is, and neither do I. Peace has found this tortured, pathetic country, peace from the inside and out, and in its serenity I finally see what it is that so many fought and died for.

I see a beginning.

I awake from my dream. Next to me my wife stirs momentarily and then drifts off back to sleep. She is accustomed to my restless nights; she has been for years. She wonders if I will ever find that part of myself that I lost in Iraq so long ago. I walk down the hall to the bedrooms of my two young daughters. They have never seen Iraq, and I wonder if my recurring dream will ever come true. In the warm glow of their night-lights I stare at them one by one, their angelic features reflecting a blissful ignorance only visible on the faces of small children who have never suffered the trauma of war. No bombs will explode outside their windows tonight; no masked gunmen will cut them down in their beds. They will remain blissfully unaware that somewhere in Iraq a different father questions if his children will survive another day. I wonder if true peace will ever find that country, and as I turn to leave I wonder what kind of world my daughters will grow up in. And then, as they frequently do, my thoughts turn to the brave young Marines with whom I have served, and I gaze at my daughters once more and remember the words often attributed to George Orwell:

"We sleep soundly in our beds because rough men stand ready in the night to visit violence upon those who would do us harm."

Iraq is far away, and my daughters will sleep soundly tonight.

So will I.

Acknowledgments

Books are collaborative ventures. Just as no commander achieves success individually, authors are similarly indebted to those around them who assist in both direct and indirect ways.

For the writing of this book I owe my greatest debt to my best friend and wife, Ashley. Her strengths are innumerable, and as always her painstaking editorial assistance made the difference between this book being a good one and a great one.

I am similarly thankful for my parents, CAPT Benjamin F. Folsom Jr., USN (Ret.), and Judith G. Folsom. Their love, support, and shameless public promotion of me and my previous work have been a constant source of encouragement for me throughout this process.

Gracious thanks go to Ron Gridley and Jeff Simpson for their assistance with the manuscript's security and policy review, as well as Curtis Williamson and Robert Miller for their public affairs and ethics guidance.

Sincere thanks to Roger Cirillo at the Association of the United States Army, as well as the editorial staff of the Naval Institute Press for their confidence in my work.

As with my previous book, the story presented here is not solely my own. Without the Marines and sailor of Military Transition Team 0733 this book could not have been written. To all of the Outlanders—Todd Hanna, Norvin Deleonguerrero, Jason Rehm, Matt Bates, Joe Davidoski, Andrew Grubb, Shaun Leek, Clarence Wolf, Theo Bowers, Olanza Frazier, Mark Hoffmier, Emiliano Rabor, Travis Wardle, and Daniel Fry—I am eternally grateful. For months you so often heard me tell you that I had nothing for you. Now I finally do.

Semper Fidelis.

Glossary

1st Lt.	First lieutenant
2nd Lt.	Second lieutenant
Aajaaz	Arabic for "sandstorm"
AH-1W	Marine Corps attack helicopter
AK-47	Russian-made 7.62-millimeter assault rifle used by the Iraqi army
Ameed	Arabic for "brigadier general"
AO	Area of operations
AQ	Camp Al Qa'im
Aqeed	Arabic for "colonel"
ATG	Advisor Training Group
Berm	Artificial sand wall used for protection or for delineating boundaries in the desert
BFT	Blue Force Tracker: digital, GPS-based system used to track and communicate with Coalition units on the battlefield
BP	Battle position
BTT	Border transition team
BZO	Battle-sight zero; calibrated settings on the sights of a rifle that allow the shooter to overcome various factors and hit accurately at a given range, used as a default before adjusting for wind or distance
Canc	Short for "cancel"
Capt.	Captain

CASEVAC	Casualty evacuation
CH-53	Marine Corps heavy-lift transport helicopter
Chai	Hot, sweet tea
CMR	Consolidated memorandum receipt
COC	Combat operations center
Col.	Colonel
Comm	Short for "communications"
COP	Combat outpost
Cpl.	Corporal
DBE	Department of Border Enforcement (Iraqi)
DHQ	District headquarters
Dishdasha	Traditional dresslike outfit worn by Arabic men
DOD	Department of Defense (U.S.)
DshK	Russian 12.7-millimeter heavy machine gun used by the Iraqi army
ECP	Entry control point
EOD	Explosive ordnance disposal
Eye-pro	Slang for "eye protection" (ballistic glasses or goggles)
FAO	Foreign area officer
FOB	Forward operating base
G-2	Brigade intelligence section; also used for brigade intelligence officer
GPS	Global Positioning System
GSR	Gunshot residue
HF	High frequency
HME	Homemade explosives
HMMWV	High-mobility multipurpose wheeled vehicle; also called Humvee
HN1	Hospitalman first class
Hobas	Arabic kiln-baked flat bread

HUMINT	Human intelligence
Humvee	*See* HMMWV
IA	Iraqi army; also used for a member of the Iraqi army
IED	Improvised explosive device
IP	Iraqi Police; also used for a member of the Iraqi Police
IRR	Individual Ready Reserve
ISF	Iraqi Security Forces
JCC	Joint Coordination Center
Jundi	Arabic for "soldier"
Junood	Plural of *jundi*
KVN	Key Volunteer Network
LAR	Light Armored Reconnaissance
LAV	Light armored vehicle
LCpl.	Lance corporal
Lt.	Lieutenant
Lt. Col.	Lieutenant colonel
LZ	Landing zone
M1114	Model number of up-armored HMMWVs
M2	.50-caliber heavy machine gun used by U.S. forces
M240	7.62-millimeter medium machine gun used by U.S. forces
M4	Carbine version of 5.56-millimeter M16 assault rifle used by U.S. forces
M9	9-millimeter sidearm used by U.S. forces
Maj.	Major
Maj. Gen.	Major general
MARSOC	Marine Special Operations Command
MEF	Marine Expeditionary Force
MiTT	Military transition team

MNC-I	Multi-National Corps-Iraq
MNF-W	Multi-National Force-West
MOD	Ministry of Defense (Iraqi)
MRAP	Mine-resistant, ambush-protected vehicle
MRE	Meals ready to eat
MSgt.	Master sergeant
MTV	Modular Tactical Vest
Mujaas	Arabic for "monthly leave cycle"
Mulaazem	Arabic for "second lieutenant"
Muqaddam	Arabic for "lieutenant colonel"
Muqaddam rukn	Arabic for "staff lieutenant colonel"
MWR	Morale, Welfare, and Recreation
NAI	Named area of interest
Naqeeb	Arabic for "captain"
NCO	Noncommissioned officer
ND	Negligent discharge
Net	Short for "network"
NVGs	Night-vision goggles
ORA	Operational readiness assessment
Oscar-Mike	Jargon for "on the move"
PAS-13	Bulky handheld thermal imaging device used by U.S. forces
Pax	Jargon for "personnel"
PBIED	Personnel-borne improvised explosive device
PKM	Russian-made 7.62-millimeter medium machine gun used by the Iraqi army
Pogue	Slang for "rear-echelon"
PPE	Personal protective equipment
PSD	Personal security detachment
PTT	Police transition team
PX	Post exchange

QRF	Quick Reaction Force (formal Iraqi army unit designation); also quick-reaction force (USMC unit)
Raad	Arabic for "major"
RCIED	Radio-controlled improvised explosive device
RCT	Regimental Combat Team
RIP	Relief in place
RPG	Rocket-propelled grenade
RSM	Regional security meeting
S-2	Battalion intelligence section; also used for battalion intelligence officer
S-3	Battalion operations section; also used for battalion operations officer
S-4	Battalion logistics section; also used for battalion logistics officer
Sadie	Arabic for "sir"
SAPI	Small-arms protective insert
SATCOM	Satellite communications
Seabee	Used for a member of the Naval Construction Battalion
SEAL	Sea, air, and land; a member of a Naval Special Warfare team
Sgt.	Sergeant
Shemagh	Checkered-pattern Arabic headwrap
Sherta	Arabic for "police"
Shukraan	Arabic for "thank you"
SITREP	Situation report
SNCO	Staff noncommissioned officer
SOP	Standing operating procedure
Souq	Arabic for "market"
SSgt.	Staff sergeant
SWA	Southwest Asia

TCN	Third-country national
Terp	Slang for "interpreter"
TQ	Taqaddum (Iraq)
TTP	Tactics, techniques, and procedures
UAV	Unmanned aerial vehicle
UH-1N	Marine Corps utility helicopter
UHF	Ultrahigh frequency
USZ	Urban security zone
VBIED	Vehicle-borne improvised explosive device
VC	Vehicle commander
VCP	Vehicle checkpoint
VHF	Very high frequency
Vic	Jargon for "vehicle"
WAG	Waste Alleviation and Gelling
Wadi	Dry riverbed or creek bed in the desert
Wasta	Arabic for "influence" or "clout"
XO	Executive officer

Index

About the Author

Major Seth W.B. Folsom, USMC, has a Bachelor's degree in international relations from the University of Virginia and a Master's degree in South Asian national security affairs from the Naval Postgraduate School. He resides in Woodbridge, VA, with his wife Ashley and his daughters Emery and Kinsey.